# THE MUNROS

## SCOTLAND'S HIGHEST MOUNTAINS

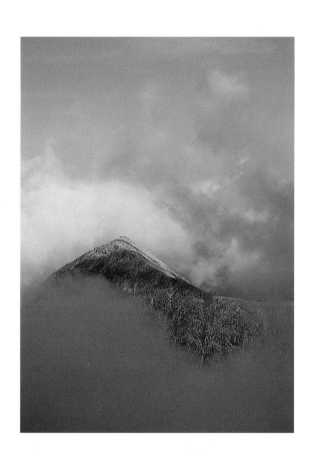

*This book is dedicated to the memory of Alan Sands,*
*Bookseller and Mountaineer.*

First published in Great Britain in 1996 for Lomond Books
36 West Shore Road, Granton
Edinburgh EH5 1QD

Reprinted 1996

Information used in the creation of the maps was kindly supplied by the
Macaulay Land Use Research Institute in Aberdeen and the Royal Commission on the
Ancient and Historical Monuments of Scotland (LCS88 Photography)

Colin Baxter Photography Ltd. gratefully acknowledges permission granted
by Neil Wilson Publishing Ltd., Glasgow, to reproduce those route summaries that
are also published in *The Munro Almanac* by Cameron McNeish

ISBN 1 900455 13 7

Printed in Hong Kong

Photography:

© Colin Baxter 1996:
Front Cover, Back Cover and Pages 6, 9, 14, 23, 24, 26, 27, 28, 42, 48, 60, 62, 65, 71, 72, 75, 78,
84, 89, 90, 93, 94, 97, 98, 100, 102, 104, 106, 114, 116, 121, 123, 124, 129, 131, 137,
140, 151, 154, 158, 165, 174, 188, 195, 212, 219, 223

© Alan Gordon 1996:
Pages 1, 31, 34, 51, 69, 76, 83, 86, 112, 132, 143, 144, 148, 157, 160, 162, 169, 172,
179, 180, 184, 192, 200 (Scotland in Focus), 203, 205, 207, 209, 210, 217, 221

© David Paterson 1996:
Pages 47, 52, 58, 186, 191, 216

© R G Elliott (Scotland in Focus) 1996: Pages 152, 215

© Alex Gillespie 1996: Pages 55, 81

© Alan O'Brien 1996: Pages 126, 183

© Jerry Rawson 1996: Pages 41, 66

© Chris Townsend 1996: Pages 39, 171

© Rab Anderson 1996: Page 146

© Jeremy Ashcroft 1996: Page 18

© Laurie Campbell (Scotland in Focus) 1996: Page 109

© R Weir (Scotland in Focus) 1996: Page 37

# THE MUNROS

## SCOTLAND'S HIGHEST MOUNTAINS

### CAMERON MCNEISH

**LOMOND BOOKS**

EDINBURGH • SCOTLAND

To Orkney

Thurso

Wick

Kinlochbervie

Tongue

*Ben Hope*

Altnaharra

*Ben Klibreck*

A838

A836

A9

Lochinver

*Ben More Assynt*

Lairg

Helmsdale

A835

A837

Stornoway

*L e w i s*

Ullapool

Dornoch

Tarbert

A835

Tain

A9

To Lochmaddy

*An Teallach*

*Seana Braigh*

Gairloch

A832

Dundonnell and Fisherfield Hills

*Ullapool Hills*

Ben Wyvis

Elgin

A98

A835

Fannaichs

Dingwall

A96

Achnashellach and Torridon Hills

*Slioch*

A832

Achnasheen

A835

A96

A95

Torridon

*Sgorr Ruadh*

A890

*Moruisg*

*Sgurr na Ruaidhe*

Inverness

A96

Portree

*Raasay*

A850

*Sgurr na Lapaich*

Glen Affric and Strathfarrar

Grantown on Spey

A939

Kyle of Lochalsh

A850

*The Cuillin*

*Bla Bheinn*

*Ben Attow*

Glen Shiel

Invermoriston

A82

Aviemore

*S k y e*

Northern Cairngorms

Ballater

A93

To Lochboisdale

*The Saddle*

A87

*Braeriach*

*Ben Avon*

*Canna*

*Ladhar Bheinn*

*Creag a' Mhaim*

Kingussie

Southern Cairngorms

Braemar

Glenshee and Lochnagar Hills

Armadale

Knoydart and Loch Quoich

A82

Laggan and the Monadh Liath

*Meall Chuaich*

Cairnwell Hills

*Mt Keen*

*Rum*

Mallaig

*Sgurr Thuilm*

Lochs Lochy Arkaig and Eil

A86

Dalwhinnie

*Beinn Dearg*

Tarff and Tilt Hills

*Glas Maol*

*Driesh*

*Eigg*

Glenfinnan

A830

Spean Bridge

Loch Ericht to Loch Laggan

Dalwhinnie Hills

A9

Glenshee

Fort William

Ben Nevis and Grey Corries

Loch Treig and Loch Ossian

Drumochter Hills

Blair Atholl

A93

*Coll*

A884

The Mamores

Schiehallion

*Schiehallion*

Tobermory

Ballachulish

Glencoe Hills

A82

Rannoch and Glen Lyon

A827

A9

Perth

A90

Lochaline

*M u l l*

Glen Etive Hills

Bridge of Orchy Hills

Lawers Group

Salen

*Ben Starav*

Mamlorn Hills

Killin

*Ben Chonzie*

A85

*Ben More*

A849

Crunachan Hills

Tyndrum

A85

Oban

A85

Tyndrum Hills

Crianlarich

*Ben Vorlich*

Comrie

Dalmally

Crianlarich Hills

A84

*Colonsay*

Arrochar Alps

A83

Inveraray

A82

A83

*Ben Lomond*

Stirling

A811

Lochgilphead

*Jura*

A83

Dunoon

M9

Edinburgh

A1

*Bute*

Glasgow

M8

*Islay*

M74

Tarbert

A702

A7

*Arran*

Brodick

0                    40 Kilometres

0          20 miles

# CONTENTS

*The Munros* — *7*

*Munro Heights and Numbers* — *10*

Ben Lomond and the Arrochar Alps — 15

The Crianlarich Hills — 20

The Tyndrum Hills — 25

The Crieff and Loch Earn Hills — 29

Rannoch and Glen Lyon — 32

The Lawers Group — 36

The Mamlorn Hills — 40

The Bridge of Orchy Hills — 44

The Cruachan Hills — 49

The Glen Etive Hills — 53

Glencoe — 61

The Mamores — 68

Ben Nevis, The Aonachs and the Grey Corries — 73

Loch Treig and Loch Ossian — 79

Loch Ericht to Loch Laggan — 85

The Drumochter Hills — 91

The Tarf and Tilt Hills — 97

The Cairnwell Hills — 103

Glenshee and Lochnagar Hills — 107

Northern Cairngorms — 115

Southern Cairngorms — 125

Laggan and the Monadh Liath — 134

Loch Lochy, Loch Arkaig and Loch Eil — 141

Knoydart and Loch Quoich — 147

Glen Shiel Hills — 159

Glen Affric and Strathfarrar — 166

The Achnashellach and Torridon Hills — 175

The Dundonnell and Fisherfield Hills — 189

The Fannaichs and Ullapool Hills — 199

Assynt and the Far North — 208

Skye and Mull — 213

*Mountain Safety and Access* — *224*

*Index* — *226*

# THE MUNROS

The Munros, the 277 mountains in Scotland over 3000ft (914m) in height, are enjoying an unprecedented popularity. Since the centenary of *Munros Tables*, the list of 3000ft mountains first compiled in 1891 by Sir Hugh Munro of Lindertis, it has become fashionable to climb the hills, with an increasing number of people stoically ticking their way through the list. I completed my first round of the Munros during the centenary year in 1991 and became Munroist No.913. Since then, several hundred other hillwalkers have added their names to the list and it looks set to grow dramatically.

So what's the appeal? There is little doubt that physical exercise has become much more popular in recent years following the great jogging/running boom of the eighties. More and more people have been seeking a greater challenge than just running around streets, and the completion of the Munros offers such a challenge. As well as the physical exertion involved, there is also the aesthetic appeal of magnificent scenery, the skills that have to be learned, the camaraderie of like-minded souls, and the added bonus of visiting parts of Scotland that you otherwise would probably ignore.

When Sir Hugh Munro drew up his tables he could scarcely have realised the consequences of his act. I wonder what he would think today if he knew that his surname had become a generic term for Scottish mountains over 3000ft? I wonder what he would think of the legions of people who refer to themselves as Munro-baggers rather than walkers, climbers or hikers? I wonder what he would think of those poor souls who have suffered premature dementia because of a continued struggle to climb mountains for the prime purpose of ticking them off in a book? I wonder what he would think if he heard his name taken in vain as the afflicted souls toil up their umpteenth Geal Charn in snow, sleet and wind for the pleasure of following their compasses all the way back down again?

I suspect Sir Hugh would probably chuckle, for he had a sense of humour. The frailties of the human mind, and the increasing desire for freedom from 20th-century living, were not his concern when he compiled his tables. Someone once likened Munro-bagging to smoking – both habits are addictive, both are socially obnoxious (Munro-baggers have been known to bore others to death with diatribes on how many Munros they have left to climb and the relative merits of Munros and lesser mountains), and both habits can be expensive.

But despite the disadvantages of being a Munro freak, the game undoubtedly has good points. The walker or climber who has never wavered from the single-mindedness of the Munro challenge will have travelled the length and breadth of the Scottish highlands, enjoying considerable exercise in the most beautiful of surroundings. He or she will have become familiar with some truly magical places and many magnificent hills – hills which the car-borne visitor will never see. Some favourites flash to mind – Seana Bhraigh, the 'old high slopes' up in the empty quarter beyond Inverlael; the castellated form of An Teallach, the forge, in shape and form one of the most appealing mountains in the land, and of course for sheer, rugged, majestic splendour, the spectacle that is the Cuillin of Skye.

The other attractive feature of the Munro challenge is the sheer volume of experience that is gained through the accumulation of the peaks. I know of many hillwalkers who are purely fair-weather climbers. Several of them have many years' experience of climbing and walking in Scotland, but the vast majority of their activities have been enjoyed in good weather. To my mind this only makes them half a walker.

*Buachaille Etive Mor, Glencoe*

It really is foul weather and winter conditions which are the givers of experience. Climb hills in good weather and all you really gain is some exercise and a good view. This is fine but it doesn't prepare you for the day when the conditions will change rapidly and you are suddenly faced with an adventure of epic proportions!

In the course of climbing 277 Munros you will inevitably be faced with more than a fair share of nasties. By the time you have completed the round you will be well prepared for almost every eventuality you can encounter in the British hills. Your navigation will have reached a high level of expertise, you will have a pretty shrewd idea of what the weather is likely to do by watching the clouds and sensing the wind, you will have become a competent scrambler if not a rock climber, and it is more than likely that you will have picked up a fair degree of experience in snow and ice. All in all, it's not a bad game, a favourable excuse, if one is needed, for going to the hills and wild places.

There are those, of course, who dislike the idea of Munro-bagging, suggesting that people shouldn't need that form of motivation to head for the high places. While the critics may be absolutely right, there is little doubt that virtually everyone who climbs all 277 of the Munros has scored a pretty high achievement, an achievement that will have been made worthwhile by a host of mountain memories that will never diminish.

This book is *not* intended to be packed away in your rucksack for quick reference. I hope it will be used to glean information on the mountains and the routes, and I believe the photographs portray the grandeur and beauty of the hills in a way which has not previously been achieved and which will encourage readers to get out there. I therefore hope the text of this book fulfills two main functions:

1. To offer a choice of route up the mountains, and in particular, ways of combining several Munros together to make a satisfying day out. It would also serve the purpose of spreading the load on the hill, taking the more adventurous away from the popular honeypot routes.

2. To form a good, substantial read which can motivate and inspire people to go out and climb the hills in question. Many people climb the hills without actually getting to know them, climbing and descending them by the shortest possible route. I would hope this book will introduce them to different aspects of the hills' characters, in a more holistic way.

The usual planning information is in sidepanels – distance of recommended routes, height climbed, translation and pronunciation of hill name, etc – but always bear in mind that this is not intended as a basic guide, but as a tool to be used in planning days or weekends away.

While I hope this book proves useful, please bear in mind that it is not the ticking off of 3000ft mountains that is important, but the 'being there' which really matters. At the end of your climb, even if you don't reach the summit, remember the mountains will always be around another day.

CAMERON McNEISH

*Braeriach and the Lairig Ghru, Cairngorms*

# MUNRO HEIGHTS AND NUMBERS

| | | | | | |
|---|---|---|---|---|---|
| 1 | Ben Nevis | 1344m/4409ft | 34 | Sgor Gaoith | 1118m/3668ft |
| 2 | Ben Macdui | 1309m/4295ft | 35 | Meall Garbh | 1118m/3668ft |
| 3 | Braeriach | 1296m/4252ft | 36 | Stob Coire Easain | 1116m/3661ft |
| 4 | Cairn Toul | 1293m/4242ft | 37 | Stob Coire an Laoigh | 1115m/3658ft |
| 5 | Cairngorm | 1245m/4085ft | 38 | Aonach Beag | 1114m/3655ft |
| 6 | Aonach Beag | 1234m/4049ft | 39 | Monadh Mor | 1113m/3652ft |
| 7 | Carn Mor Dearg | 1223m/4012ft | 40 | Tom a' Choinich | 1111m/3645ft |
| 8 | Aonach Mor | 1221m/4006ft | 41 | Sgurr Mor | 1110m/3642ft |
| 9 | Ben Lawers | 1214m/3983ft | 42 | Sgurr nan Conbhairean | 1110m/3642ft |
| 10 | Beinn a' Bhuird (North Top) | 1196m/3924ft | 43 | Meall a' Bhuiridh | 1108m/3635ft |
| 11 | Carn Eige | 1183m/3881ft | 44 | Stob a' Choire Mheadhoin | 1106m/3629ft |
| 12 | Beinn Mheadhoin | 1182m/3878ft | 45 | Beinn Ghlas | 1103m/3619ft |
| 13 | Mam Sodhail | 1180m/3871ft | 46 | Mullach Fraoch-choire | 1102m/3615ft |
| 14 | Stob Choire Claurigh | 1177m/3861ft | 47 | Beinn Eibhinn | 1100m/3609ft |
| 15 | Ben More | 1174m/3852ft | 48 | Creise | 1100m/3609ft |
| 16 | Ben Avon | | 49 | Sgurr a' Mhaim | 1099m/3606ft |
| | (Leabaidh an Daimh Bhuidhe) | 1171m/3842ft | 50 | Sgurr Choinnich Mor | 1095m/3592ft |
| 17 | Stob Binnein | 1165m/3822ft | 51 | Sgurr nan Clach Geala | 1093m/3586ft |
| 18 | Beinn Bhrotain | 1157m/3796ft | 52 | Bynack More | 1090m/3576ft |
| 19 | Lochnagar (Cac Carn Beag) | 1155m/3789ft | 53 | Beinn a' Chlachair | 1088m/3570ft |
| 20 | Derry Cairngorm | 1155m/3789ft | 54 | Stob Ghabhar | 1087m/3566ft |
| 21 | Sgurr nan Ceathreamhnan | 1151m/3776ft | 55 | Beinn Dearg | 1084m/3556ft |
| 22 | Sgurr na Lapaich | 1150m/3773ft | 56 | Sgurr a' Choire Ghlais | 1083m/3553ft |
| 23 | Bidean nam Bian | 1150m/3773ft | 57 | Schiehallion | 1083m/3553ft |
| 24 | Ben Alder | 1148m/3766ft | 58 | Beinn a' Chaorainn | 1082m/3550ft |
| 25 | Geal-Charn | 1132m/3714ft | 59 | Beinn a' Chreachain | 1081m/3547ft |
| 26 | Creag Meagaidh | 1130m/3707ft | 60 | Ben Starav | 1078m/3537ft |
| 27 | Ben Laoigh (Ben Lui) | 1130m/3707ft | 61 | Beinn Heasgarnich | 1076m/3530ft |
| 28 | An Riabhachan | 1129m/3704ft | 62 | Beinn Dorain | 1076m/3530ft |
| 29 | Carn nan Gabhar (Beinn a'Ghlo) | 1129m/3704ft | 63 | Braigh Coire Chruinn-bhalgain | |
| 30 | Binnein Mor | 1128m/3701ft | | (Beinn a' Ghlo) | 1070m/3510ft |
| 31 | Ben Cruachan | 1126m/3694ft | 64 | An Socach | 1069m/3507ft |
| 32 | A' Chralaig | 1120m/3674ft | 65 | Meall Corranaich | 1069m/3507ft |
| 33 | Carn a' Coire Boidheach | | 66 | Sgurr Fhuaran | 1068m/3504ft |
| | (White Mounth) | 1118m/3668ft | 67 | Glas Maol | 1068m/3504ft |

| | | | |
|---|---|---|---|
| 68 | Cairn of Claise | 1064m/3491ft | |
| 69 | An Teallach | | |
| | (Bidein a' Ghlas Thuill) | 1062m/3484ft | |
| 70 | An Teallach (Sgurr Fiona) | 1059m/3474ft | |
| 71 | Na Gruagaichean | 1055m/3461ft | |
| 72 | Liathach | | |
| | (Spidean a' Choire Leith) | 1054m/3458ft | |
| 73 | Toll Creagach | 1054m/3458ft | |
| 74 | Sgurr a' Chaorachain | 1053m/3455ft | |
| 75 | Stob Poite Coire Ardair | 1053m/3455ft | |
| 76 | Beinn a' Chaorainn | 1052m/3451ft | |
| 77 | Glas Tulaichean | 1051m/3448ft | |
| 78 | Geal Charn | 1049m/3442ft | |
| 79 | Sgurr Fhuar-thuill | 1049m/3442ft | |
| 80 | Creag Mhor | 1048m/3438ft | |
| 81 | Carn an t-Sagairt Mor | 1047m/3435ft | |
| 82 | Chno Dearg | 1047m/3435ft | |
| 83 | Ben Wyvis (Glas Leathad Mor) | 1046m/3432ft | |
| 84 | Cruach Ardrain | 1046m/3432ft | |
| 85 | Beinn Iutharn Mhor | 1045m/3428ft | |
| 86 | Stob Coir' an Albannaich | 1044m/3425ft | |
| 87 | Meall nan Tarmachan | 1043m/3422ft | |
| 88 | Carn Mairg | 1041m/3415ft | |
| 89 | Sgurr na Ciche | 1040m/3412ft | |
| 90 | Meall Ghaordie | 1039m/3409ft | |
| 91 | Beinn Achaladair | 1039m/3409ft | |
| 92 | Sgurr a' Bhealaich Dheirg | 1038m/3405ft | |
| 93 | Carn a' Mhaim | 1037m/3402ft | |
| 94 | Gleouraich | 1035m/3396ft | |
| 95 | Carn Dearg | 1034m/3392ft | |
| 96 | Am Bodach | 1032m/3386ft | |
| 97 | Beinn Fhada | 1032m/3386ft | |
| 98 | Carn an Righ | 1029m/3376ft | |
| 99 | Ben Oss | 1029m/3376ft | |
| 100 | Carn Gorm | 1028m/3373ft | |
| 101 | Sgurr a' Mhaoraich | 1027m/3369ft | |
| 102 | Sgurr na Ciste Duibhe | 1027m/3369ft | |
| 103 | Ben Challum | 1025m/3363ft | |
| 104 | Beinn a' Bheithir (Sgorr Dhearg) | 1024m/3360ft | |
| 105 | Liathach (Mullach an Rathain) | 1023m/3356ft | |
| 106 | Buachaille Etive Mor | | |
| | (Stob Dearg) | 1022m/3353ft | |
| 107 | Aonach air Chrith | 1021m/3350ft | |
| 108 | Ladhar Bheinn | 1020m/3346ft | |
| 109 | Mullach Coire Mhic Fhearchair | 1019m/3343ft | |
| 110 | Beinn Bheoil | 1019m/3343ft | |
| 111 | Mullach Clach a' Bhlair | 1019m/3343ft | |
| 112 | Carn an Tuirc | 1019m/3343ft | |
| 113 | Garbh Chioch Mhor | 1013m/3323ft | |
| 114 | Cairn Bannoch | 1012m/3320ft | |
| 115 | Beinn Ime | 1011m/3317ft | |
| 116 | Sgurr an Doire Leathain | 1010m/3314ft | |
| 117 | Beinn Eighe (Ruadh-stac Mor) | 1010m/3314ft | |
| 118 | The Saddle | 1010m/3314ft | |
| 119 | Beinn Udlamain | 1010m/3314ft | |
| 120 | Sgurr Eilde Mor | 1008m/3307ft | |
| 121 | Beinn Dearg | 1008m/3307ft | |
| 122 | Maoile Lunndaidh | 1007m/3304ft | |
| 123 | Carn Liath | 1006m/3301ft | |
| 124 | An Sgarsoch | 1006m/3301ft | |
| 125 | Beinn Fhionnlaidh | 1005m/3297ft | |
| 126 | Sgurr an Lochain | 1004m/3294ft | |
| 127 | The Devil's Point | 1004m/3294ft | |
| 128 | Sgurr Mor | 1003m/3291ft | |
| 129 | Aonach Meadhoin | 1003m/3291ft | |
| 130 | Beinn an Dothaidh | 1002m/3287ft | |
| 131 | Sail Chaorainn | 1002m/3287ft | |
| 132 | Beinn a' Bheithir | | |
| | (Sgorr Dhonuill) | 1002m/3284ft | |
| 133 | Sgor an Iubhair | 1001m/3284ft | |
| 134 | Meall Greigh | 1001m/3284ft | |
| 135 | Sgurr Breac | 1000m/3281ft | |
| 136 | Sgurr Choinnich | 999m/3278ft | |
| 137 | A' Chailleach | 999m/3278ft | |
| 138 | Stob Ban | 999m/3278ft | |
| 139 | Broad Cairn | 998m/3274ft | |

| 140 | Ben More Assynt | 998m/3274ft | 176 | Stuc a' Chroin | 975m/3199ft |
|-----|----------------|-------------|-----|----------------|-------------|
| 141 | Stob Diamh | 998m/3274ft | 177 | Carn a' Gheoidh | 975m/3199ft |
| 142 | Glas Bheinn Mhor | 997m/3271ft | 178 | A' Mharconaich | 975m/3199ft |
| 143 | Spidean Mialach | 996m/3268ft | 179 | Ben Lomond | 974m/3196ft |
| 144 | An Caisteal | 995m/3264ft | 180 | Beinn Sgritheall | 974m/3196ft |
| 145 | Carn an Fhidhleir | 994m/3261ft | 181 | Sgurr a' Ghreadaidh | 973m/3192ft |
| 146 | Sgor na h-Ulaidh | 994m/3261ft | 182 | Meall Garbh | 968m/3176ft |
| 147 | Sgurr Alasdair | 993m/3258ft | 183 | Sgor nam Fiannaidh | |
| 148 | Sgurr na Ruaidhe | 993m/3258ft | | (Aonach Eagach) | 967m/3173ft |
| 149 | Carn nan Gobhar | 992m/3255ft | 184 | A' Mhaighdean | 967m/3173ft |
| 150 | Carn nan Gobhar | 992m/3255ft | 185 | Ben More | 966m/3169ft |
| 151 | Sgairneach Mhor | 991m/3251ft | 186 | Sgurr na Banachdich | 965m/3166ft |
| 152 | Beinn Eunaich | 989m/3245ft | 187 | Sgurr nan Gillean | 965m/3166ft |
| 153 | Sgurr Ban | 989m/3245ft | 188 | Carn a' Chlamain | 963m/3159ft |
| 154 | Conival | 987m/3238ft | 189 | Sgurr Thuilm | 963m/3159ft |
| 155 | Druim Shionnach | 987m/3238ft | 190 | Ben Klibreck (Meall nan Con) | 961m/3153ft |
| 156 | Gulvain | 987m/3238ft | 191 | Sgorr Ruadh | 960m/3150ft |
| 157 | Creag Leacach | 987m/3238ft | 192 | Beinn nan Aighenan | 960m/3150ft |
| 158 | Lurg Mhor | 986m/3235ft | 193 | Meall Glas | 960m/3150ft |
| 159 | Inaccessible Pinnacle | | 194 | Stuchd an Lochain | 960m/3150ft |
| | (Sgurr Dearg) | 986m/3235ft | 195 | Saileag | 959m/3146ft |
| 160 | Beinn Alligin (Sgurr Mhor) | 985m/3232ft | 196 | Beinn Fhionnlaidh | 959m/3146ft |
| 161 | Ben Vorlich | 985m/3232ft | 197 | Buachaille Etive Beag | |
| 162 | An Gearanach | 982m/3222ft | | (Stob Dubh) | 958m/3143ft |
| 163 | Ciste Dhubh | 982m/3222ft | 198 | Bruach na Frithe | 958m/3143ft |
| 164 | Mullach na Dheiragain | 982m/3222ft | 199 | Tolmount | 958m/3143ft |
| 165 | Stob Coire a' Chairn | 981m/3218ft | 200 | Tom Buidhe | 957m/3140ft |
| 166 | Maol Chinn-dearg | 981m/3218ft | 201 | Carn Ghluasaid | 957m/3140ft |
| 167 | Creag Mhor | 981m/3218ft | 202 | Sgurr nan Coireachan | 956m/3136ft |
| 168 | Beinn a' Chochuill | 980m/3215ft | 203 | Sgor Gaibhre | 955m/3133ft |
| 169 | Slioch | 980m/3215ft | 204 | Beinn Liath Mhor Fannaich | 954m/3130ft |
| 170 | Cona' Mheall | 980m/3215ft | 205 | Beinn Mhanach | 954m/3130ft |
| 171 | Beinn Dubhchraig | 978m/3209ft | 206 | Am Faochagach | 954m/3130ft |
| 172 | Meall nan Ceapraichean | 977m/3205ft | 207 | Sgurr nan Coireachan | 953m/3127ft |
| 173 | Stob Ban | 977m/3205ft | 208 | Meall Dearg (Aonach Eagach) | 953m/3127ft |
| 174 | Stob Coire Sgriodain | 976m/3202ft | 209 | Meall Chuaich | 951m/3120ft |
| 175 | Carn Liath (Beinn a' Ghlo) | 975m/3199ft | 210 | Meall Gorm | 949m/3113ft |

| | | | |
|---|---|---|---|
| 211 | Sgurr Mhic Choinnich | 948m/3110ft | |
| 212 | Beinn Bhuidhe | 948m/3110ft | |
| 213 | Driesh | 947m/3107ft | |
| 214 | Creag a' Mhaim | 947m/3107ft | |
| 215 | Meall Buidhe | 946m/3104ft | |
| 216 | Carn Bhac | 946m/3104ft | |
| 217 | Beinn Tulaichean | 946m/3104ft | |
| 218 | Bidein a' Choire Sheasgaich | 945m/3100ft | |
| 219 | Carn Dearg | 945m/3100ft | |
| 220 | Sgurr na Sgine | 945m/3100ft | |
| 221 | An Socach (West Summit) | 944m/3097ft | |
| 222 | Sgurr Dubh Mor | 944m/3097ft | |
| 223 | Stob a' Choire Odhair | 943m/3094ft | |
| 224 | Ben Vorlich | 943m/3094ft | |
| 225 | Carn Dearg | 941m/3087ft | |
| 226 | Carn na Caim | 941m/3087ft | |
| 227 | Beinn a' Chroin | 940m/3084ft | |
| 228 | Binnein Beag | 940m/3084ft | |
| 229 | Mount Keen | 939m/3081ft | |
| 230 | Luinne Bheinn | 939m/3081ft | |
| 231 | Mullach nan Coirean | 939m/3081ft | |
| 232 | Beinn na Lap | 937m/3074ft | |
| 233 | Beinn Sgulaird | 937m/3074ft | |
| 234 | Beinn Tarsuinn | 936m/3071ft | |
| 235 | A' Bhuidheanach Bheag | 936m/3071ft | |
| 236 | Am Basteir | 935m/3068ft | |
| 237 | Sron a' Choire Ghairbh | 935m/3068ft | |
| 238 | Sgiath Chuil | 935m/3068ft | |
| 239 | Meall a' Chrasgaidh | 934m/3064ft | |
| 240 | Fionn Bheinn | 933m/3061ft | |
| 241 | Maol Chean-dearg | 933m/3061ft | |
| 242 | The Cairnwell | 933m/3061ft | |
| 243 | Beinn Chabhair | 933m/3061ft | |
| 244 | Meall Buidhe | 932m/3058ft | |

| | | | |
|---|---|---|---|
| 245 | Beinn Bhreac | 931m/3054ft | |
| 246 | Ben Chonzie | 931m/3054ft | |
| 247 | A' Chailleach | 930m/3051ft | |
| 248 | Mayar | 928m/3045ft | |
| 249 | Eididh nan Clach Geala | 928m/3045ft | |
| 250 | Meall nan Eun | 928m/3045ft | |
| 251 | Bla Bheinn (Blaven) | 928m/3045ft | |
| 252 | Moruisg | 928m/3045ft | |
| 253 | Ben Hope | 927m/3041ft | |
| 254 | Seana Bhraigh | 927m/3041ft | |
| 255 | Beinn Narnain | 926m/3038ft | |
| 256 | Geal Charn | 926m/3038ft | |
| 257 | Meall a' Choire Leith | 926m/3038ft | |
| 258 | Beinn Liath Mhor | 925m/3035ft | |
| 259 | Sgurr nan Eag | 924m/3031ft | |
| 260 | Creag Pitridh | 924m/3031ft | |
| 261 | An Coileachan | 923m/3028ft | |
| 262 | Sgurr nan Each | 923m/3028ft | |
| 263 | Carn Sgulain | 920m/3018ft | |
| 264 | An Socach | 920m/3018ft | |
| 265 | Gairich | 919m/3015ft | |
| 266 | Sgurr a' Mhadaidh | 918m/3012ft | |
| 267 | Ruadh Stac Mor | 918m/3012ft | |
| 268 | Creag nan Damh | 918m/3012ft | |
| 269 | A' Ghlas-bheinn | 918m/3012ft | |
| 270 | Carn Aosda | 917m/3008ft | |
| 271 | Meall na Teanga | 917m/3008ft | |
| 272 | Geal Charn | 917m/3008ft | |
| 273 | Beinn a' Chleibh | 916m/3005ft | |
| 274 | Ben Vane | 915m/3002ft | |
| 275 | Beinn a' Chlaidheimh | 915m/3002ft | |
| 276 | Beinn Teallach | 915m/3002ft | |
| 277 | Sgurr nan Ceannaichean | 914m/3000ft | |

Munro numbers appear in brackets after each mountain name in the text

# BEN LOMOND
# AND THE ARROCHAR ALPS

## The Munros:

### Ben Lomond   Ben Vane   Beinn Ime   Beinn Narnain
### Ben Vorlich   Beinn Bhuidhe

Dominating the wild eastern shore of Loch Lomond, the view from the summit of the Ben is in turn dominated by the craggy outline of The Cobbler and its higher cousins of the Arrochar Alps. This is a tight clutch of high individual hills, all fine peaks in themselves, which tend to be steeper and more rugged than most other hills in the Southern Highlands. There is a wonderful sense of history in these hills and Arrochar is indisputably one of the early centres of climbing development in the country. This was entirely due to The Cobbler, the lowly yet extraordinary peak which most hill-goers would put amongst their top dozen hills. The Munroist who ignores the wonders of The Cobbler, at 883m (2899ft), is the undoubted loser. The best base for the Arrochar Alps is either Arrochar itself or Tarbet, and for Ben Lomond, there is a Youth Hostel at Rowardennan and bed and breakfasts, guest houses and hotels in Drymen and Balmaha.

## Ben Lomond (179), 974m/3196ft

Ben Lomond, the beacon hill. Glasgow's hill. This, the most southerly of all the Munros, has indeed been a beacon to genera-tions of Clydesiders, summoning them from the urban sprawl of Scotland's biggest conurbation to the gateway that it represents on the very edge of that old geological fault, the Highland Boundary.

   Dominating the eastern shore of Loch Lomond, Ben Lomond rises from a skirt of forestry into a mountain of some grandeur, and when glimpsed through the trees which surround Loch Katrine in the north east, the great north-east face can look positively Alpine.

   The summit itself is formed by a fairly short, level ridge, curving gently round the head of the north-east corrie. To the north it falls away into a high plateau of extensive moorland which falls steep-sided toward Loch Lomond, while to the south it throws out a broad and bulging ridge for some kilometres. The normal route

**Route Summary:** Follow the signposted path through the woods to the lower slopes of the S ridge. Climb to the ridge and follow it N to the summit cone. An obvious path leads to the summit

**Map:** OS Sheet 56

**Access Point:** Rowardennan Hotel, GR360983

**Distance:** 11km, 974m ascent

**Approx Time:** 4-6 hours

**Translation:** beacon hill

**Pronunciation:** Low-mond

*Ben Lomond from the east across Loch Ard*

of approach follows this ridge, approaching it through the forest from Rowardennan following a well used and fairly well maintained footpath. On the ridge itself the path deteriorates into a claggy quagmire but improves again once the summit ridge is reached where the path ascends in a series of tight zigzags.

A scenic alternative ascent route is via the Ptarmigan ridge which begins at the private road just north of Ardess. A steep hillside leads to the obvious ridge which is then followed along narrow tracks all the way to Ptarmigan. From there follow the ridge north-east across an obvious bealach (*bee-all-ach*, a saddle between two hills) to gain the north-west ridge of Ben Lomond. Follow the path to the top.

## Ben Vane (274), 915m/3002ft, Beinn Ime (115), 1011m/3317ft, Beinn Narnain (255), 926m/3038ft

**Route Summary:** From Coiregrogain (Route A) take the ESE ridge of Ben Vane to summit. Drop down to the bealach to the W and climb slopes of Beinn Ime. Descend S to another bealach and climb slopes of Beinn Narnain. Descend N to the footpath in the glen and return to Coiregrogain

**Map:** OS Sheet 56: GR272067 and GR255085

**Access Point:** Inveruglas

**Distance:** 20km, 1550m ascent

**Approx Time:** 6-8 hours

**Translation:** unknown; butter hill; middle hill

**Pronunciation:** as spelt

NB: Parking at the foot of the Hydro Board road is discouraged. Park opposite Loch Sloy Power Station to the north

Bagging Munros from my home in the central Highlands creates something of a topsy-turvy world. Those hills which to the vast majority of those climbing the Munros are considerably remote in terms of distance, are virtually on my doorstep, and those hills which are handy for those living in the Central Belt take on the proportions of a major expedition for someone travelling from Badenoch. But the Arrochar Alps are the hills of my youth, and many a time I've walked in from Inveruglas to Coiregrogain with the huge conical frame of Ben Vane pulling me onwards. It is logical to climb Ben Vane, Beinn Ime and Beinn Narnain straight away in one big round of about 19km with some 1550m of climbing, leaving Ben Vorlich for the next day.

Ben Vane sits more or less in the middle of this group of hills, separated from Ben Vorlich by the waters of Loch Sloy. To the west, a high bealach separates the long rough slopes of Ben Vane from Beinn Ime and involves a fair descent and re-ascent to reach the summit slopes of Ime, a hill that is more often climbed together with The Cobbler in the south, or from Butterbridge in the west. This fact becomes clear as you struggle up Beinn Ime from that high bealach. The obvious, badly eroded footpath which leads you up Ben Vane vanishes and all that is left is a fairly sketchy path up the higher slopes towards Ime's summit.

It's interesting that the Scottish Rights of Way Society have proposed that the major routes up the popular hills should be made rights of way, in a bid to encourage walkers to stick with one line – the honeypot concept which means only one route becomes badly eroded. It's a proposal I disagree with, as my experience shows that hills with a number of choices of ascent usually have least damage done to them. Spreading the load works.

It's a straightforward grassy descent to the bealach that separates Beinn Ime from The Cobbler and Beinn Narnain and it's always good to lie among the rocks for a while and just soak it in before tackling the 300m climb to Beinn Narnain, the last summit of the day, with its wonderful views down Loch Long to the Kyles of Bute and across to the jagged peaks of Arran.

To Crianlarich

Ben Vorlich 943

Coire na Baintighearna

Allt Ardvorlich

Loch Sloy

Route B

Coire nan Each

Beinn Dubh 773

Ben Vane 915

Lag Uaine

Route A

Beinn Chorranach 885

Coiregrogain

Inveruglas

A82

Loch Lomond

Inveruglas Water

Allt Coiregrogain

Beinn Ime 1011

A Chrois 849

Beinn Luibhean 857

Creag Tharsuinn

Bealach a' Mhaim

Beinn Narnain 926

Allt Sugach

To Inveraray

To Tarbet

Glen Loin

The Cobbler (Ben Arthur) 881

Narnain Boulders

Allt a' Bhalachain

Succoth

To Tarbet

Glen Croe

A83

Loch Long

Arrochar

N

0        1 mile
0        1 kilometre

*The Arrochar Alps from Ben Vorlich*

## Ben Vorlich (224), 943m/3094ft

**Route Summary:** Either climb the steep slopes NE of the Loch Sloy dam to the summit ridge (Route B) or by Coire Creagach to the N. Follow the NW side of the stream to the upper corrie where the main ridge will be reached NNE of the summit

**Map:** OS Sheets 56 and 50: GR295124

**Access Point:** Inveruglas to Loch Sloy Dam

**Distance:** 10km, 900m ascent

**Approx Time:** 4-6 hours

**Translation:** hill of the bay

**Pronunciation:** as spelt

Ben Vorlich is a solitary hill which boasts no single line of ascent. Some folk climb Vorlich from Inveruglas, others by its big eastern corrie, while many climb it from the road leading to Loch Sloy. However you climb it, it offers a long, hard pull up steep slopes and it's always good to reach the long ridge, even though, as you'll quickly discover, this is fairly undulating in itself. It's not until you reach the final stretch to the summit that you'll come across any real erosion and I can safely say that Ben Vorlich is one of the least damaged hills I have walked on. I'm sure this is simply because there is no single route of ascent, the load has been well and truly spread, to the benefit of the hill. Sorry, Scottish Rights of Way Society, I think your proposals to make the major routes rights of way are wrong and will eventually restrict walkers to linear routes.

## Beinn Bhuidhe (212), 948m/3110ft

This is an isolated mountain which rises near the head of Loch Fyne between Glen Fyne and Glen Shira. The hill itself is a long triple-topped ridge with its highest point roughly in the middle. Although you can't really get decent views of it from the south, it does appear as a fairly steep-sided cone from Ben Oss in the north-east. As vehicles are only allowed up the Glen Fyne road on official business (push bikes are allowed), park in the loop road between the A83 and the old Fyne bridge and continue on foot to Inverchorachan, then take to the slopes due west, climbing up a fairly steep and wooded gully above the house.

Follow the south bank of the stream to its source, then bear north west up steep grass and bracken into the upper corrie. Climb one of the gullies to the ridge. The summit cone and trig point are about halfway along the ridge.

**Route Summary:** Park in the loop road between the A83 and the old Fyne bridge. Continue on foot, or bike, to Inverchorachan, then take to the slopes due W. Follow the S bank of the stream to its source then bear NW up steep grass and bracken into the upper corrie. Climb one of the gullies to the ridge. The summit cone is about halfway along the ridge

**Map:** OS Sheet 50: GR204187

**Access Point:** Glen Fyne, GR228160

**Distance:** 10km, 940m ascent

**Approx Time:** 4-6 hours

**Translation:** yellow hill

**Pronunciation:** byn voo-ee

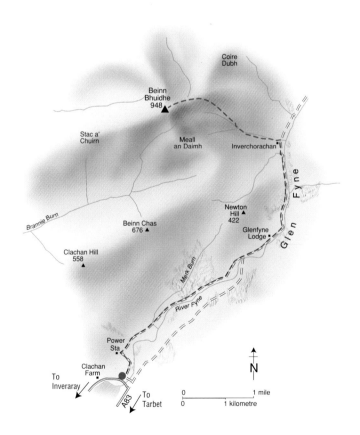

# THE CRIANLARICH HILLS

## The Munros:

### Beinn Chabhair    An Caisteal    Beinn a' Chroin
### Cruach Ardrain    Beinn Tulaichean    Ben More    Stob Binnein

The long pass of Glen Falloch runs from the head of Loch Lomond to Crianlarich, rising from the magnificently wooded lower glen to an increasingly wilder landscape characterised by windblown Scots pines. To the east of the road rise the lower slopes of a mountain range dominated by no less than seven Munros and fourteen tops, the highest group of hills in Britain south of Tayside. The best base is Crianlarich which has a Youth Hostel, a hotel and several bed and breakfast establishments.

## Beinn Chabhair (243), 933m/3061ft

Like An Caisteal and Beinn a' Chroin, Beinn Chabhair is best climbed from Glen Falloch by its long north-westerly ridge. It's a shy mountain, sitting well back from the road, and thankfully the lower approaches have not been spoiled by mass coniferisation, unlike the upper reaches of Glen Falloch.

The starting point is Beinglas Farm which can be avoided by following the West Highland Way signs around it. Behind the farm a slanting path climbs up through birch and hawthorn and eventually reaches a flatter stretch above the Ben Glas Falls. Follow the burn as far as the lochan where something of the rugged grandeur of Beinn Chabhair is first seen, a steep face made up of rocky outcrops and grass terraces.

Those of a more adventurous disposition will be happy to thread their way up this broken face to the summit, but most tend to head north-east to an obvious bealach on the north-west ridge. From there a path leads past a small cairn to the summit, perched precariously on top of its own little crag.

**Route Summary:** Climb steeply behind Beinglas Farm to above the falls of the Ben Glas Burn (Route A). Follow the burn to Lochan Beinn Chabhair then climb diagonally NE to the NW ridge. Follow ridge to summit.

**Map:** OS Sheets 50 and 56

**Access Point:** Beinglas Farm, GR319188

**Distance:** 13km, 869m ascent

**Approx Time:** 4-6 hours

**Translation:** possibly hill of the hawk

**Pronunciation:** byn chav-aar

## An Caisteal (144), 995m/3264ft
## Beinn a' Chroin (227), 940m/3084ft

Like Beinn Chabhair, these two craggy hills are made up of rocky outcrops above lower grassy slopes and their dual ascent offers a fine day's hill walking. An Caisteal can be attacked directly from Glen Falloch from where the prominent tor which gives the hill its name is easily identified. The best approach is from Derrydarroch Farm from where the hill can be climbed by either of the ridges which flank the corrie of the Allt Andoran. To make more of a circuit, cross the mouth of the corrie to the hill's north ridge where grassy rakes lead to a more scree-covered ridge known as Twistin' Hill above Sron Garbh. The rocky tor known as the castle, from where the hill gets its name, seems to bar further progress up this ridge but a path cuts its way across the top. If necessary, you can avoid the rather exposed route by passing the outcrop on its right. The bald pate of the summit is a little distance further on from where the SSE ridge drops down grassy slopes and then through rocky ground to a level col.

Beinn a' Chroin has two tops separated by a 60m drop. Its western top is the start of a short rocky ridge which leads to the higher, eastern top. To return to Glen Falloch go back to the col below An Caisteal and descend the hill's north-west ridge via Sron Garbh.

**Route Summary:** (Route B) From Derrydarroch cross the river by a bridge and up its W bank. Climb slopes of Sron Garbh and follow the ridge, Twistin' Hill, to An Caisteal. Descend SSE ridge to col and climb rocky NW end of Beinn a' Chroin's summit ridge. Continue along crest to summit

**Map:** OS Sheets 50 and 56

**Access Point:** Glen Falloch, GR368238

**Distance:** 14.4 km, 792m ascent

**Approx Time:** 4-6 hours

**Translation:** the castle; hill of danger

**Pronunciation:** aan kastail; byn a chroin

## Cruach Ardrain (84), 1046m/3432ft, Beinn Tulaichean (217), 946m/3104ft

I've lost count of the number of times I've driven down the hill into Tyndrum from Bridge of Orchy and looked east towards the Crianlarich hills with Cruach Ardrain reflecting the setting sun from the snow-filled Y-gully of its northern corrie. Its ridges make up a fine peak which stands proudly beside its bigger neighbours, Ben More and Stob Binnein, separated by the long rough ridge of Stob Garbh.

The ascent of the hills from Glen Falloch starts just south of Crianlarich where a bridge crosses the railway line and gives access to the dense forest which covers much of this side of upper Glen Falloch. A footpath goes through a clearing in the trees to reach a broken fence. A narrow gap offers a way up through the dense forest and eventually leads to the tree-line below Grey Height.

From here, a footpath climbs up over Grey Height and over Meall Dhamh from where a high col leads to the north-west ridge of Cruach Ardrain. Climb this steep ridge to a subsidiary top adorned by two small cairns and then on across a shallow col to the true summit.

Beinn Tulaichean can easily be reached from here – return past the twin cairns and descend in a SW direction to a grassy ridge. Turn south along the ridge to the summit.

Beinn Tulaichean can also be climbed from the south, from Inverlochlarig. This was the farm where Rob Roy spent his last years, dying here on 27 December 1734. Other than paying your last respects to the Macgregor, there isn't really a lot to recommend an ascent from this side. From the farm, long grassy slopes are climbed in a north-westwards direction to the ridge just south of the summit of Beinn Tulaichean. From here it's a straightforward walk to Cruach Ardrain.

## Ben More (15), 1174m/3852ft, Stob Binnein (17), 1165m/3822ft

These hills are the Castor and Pollux of the Scottish highlands, heavenly twins joined together by a high bealach. The highest peaks south of the Tay, they are clearly visible from mountain vantage points throughout the Southern and Central Highlands. Although Ben More is the higher of the two, there is little doubt that Stob Binnein is the more shapely, its long and elegant slopes rising from long, sweeping ridges to a tiny tabled summit.

Ben More's northern slopes sweep down virtually continuously from its summit all the way to Glen Dochart and I vividly recall as

*Stob Binnein (left) and Ben More (right) from the air, with Ben Laoigh and Ben Cruachan in the background*

a teenager sliding down almost all the way back to Benmore Farm. I think we descended from the summit in under an hour. Care is needed though, for a hanging corrie, immediately below the summit facing north-west, has a steep upper section which is liable to avalanche in snowy conditions – sadly it's been the site of several fatalities so avoid it if you can.

The normal route of ascent follows the Sron nam Forsairean ridge virtually all the way from Benmore Farm to the summit. It is a long and strenuous climb and it's a welcome descent from the summit down to the flat Bealach-eader-dha-Beinn. Stob Binnein is climbed from here by way of its north ridge.

An alternative route, which avoids the long pull up the Sron nam Forsairean, follows the Benmore Burn southwards. From the head-waters of the burn a diagonal line can be taken across the slopes to reach the spur of Creagan Liatha. Climb to the top of this spur and follow the ridge to Stob Coire an Lochain. Follow the south-south-east ridge of Stob Binnein to the summit, and then climb Ben More by way of the Bealach-eader-dha-Beinn.

**Approx Time:** 6-8 hours

**Translation:** big hill; hill of the anvil

**Pronunciation:** byn moar; stop binyan

# THE TYNDRUM HILLS

## The Munros:

## Beinn Laoigh    Beinn a' Chleibh    Ben Oss    Beinn Dubhchraig

These hills can be reached from Glen Falloch but a better approach is by the River Cononish just south of Tyndrum. From this approach Beinn Laoigh (Ben Lui) in particular is seen to best advantage, probably the most Alpine-looking mountain in the Southern Highlands. Its great NE corrie, Coire Gaothaich, holds snow until well into the spring. Unfortunately, extensive gold mining has hideously disfigured what was once a most scenic walk up to Cononish Farm.

## Beinn Laoigh (Ben Lui) (27), 1130m/3707ft,
## Beinn a' Chleibh (273), 916m/3005ft

I've often heard Beinn Laoigh, or Ben Lui, described as the 'Queen of Scottish Mountains', a sobriquet which describes the regal lines of this, one of the most beautiful mountains in the country. With this aspect of the mountain drawing you onwards, the approach down Glen Cononish is without doubt the most aesthetic. Eight kilometres from the Tyndrum/Crianlarich road the route climbs right up into the eastern corrie and then on to the north-east spur which leads to one of the two summits of the hill.

These two summits drop twin spurs which enclose a high round-bottomed corrie, 300 metres deep. At the back of this high corrie, a central gully splits the wall, a route which offers a classic snow climb in winter, often topped by an equally classic cornice. A word of warning – it's also a route which is frequently avalanched!

A shorter and less aesthetic route, which nevertheless appears to satisfy most Munro-baggers with little inclination towards rock scrambling or snow climbing, leaves a car park on the A85 in Glen Lochy (GR239278). Stepping stones lead across the river where a path follows the Eas Daimh through the conifers. After 500m or so cross the burn and follow the path to the stile in the fence which leads to the open hillside. From here it's an easy climb up to the broad north-north-west ridge which is followed to the summit of Beinn Laoigh.

From the summit cairn wide slopes lead down south-west to the col at the head of the Fionn Choirein from where another broad ridge leads to the summit of Beinn a'Chleibh.

*Ben Laoigh from just below the summit of Ben Oss*

**Route Summary:** Follow path (Route A) on the E side of the Eas Daimh through conifer forest to a stile in the fence which leads to open hillside. Climb NNW ridge of Ben Laoigh to summit. Descend SW to the bealach at the head of Fionn Choirein and follow flat ridge to the summit of Beinn a' Chleibh

**Map:** OS Sheet 50: GR251256

**Access Point:** Glen Lochay, GR239278

**Approx Time:** 4-7 hours

**Distance:** 11.2km, 1006m ascent

**Translation:** hill of the calf; hill of the chest

**Pronunciation:** byn loo-ee; byn a chlayv

*Ben Laoigh (left) and Ben Oss (right) from the air*

## Ben Oss (99), 1029m/3376ft, Beinn Dubhchraig (171), 978m/3209ft

**Route Summary:** Leave Dailrigh in Strathfillan (Route B) and follow rough road on S side of river to a bridge over the railway. Head W and cross the Allt Coire Dubhchraig. Follow path through woods to open hillside and continue SW up grassy corrie to the shoulder of Beinn Dubhchraig. Follow broad stony ridge to summit. From Dubhchraig follow ridge NW and W to Ben Oss

**Map:** OS Sheet 50

**Access Point:** Dailrigh, GR344290

**Distance:** 19.2km, 1006m ascent

**Approx Time:** 4-7 hours

**Translation:** loch outlet hill; black rock hill

**Pronunciation:** byn oss; byn doo-craig

Although overshadowed by the beauty of Beinn Laoigh, these two hills offer a high knobbly traverse with stunning views down the length of Glen Falloch to the Crianlarich hills and Loch Lomond. From the south Ben Oss appears as a fine pointed peak and Beinn Dubhchraig more rounded but presenting a craggy well broken face, but from the north-east, the usual approach, Oss presents steep slopes above Coire Buidhe while the summit of Beinn Dubhchraig sits over the wide and open Coire Dubhchraig above recent forestry plantations. Just below the conifers, as a form of consolation, ancient remnants of the pine woods of Caledon stand proudly, wind blown, twisted and gnarled. This wood, the Coile Coire Chuilc, fills the confluence of the River Cononish and the Allt Gleann Auchreoch.

Our route begins at Dailrigh, the King's Field in Glen Fillan, commemorating a battle between the MacDougalls of Lorn and the forces of Robert the Bruce in 1306. The route to Beinn Dubhchraig follows the track across the railway line then a path into the pines of the old

*The Crianlarich Hills from Ben Oss (Ben More on the far left and Ben Chabhair on the far right)*

Caledonian Forest. Follow paths on the north-west side of the burn to the edge of the wood where a stile crosses a deer fence and continue south-west up the wide, grassy slopes of the corrie to reach the upper ridge of Beinn Dubhcraig just north-west of the summit, which is easily reached from here along a broad rocky ridge. From the summit return along this ridge and continue steeply westwards down to the col. From here the route follows a wide ridge over a knobbly summit and then onwards in a south-west direction to the true summit of Ben Oss. It is possible to descend immediately north into Glen Cononish but the ground is steep and broken in places. It's probably best to return over the knobbly summit and back on to Beinn Dubhcraig where the north ridge can be followed back down to the lower reaches of Glen Cononish, where the track returns to Dailrigh.

# THE CRIEFF AND LOCH EARN HILLS

## The Munros:

## Ben Vorlich    Stuc a' Chroin    Ben Chonzie

These three mountains lie just to the north of the Highland fault line which runs from the southern shores of Loch Lomond to Stonehaven just south of Aberdeen. As such they form something of a dividing line between the Central Highlands and lowland Scotland and needless to say, the best views are to the north and west. Ben Vorlich and Stuc a' Chroin, because of their proximity to the Central Belt, are very popular hills indeed and tend to suffer the ravages of sponsored walks and the like. Ben Chonzie is far less popular, having a reputation of being one of the dullest Munros in the land. Nevertheless, because of its position it can catch some bad weather and offer a challenging walk. In good summer weather it makes a delightful evening stroll.

The best bases are Callander, Comrie, St. Fillans or Lochearnhead, and there are camp sites at Callander, Crieff and Comrie. The nearest Youth Hostel is at Killin.

## Ben Vorlich (161), 985m/3232ft, Stuc a' Chroin (176), 975m/3199ft

Not to be confused with Ben Vorlich which frowns down on the head of Loch Lomond, this Perthshire Ben Vorlich nevertheless shares the same name origin. It comes from the Gaelic Mur-Bhalg, meaning sea-bay, and refers to small bays in the lochs which sit at their respective feet. Ardvorlich, at the beginning of this hill walk, is therefore Ard-Mhurlaig, the Promontory of the Sea-bay, and is the home of the Stewarts of Ardvorlich, an ancient family who have held these lands for some 400 years.

For many years a stone was kept in Ardvorlich House, the Clach Dhearg, or the Red Stone, which was believed to have miraculous properties. If you dipped it in a pail of water and moved it three times sun-wise around the pail, the water would then contain healing powers which could be used to treat sick cattle. So famous was this stone that it attracted people from all around the area, who came with their own buckets to carry home some of the miraculous water which had been swilled over the stone. It was said that the stone had been brought back to Ardvorlich House in the fourteenth century after a crusade.

Beyond the house, away up Glen Vorlich lie the high slopes of Ben Vorlich, at 985m. Take the private road from the east gate of Ardvorlich

**Route Summary:** Follow the track past Ardvorlich House on to the open hillside in Glen Vorlich. Follow the track to the foot of Coire Buidhe and then the SE side of the corrie to reach the NNE ridge of Ben Vorlich and the summit. Follow the line of fence posts down to the Bealach an Dubh Choirein and take the steep path which avoids the obvious steep, and loose buttress. From the cairn at the top of the buttress head S to summit of Stuc a' Chroin

**Map:** OS Sheet 51 and 57

**Distance:** 17km, 1200m ascent

**Approx Time:** 5-6 hours

**Access Point:** Ardvorlich, GR633232

**Translation:** hill of the bay; peak of danger

**Pronunciation:** byn vorlich; stook a kroin

*Ben Vorlich from above Balquhidder, rising behind the slopes of Meall nan Oighreag*

House on the south side of Loch Earn. There are few parking places so be careful where you leave your car so that you don't interfere with passing vehicles. As you enter through the gates of the estate follow the road south, past the farm, where a signpost points to the right. Cross a stone bridge, and find another sign, this time pointing to the left. The track now wanders up through Glen Vorlich, a lovely spot with a tree lined burn and good views opening up across Loch Earn towards the mighty Lawers hills.

About one-and-a-half kilometres further on a wooden bridge crosses the Allt a' Coire Buidhe. The real walking begins now, a stony footpath which heads right across the bare moorland and begins to climb onto the steeper and stonier north-north-east ridge of Ben Vorlich itself. Although well eroded, the path continues upwards to the 100m long summit ridge which is crowned by a small cairn. The OS trig point at its north-west end indicates the true summit.

Most walkers will want to add the ascent of Stuc a' Chroin, Vorlich's neighbouring Munro, to their day's climb. While the ascent of Stuc a' Chroin from Ben Vorlich is straightforward enough, it does involve some fairly loose scrambling from the adjoining Bealach an Dubh Choirein. The steeper ground can be avoided by ascending in a south-west direction from the Bealach, avoiding the obvious rocky buttress by traversing about 15m to the right (north-west) and following a steep path up through some broken rocks. The direct route up the north east buttress offers some fine scrambling for those used to such things, but is definitely not for the inexperienced.

At the top of the buttress you'll reach a small cairn and the summit of Stuc a' Chroin is only about 180m away along a line of fence posts.

To return to Ardvorlich (from Stuc a' Chroin), simply descend to the Bealach an Dubh Choirean and then traverse north-west across a grassy hillside to reach another bealach at the head of Coire Buidhe. Descend the east ridge of the corrie to regain the footpath in Glen Vorlich.

*Looking north from Ben Chonzie towards Schiehallion and the Grampian mountains*

## Ben Chonzie (246), 931m/3054ft

Can this hill lay claim to be the dullest Munro in the land? A friend of mine, Jim Crumley, once wrote that there is no such thing as a dull hill, only dull people and on three ascents of Ben Chonzie, twice on skis, I've found it anything but dull, but that was largely due to some wild weather rather than the hill itself.

It's an isolated lump, the high point in a huge area of hill and moorland between Strath Earn and Loch Tay and probably because of that position it catches a lot of snow. This big mound of a hill lacks any immediate notable feature other than its long and broad ridge and its eastern corrie.

From Invergeldie in Glen Lednock take the right of way up the west side of the burn. At a track junction just beyond a gate take the right hand track and follow it across the burn and ENE up the hillside then NE to the broad summit ridge. Follow the fence NW then NE to the summit.

**Route Summary:** Take the right of way up the W side of the burn. At a track junction take the right hand track, cross the burn and head ENE up the hillside then NE to broad summit ridge. In bad weather you can follow the line of fence NW then NE to the summit

**Map:** OS Sheets 51 and 52

**Access Point:** Invergeldie, GR743272

**Distance:** 12.8km, 67m ascent

**Approx Time:** 3-5 hours

**Translation:** possibly hill of moss

**Pronunciation:** byn ee hoan; locally honzee

# RANNOCH AND GLEN LYON

## The Munros:

## Schiehallion  Carn Gorm  Meall Garbh  Carn Mairg
## Creag Mhor  Stuchd an Lochain  Meall Buidhe

With the exception of Schiehallion, these hills tend to be flat topped, heather clad and featureless, although Stuchd an Lochain's Lochan nan Cat is rather fine. Having said that, the western end of Loch an Daimh, below the steep slopes of the Corbett Sron a' Choire Chnapanich, has a quality of wilderness unequalled in the Southern Highlands. For that reason I would recommend a long link around the head of the loch when climbing Stuchd an Lochain and Meall Buidhe.

Schiehallion, a superb cone when seen from Rannoch-side, has been tamed by a dreadfully eroded path up its easiest route and perhaps walkers should consider other ways of ascent. My first visit to the hill was on a multi-day Trans-Scotland walk from Oban to Montrose and we climbed Schiehallion immediately after traversing the Carn Mairg hills. On another occasion I climbed it from Tempar, north west of the mountain. Both of these alternative routes were far preferable to the trudge up from Braes of Foss.

Aberfeldy makes a good base for this group, although Fortingall, reputedly the birthplace of Pontius Pilate, is closer to the hills. Local legend claims that the Roman Governer was born in Dun Geal, an old fort not far from the village where Pilate's father was on a mission of peace between Ceasar Augustus and Metallanus, King of Scotland. There is a Youth Hostel in Killin.

**Route Summary:** The 'trade route' follows the track W from the car park at Braes of Foss (Route A). This is one of the most eroded footpaths in the Highlands although higher up things improve where the ground becomes stony. Continue on E ridge to the summit.

Alternatively, start at Tempar and follow the E side of the Tempar Burn which leads to a bothy. From there climb the increasingly rocky W slopes to the summit

**Map:** OS Sheet 51: GR714548

**Access Point:** Braes of Foss, GR750559 or Tempar, GR691575

**Distance:** 8 km, 753m ascent

## Schiehallion (57), 1083m/3553ft

Walking this hill with Hamish Brown a few years ago he commented that he wished people would begin to act more like goats than sheep. He was criticising the fact that everyone tended to climb hills by the same route, rather than discover their own way to the summits. In this case the problem is exacerbated by the provision of a large car park at Braes of Foss which positively encourages walkers to take the same route, in this case causing disastrous erosion of the footpath.

Let me offer two alternative and interesting routes. Leave Braes of Foss and follow the track southwards into Gleann Mor. From the end of the track cross the slopes to the riverside and explore the length of the glen (there are numerous shielings and with some searching you can find some old cup-and-saucer ring markings). From the upper glen follow the burn in a north-west direction to

32

the building at the end of the Tempar track. Climb Schiehallion by its western slopes.

The other, simpler, route follows the Tempar Burn from the Braes of Foss/Kinloch Rannoch road up towards the bothy at GR699546. Leave the track just north of the bothy and climb the west slopes of the hill, slopes which become increasingly rocky as you ascend.

**Approx Time:** 3-5 hours

**Translation:** Fairy Hill of the Caledonians

**Pronunciation:** shee-haal-yan

## Carn Gorm (100), 1028m/3373ft, Meall Garbh (182), 968m/3176ft, Carn Mairg (88), 1041m/3415ft, Creag Mhor (167), 981m/3218ft

As I mentioned, my first traverse of these hills was part of a Trans-Scotland walk from Oban to Montrose and my abiding memory was of a series of high plateau-like hills with little to commend them. Return visits, especially on skis, have changed my opinion.

From the top of the forest steep moorland and grassy slopes lead to Carn Gorm and the beginning of a long, broad and easy ridge walk to An Sgorr (which can be avoided by a traverse across its north-west slopes) and the flattish summit of Meall Garbh. The north-west top is the highest. A long line of fencing now leads past a tiny lochan to a wide bealach before the slopes begin to rise towards Meall a' Bharr at 1004m. The ridge now descends and narrows considerably for its ascent of Carn Mairg and its great cairn. The slopes north-east of Carn Mairg lead down into Gleann Mor and form a front to an unusual view of Schiehallion: no fine conical shape from this angle, but a long whalebacked

**Route Summary:** (Route B) Follow the Invervar Burn to the top of the forest and follow steep grassy slopes W then N to the summit of Carn Gorm. Follow broad ridge NNE to An Sgor and the summit of Meall Garbh. Follow the march fence to Meall a' Bharr then E and SE to Carn Mairg. Follow ridge east of summit to Meall Liath then S on a wide grassy ridge around the head of Gleann Muillin to Creag Mhor

**Map:** OS Sheet 51: GR635501,

*From Creag Mhor summit above Glen Lyon, looking east across Strath Tay*

GR646517, GR684513, GR695496

**Access Point:** Invervar, GR666483

**Distance:** 17.6km, 1387m ascent

**Approx Time:** 6-8 hours

**Translation:** blue hill; rough hill; hill of sorrow or boundary hill; big rock

**Pronunciation:** kaarn gor-om; myowl gaarv; kaarn mairg; crayk vore

**Route Summary:** From the dam climb the steep grassy hillside S to reach the ridge above Coire Ban. Follow fence posts W to Creag an Fheadain, then SSW to Sron Chona Choirein then W and NW to summit of Stuchd an Lochain. Continue W to Meall an Odhar, drop down its SW slopes to a wide bealach and climb the S slopes of the Corbett, Sron a' Choire Chnapanich. From the summit head N for a short distance and descend the very steep NW slopes to the Feith Thalain. From the W end of Loch an

ridge rising to its western summit.

The route from Carn Mairg to Meall Liath is fairly obvious but you can avoid the latter top by turning south down grassy slopes from the bealach. These slopes lead to a wide col, a deer-infested place in summer, then another broad ridge to the summit of Creag Mhor. The summit is the rock-capped north-east top. Finally, descend due west to the grassy ridge on the south side of the Allt Coire Chearcaill and follow this ridge back to the footpath above Invervar.

## Stuchd an Lochain (194), 960m/3150ft, Meall Buidhe (244), 932m/3058ft

Most walkers combine these two hills by climbing Stuchd an Lochain, returning to their starting point by the Loch an Daimh dam, climbing Meall Buidhe and returning by the same route. How boring! A circuit of Loch an Daimh starting and finishing at the dam makes a superb circular walk and adds an excellent Corbett, Sron a' Choire Chnapanich, 837m (2746ft), to the itinerary. In addition, the head of Loch an Daimh is a wonderful spot, splendidly remote.

Stuchd an Lochain can also be climbed from Cashlie at the western end of the Stronuich Reservoir in Glen Lyon via the Allt Cashlie which leads to the plateau between Sron Chona Choirein and the summit, but this route of ascent lacks the character of the north side of the hill.

Better to start from the Loch an Daimh dam, where a faint path climbs grassy slopes southwards to reach the ridge above Coire Ban. A line of fence posts can be followed westwards to Creag an Fheadain from where a descent into a bealach is followed by an easy climb to Sron Chona Choirein. A broad mossy ridge now leads round the cliffs above Lochan nan Cat to the summit. (It seems that in 1590, a local laird, Mad Colin Campbell of Meggernie, took a perverse delight in climbing the hill and chasing a herd of goats over the edge into Lochan nan Cat. Apparently the shepherd only just escaped a similar fate!)

From Stuchd an Lochain a descent down a broad ridge leads to a col then an easy climb to Meall an Odhar whose south-west ridge leads down to a rather wet and boggy bealach. From here climb almost due north to the Corbett of Sron a Choire Chnapanich, the Nose of the Lumpy Corrie!

Steep slopes drop down to the head of Loch an Daimh, a place of great atmosphere which I would never have associated with these southern hills. It's a spot which feels as remote as any, hemmed in on three sides by high, steep hills, with the long slim trench of Loch an Daimh creating a long funnel for the wind.

Steep slopes lead to Meall Cruinn and a long undulating tramp over high moorland leads to our other Munro, Meall Buidhe. From here follow the rim of the Glas Choire to just before Meall a' Phuill before dropping southwards to pick up the broad ridge of Druim Chaluim and the return to the dam.

Daimh climb steeply to Meall Cruinn and follow the rolling moorland in a rough NE direction to Meall Buidhe. Descend back to the dam via Meall a' Phuill and the Druim Chaluim

**Map:** OS Sheet 51: GR483448 and GR498499

**Access Point:** Loch an Daimh, GR510436

**Distance:** 20km, 1067m ascent

**Approx Time:** 6-8 hours

**Translation:** peak of the small loch; yellow hill

**Pronunciation:** stoochk an lochan; myowl boo-ee

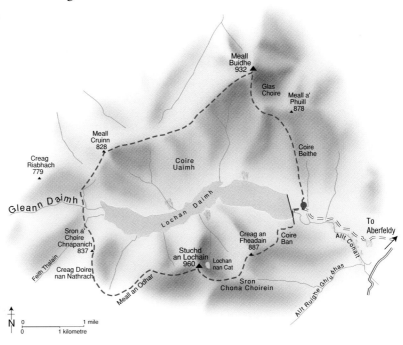

# THE LAWERS GROUP

## The Munros:

Meall Corranaich     Meall a' Choire Leith     Meall Greigh
Meall Garbh     Ben Lawers     Beinn Ghlas     Meall nan Tarmachan

This is one of the most popular mountain walking areas in Scotland, owing to the proximity of the Central Belt and the fact that there is easy access to the hills from the National Trust for Scotland car park on the Lochan na Lairige road. Because of the rich lime-loving calcareous soil of this area, caused by the very friable schist, Arctic-Alpine plants grow here in profusion and the whole area is a National Nature Reserve. Lawers is the highest point in a long and easy winding ridge which aids the walker, while the Tarmachan ridge, particularly in winter conditions, offers a traverse of great character.

A complete traverse of the Lawers massif is a long and arduous expedition (25km, 2500m ascent), but is well worth while, especially if you can arrange for a car to be left at the NTS car park to return you to your starting point on Loch Tayside. Most walkers, though, are content to tackle these hills in two, or even three groupings.

Killin is undoubtedly the best base for these hills.

*Ben Lawers from the east*

## Meall Corranaich (65), 1069m/3507ft, Meall a' Choire Leith (257), 926m/3038ft

I have to confess that these are not my favourite hills – I've always felt that Loch Tay is not the most scenic of Scottish lochs and the views south extend over some of the most featureless areas in the Highlands. Add to that a grossly eroded trail from the National Trust for Scotland car park on the Lochan na Lairige road. Winter is probably the best time for these over-visited hills and they are ideal Munros for touring on skis; in fact some of the earliest downhill ski-ing in Scotland was enjoyed here.

In an attempt to avoid the duckboarding and erosion of the NTS footpath, start this walk just north of the Lochan na Lairige near the prominent cairn at the end in the road. Leave the road and take to the rough hillside, crossing peat hags and boggy sections to reach the upper Allt Gleann Da-Eig. Follow the stream's shallow corrie south-east and climb the slopes above its source to reach the narrow south-west ridge of Meall Corranaich. Follow the ridge north-north-east to the summit and then beyond, down a broad grassy ridge for a kilometre or so to where the ridge bifurcates to form two ridges enclosing the high Coire Gorm. Follow the right-hand ridge, the north one, passing close to the edge of the steep Coire Liath. Beyond the corrie lip the ridge narrows to a col and then broadens to form the flattish summit of Meall a' Choire Leith.

To return to your starting point descend the south-west slopes of Meall a' Choire Leith, cross the stream in Coire Gorm and the Allt Gleann Da-Eig, cross open, peat-hag ridden ground and pass through the shallow col immediately south-east of Meall nan Eun. From there it's a short drop to your starting point.

**Route Summary:** Leave road just N of Lochan (Route A) and cross rough moorland SE over peat hags. Reach the Allt Gleann Da-Eig and follow it uphill to SW ridge of Meall Corranaich. Leave the summit and head N down the easy angled ridge. Keep to the NNE ridge, drop to a col then follow ridge on the flat topped summit plateau of Meall a' Choire Leith

**Map:** OS Sheet 51: GR616410, GR612439

**Access Point:** Summit of Lochan na Lairige Road

**Distance:** 12.8km, 716m ascent

**Approx Time:** 4-6 hours

**Translation:** notched hill or hill of lamenting; hill of the grey corrie

**Pronunciation:** myowl kora-neech; myowl kora lay

## Meall Greigh (134), 1001m/3284ft, Meall Garbh (35), 1118m/3668ft, Ben Lawers (9), 1214m/3983ft, Beinn Ghlas (45), 1103m/3619ft

**Route Summary:** From Machuim Farm follow track E of the Lawers Burn (Route B) and climb due N to Meall Greigh on easy grassy slopes. Follow W ridge to Meall Garbh. Follow ridge around the head of Coire nan Cat over the subsidiary tops of An Stuc and Creag an Fhithich to steep slopes which lead to Ben Lawers. From summit follow E ridge down to Beinn Ghlas then obvious footpath which leads SW to the National Trust for Scotland centre. Better still take the S ridge of Beinn Ghlas down to the public road just E of the Edramucky Burn, avoiding the NTS car park. Follow public road back to A827 at Erdamucky

**Map:** OS Sheet 51: GR674438, GR644437, GR636414, GR626404

**Access Point:** Lawers on A827

**Distance:** 19.2km, 1753m ascent

**Approx Time:** 7-10 hours

**Translation:** hill of the horse studs; rough hill; possibly loud hill or hoofed hill; green/grey hill

**Pronunciation:** myowl gray; myowl garv; ben lors; ben glas

You can tackle these hills without going near the dreadful Visitor Centre car park, but the easiest method is to leave a car there and take another to Machuim Farm near the tiny hamlet of Lawers. It is possible to climb Meall Greigh, Meall Garbh and Ben Lawers from Machuim Farm, returning there by the north-west ridge and the Lawers Burn, but that route, of course, leaves Beinn Ghlas in limbo to be completed on another day.

From the farm the Lawers Burn offers a long and curving route all the way to Lochan nan Cat below the beetling crags of Lawers's east face. Follow the path beside the burn for about two kilometres, then leave it and climb north-eastwards to reach the broad south ridge of Meall Greigh; follow this to the summit. As you tramp over pretty featureless terrain westwards enjoy the views of Ben Lawers rising above its archetypal hanging corrie and lochan and you can follow the skyline that you will shortly be walking. Continue up the grassy shoulder of Meall Garbh, turning on to the north-east ridge which then narrows as you approach the summit and the small cairn. Descend to the col below An Stuc, the next top on the round and climb very steep grassy slopes to the small table of a summit. These slopes have been known to cause problems in winter conditions when great icy sheets form very quickly indeed. It's then a place for crampons.

A fairly straightforward ridge walk takes you to Ben Lawers, following the lip of the crags which line the huge Coire nan Cat below. An obvious footpath runs its merry way down to Beinn Ghlas – you're now in tourist territory but you can escape from it by descending the south ridge of Beinn Ghlas rather than follow the erosion all the way to the Visitor Centre. This ridge leads down to some rough moorland just north of the Lochan na Lairige road which can then be followed back down to the A827. It's slightly longer, and certainly rougher than the tourist route, but maybe I'm just being paranoid!

## Meall nan Tarmachan (87), 1043m/3422ft

**Route Summary:** Leave the bridge, cross the rough moorland and pick up the S ridge of Meall nan Tarmachan (Route C). Climb easy grass slopes to a prominent knoll. Turn NW and

I wouldn't swap Meall nan Tarmachan for all the Ben Lawers in the world. Although virtually neighbours there is a world of a difference between the overly popular Lawers and the entertaining Tarmachans,

*Ben Lawers across Lochan nan Cat*

the latter being rough and rocky, a wonderful tonic after the smooth grassy slopes of the Lawers massif. As if that's not enough the Tarmachans represent a long switchback of a ridge which is at times chronically tortuous, winding its way over rocky bluffs, rock-covered hollows and often high above steep cliffs, the like of which you won't find in all Breadalbane.

Another bonus is that this walk starts at about 500m above sea level, at a point just north of the NTS Visitor Centre where a bridge crosses the Allt a' Mhoirneas. From here make your way westwards over the rising moorland to reach the south ridge of Meall nan Tarmachan. The going is fairly difficult here over peat hags and tussocky grass but once you reach the ridge life becomes more bearable. Follow the ridge northwards over its prominent knoll and follow a distinct grassy rake up, below and then through the crags to reach the Tarmachan ridge itself just slightly north of the summit of Meall nan Tarmachan. Climb to the summit and then enjoy this tortuously winding ridge as it crosses above the cliffs of Cam Chreag, over Meall Garbh, Beinn nan Eachan and finally Creag na Caillich. This latter top sits above a long line of steep cliffs and to reach the Coire Fionn Lairige and the return to the starting point you'll have to backtrack a few hundred metres to the col between Caillich and Beinn nan Eachan. From here you can safely drop down into the corrie and pick up a Land Rover track which takes you all the way back to the start.

climb various raked terraces to the ridge just N of the summit of Meall nan Tarmachan. Follow the ridge SW

**Map:** OS Sheet 51: GR585390

**Access Point:** Bridge over Allt a' Mhoirneas, GR603382

**Distance:** 12.8km, 744m ascent

**Approx Time:** 4-6 hours

**Translation:** hill of the ptarmigan

**Pronunciation:** myowl nan tar-mach-an

# THE MAMLORN HILLS

## The Munros:

## Meall Ghaordie    Beinn Heasgarnich    Creag Mhor
## Ben Challum    Sgiath Chuil    Meall Glas

In many ways these hills which surround the lonely western extremity of Glen Lochay are undistinguished mountains and tend to be visited only by the enthusiast. Lacking any really distinctive feature, they nevertheless offer a degree of wildness and remoteness lacking in the less subtle delights of Ben Lawers, Beinn Laoigh or Ben More. All the hills are accessible from Glen Lochay but Ben Challum is more usually climbed by the less scenic route from Strath Fillan. Likewise, Meall Glas and Sgiath Chuil can be climbed from the south. Killin makes a convenient base for ascents of all the hills.

**Route Summary:** From near the farm of Tullich climb easy slopes in a N then NW direction. Pass some small rock outcrops and reach the summit soon afterwards. The OS trig point stands inside a circular cairn

**Map:** OS Sheet 51: GR514397

**Access Point:** Tullich in Glen Lochay, GR516369

**Distance:** 6.4km, 823m ascent

**Approx Time:** 3-5 hours

**Translation:** Possibly rounded hill of the shoulder, arm, hand

**Pronunciation:** myowl girday

## Meall Ghaordie (90), 1039m/3409ft

In the whole list of Munros there are a number of hills which are so isolated from other Munros that, by necessity, they have to be climbed on their own. A handful of them fall into the less interesting category and Meall Ghaordie is one of them. The hill is basically a blunt nose which lifts itself above the rough moorland of the long, broad ridge which separates Glen Lochay from Glen Lyon. Normally climbed via long grassy slopes from Glen Lochay, the route from the north, from Glen Lyon, is marginally more attractive, thanks to a couple of rocky spurs, Creag an Tulabhain and Creag Laoghain. A straightforward route follows the Allt Laoghain high into its corrie from where grassy slopes lead to the summit cairn.

The Glen Lochay ascent is even more simple and

*Ben Challum from its southern top*

straightforward. A long trudge of some 820m from Tullich follows grassy slopes, the monotony of which is only broken by some rocky outcrops near the summit ridge, but Meall Ghaordie can be made more bearable by climbing it in the morning, driving round to the Lochan na Lairige and climbing the Tarmachan ridge in the after-noon/evening. That gives a full summer's day with the anticipation of the delightful Tarmachan ridge to keep you going on Ghaordie's interminable slopes.

## Beinn Heasgarnich (61), 1076m/3530ft, Creag Mhor (80), 1048m/3438ft, Ben Challum (103), 1025m/3363ft

I first climbed these three Munros on a very wet and misty day and found them challenging – subsequent ascents have shown them to be fairly remote hills of tremendous character – big, steep and muscle-bound. The highest hills in the old hunting Forest of Mamlorn, they dominate the head of Glen Lochay. The three hills can be climbed together in one outing in a rather long day of 22km with some 1800m of climbing, although many walkers climb Ben Challum by itself, from St Fillans Chapel in the south. That gives a rather straightforward outing of 11km with 914m of ascent.

Beinn Heasgarnich, despite its wonderful name (Hamish Brown translates it as the 'peak of the roaring waterfall of the horses'. Peter Drummond, in his excellent *Scottish Hill and Mountain Names*,

**Route Summary:** Leave the cottage of Badour (Route A, p.43) and follow grassy slopes in a NW direction making for the top of Stob an Fhir-bhogha. A broad ridge leads N to the summit hump of Beinn Heasgarnich. Return to Stob an Fhir-bhogha and take the SW ridge to the boggy Bealach na Baintighearna. Find the lochan on the bealach which gives a good line for the steep but direct ascent to the top of Creag Mhor. Follow the rim of Coire-cheathaich to Stob nan Clach, descend into the Lairig Mhic Bhaidein, cross the spur of Cam Chreag and climb Challum's NW ridge to the summit

*Meall Glas (right) and Beinn Cheathaich above Glen Lochay*

**Map:** OS Sheets 50 and 51: GR413383, GR390361 and GR387323

**Access Point:** Badour in Glen Lochay, GR431351

**Distance:** 23km, 1800m ascent.

**Approx Time:** 7-10 hours

**Translation:** peak of the roaring waterfall of the horses; big rock; Callum's peak

**Pronunciation:** byn heskarneech; craig vore; byn cha-lam

suggests the more prosaic 'peaceful or sheltering mountain, from seasgairneach'. I prefer Hamish's translation!) is basically a great grassy whaleback and is reached from Badour, at the end of the public road in Glen Lochay, via the subsidiary top of Stob an Fhir-bhogha.

The descent to the Bealach na Baintighearna returns over Stob an Fhir-bhoga and follows its south-west ridge down into the boggy depths between the two Munros. Look out for a tiny lochan which can be used to line up the route of ascent, a steep one, all the way to the summit of Creag Mhor.

This Munro is more shapely than Heasgarnich, and has steeper slopes. It forms the blunt apex of three distinct ridges. Its minor top, Stob nan Clach, is easily reached by following the rim of Coire-cheathaich from where you should drop down steep southerly slopes to reach the Lairig Mhic Bhaidein. Ben Challum can be climbed from here by crossing the south-east spur of Cam Chreag and negotiating the steep slopes of Challum's north-west ridge. Return to Glen Lochay by the east-north-east ridge.

## Sgiath Chuil (238), 935m/3067ft, Meall Glas (193), 960m/3150ft

While these hills can be climbed from Glen Dochart in the south, via Auchessan at the east end of Loch Iubhair and the waters of the Allt Riobain, the route from Glen Lochay is marginally more interesting.

Both hills are unexceptional but do offer some pretty wide views, particularly of Ben More and Stob Binnein in the south and near neighbours Creag Mhor and Beinn Heasgarnich in the north. The best route from Glen Lochay starts at Lubchurrin and climbs onto the north ridge of Meall a' Churain. A broad and fairly level ridge now leads to the summit rise of Sgiath Chuil, a fairly undistinguished top, although there is a hint of promise in some rocky outcrops to the south and west. The promise is shortlived, however, as we have to retrace our steps almost all the way back to Meall a' Churain. To the west of this ridge steep, stony slopes drop a good 300m to the bealach from where easier slopes climb to the rocky summit of Beinn Cheathaich. This is probably the best part of the walk as the ridge begins to form a gentle curve around the head of Coire Cheathaich. Pass a small cairned top and then follow the broad ridge which rises gently to the cairn of Meall Glas. The north-west ridge provides an obvious return to Glen Lochay although you could return to Meall a' Churain and follow its north-east ridge for a more direct descent back to Lubchurrin.

**Route Summary:** Follow the stream S of Lubchurrin cottage (Route B). Keep E of the stream and follow the broad ridge which leads to Meall a' Churain. Follow the obvious ridge to the summit of Sgiath Chuil. Return almost to Meall a' Churain, and descend the steep, stony slopes W 500m to the bealach. Continue W up slopes to the summit of Beinn Cheathaich. Follow the ridge SW to a small cairned top then continue along a broad slightly curved ridge around the rim of Coire Cheathaich. A gentle rise leads to the summit of Meall Glas

**Map:** OS Sheets 51: GR463318, GR431322

**Access Point:** Lubchurrin in Glen Lochay, GR453357

**Distance:** 12.8km, 1158m ascent

**Approx Time:** 4-7 hours

**Translation:** back wing; grey-green hill

**Pronunciation:** skeea-chool; myowl glas

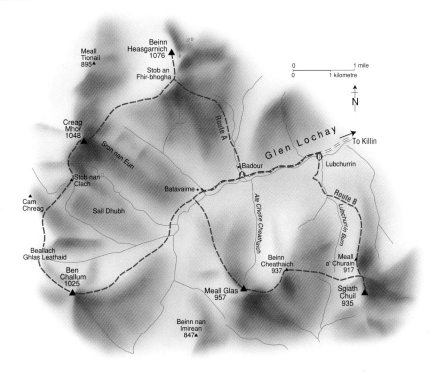

# THE BRIDGE OF ORCHY HILLS

## The Munros:

### Beinn Dorain    Beinn an Dothaidh    Beinn Mhanach
### Beinn Achaladair    Beinn a' Chreachain

Although geographically these hills are in the Southern Highlands, most walkers feel that they are entering the Highlands proper once they drive up the long winding pull out of Tyndrum towards Bridge of Orchy with the immaculate conical shape of Beinn Dorain filling the horizon. To add credence to that feeling, as soon as you set foot on these hills you become aware that they are generally rockier and steeper than their heather- and grass-clad cousins of the Southern Highlands. In effect Beinn Dorain, Beinn an Dothaidh, Beinn Achaladair and Beinn a' Chreachain form a gentle curve with Beinn Mhanach in their grasp, with Dothaidh, Achaladair and Chreachain showing broken and cliff-girt faces to the flat wilderness of the Rannoch Moor.

Bridge of Orchy, with its hotel and bunkhouse, is the obvious base, but there is a greater choice of accommodation in Tyndrum.

## Beinn Dorain (62), 1076m/3530ft,
## Beinn an Dothaidh (130), 1002m/3287ft

Forming part of the Great Wall of Rannoch, these two hills, along with Beinn Achaladair and Beinn a' Chreachain, form the boundary between the old Pictish Kingdom of Alba to the east and the Dalriadic Kingdom of the Scots in the west and while all four hills can be climbed in a long day of some 25km and 1800m of climbing they are probably more conveniently broken down into two days.

Bridge of Orchy railway station offers the best starting point, with plenty of car parking. You may, of course, wish to arrive by train, timing your descent to catch a later train home. From the underpass beneath the railway line a gate gives access to the open moorland. A fairly well-used path runs up alongside the Allt Coire an Dothaidh; higher up it becomes very faint indeed, although the bealach between the two hills is obvious enough in clear weather. The last few hundred metres to the bealach steepen considerably, although there are no real difficulties. From the cairn on the bealach another path weaves its southerly way up a fairly easy angled ridge, avoiding the worst of the outcrops and rocky slabs. This soon gives way to grassy slopes, with a big drop to your right and some wonderful views across to Glen Orchy. Pass a bouldery summit and a large cairn, which fools many into believing this is the summit, and continue a couple of hundred metres further south across a shallow dip in the ridge to the true summit. The views from here are a bit disappointing, although you can gaze down into the Auch Gleann below, a place long associated with Rob Roy and the Macgregors. They used to walk through from Glen Lyon to bury their dead here – a long way for a wake!

Retrace your steps to the bealach, taking care not to wander too far west into steep and rocky ground, and take a steeper north-north-east line up the grassy flank of Beinn an Dothaidh to the first of three summit tops. The middle one is the true summit. Take care as you descend to the bealach for steep crags, offering some excellent winter climbing, guard the hill on its western and northern flanks.

**Route Summary:** Leave the railway station (Route A) and make for the obvious bealach on the skyline between the two hills. Once there climb due S following an obvious path up an easy angled ridge then along the edge of a rocky escarpment. Continue up broad grassy slopes to a bouldery summit. The real summit of Beinn Dorain lies about 200m further S. Return to the col and climb a diagonal line NNE to the summit of Beinn an Dothaidh. The highest top is the central one

**Map:** OS Sheet 50: GR326378, GR332408

**Access Point:** Bridge of Orchy Station, GR301394

**Distance:** 12.8km, 1097m ascent

**Approx Time:** 5-7 hours

**Translation:** hill of the otter or small stream; hill of the scorching

**Pronunciation:** doa-ran; daw-ee

## Beinn Mhanach (205), 954m/3130ft

This hill is awkwardly placed in the grasp of its four near neighbours and it's difficult to connect it to ascents of the other hills. It's a double topped hill with the lower of the two tops, Beinn a' Chuirn (924m), closer to the hills of the Wall of Rannoch. On one memorable excursion a friend and I skied in from Bridge of Orchy over the bealach between Beinn Dorain and Beinn an Dothaidh. Deep snow gave us good running down to the very head of the Auch Gleann from where we cut round into the head of Gleann Cailliche. A long rising traverse took us to the shallow col between the two tops and from there it was an easy glide to the summit of Beinn Mhanach. The return was even better in first-class snow conditions and I recall a long, easy schuss from the pass between Gleann Cailliche and the Auch Gleann before we had to climb back to the Beinn an Dothaidh bealach and a descent in fast diminishing light back to Bridge of Orchy.

While it's possible to follow this route on foot, rather than on skis, a more interesting route follows the Auch Gleann past Ais-an t-Sidhean, once the home of the 18th-century Gaelic bard Duncan Ban MacIntyre. It's ironic that the ruin is now used as a sheep fank – MacIntyre hated the sheep which caused so many people to be cleared from their homes, a hatred which is explained in one of his poems, 'Oran Nam Balgairean', the Song of the Foxes:
'My blessing be upon the foxes, because that they hunt the sheep,
The sheep with the brockit faces that have made confusion in all the world.'

About a kilometre beyond the ruin leave the track and climb the steep grassy slopes to the summit of Beinn a' Chuirn. From there it's an easy stroll to the summit of the Munro.

## Beinn Achaladair (91), 1039m/3409ft,
## Beinn a' Chreachain (59), 1081m/3547ft

Achallader Farm has an interesting history. It was on this spot that Black Duncan of Cowal, Campbell of Glenorchy, built one of his seven castles – the remains can still be seen next to the farmhouse. And it was here that Robert Campbell of Glenlyon rested as he made his way north to Glen Coe before the infamous massacre.

Nowadays it's a working farm and the farmer has kindly built a large car park – it's good manners to ask permission to leave your car though!

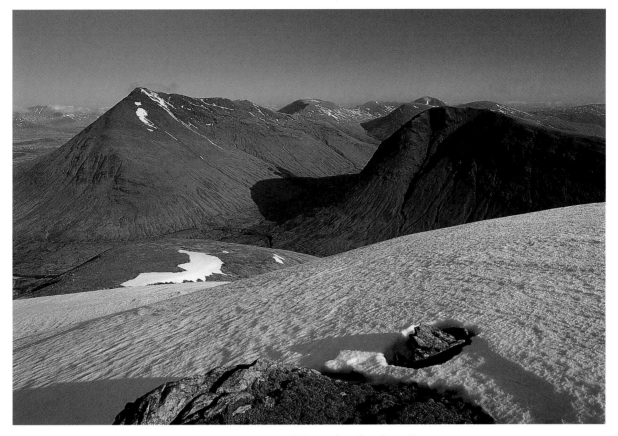

*Beinn Dorain and the Bridge of Orchy Hills*

These two hills show their best faces northwards over the great blanket of Rannoch Moor and you can enjoy the anticipation as you head south from the farm along a track which crosses the railway line and continues up into Coire Achaladair. You can either climb directly to the col at the head of the corrie, or climb south-east between the crags to reach the ridge between Achaladair and its south top.

From the airy perch which heralds the summit of Beinn Achaladair enjoy the high-level promenade eastwards to Meall Buidhe, with the flatness of Rannoch Moor on your left accentuating the height and spaciousness of your situation. A descent to a col above Loch a' Chreachain and then a steeper, stony climb leads to the summit of Beinn a' Chreachain.

Descend the north-east ridge of the hill, a narrow and interesting route, and when the gradient of the grassy slopes begins to lessen turn due north, cross the railway line, drop through the scattered birches and pick up the track which returns you to Achallader Farm.

slopes of Beinn a' Chreachain. Descend by the NE ridge and once the crags are avoided turn N to descend grassy slopes, over the railway, past scattered birches to the track back to the farm

**Map:** OS Sheet 50: GR345434, GR373441

**Access Point:** Achallader Farm car park

**Distance:** 4.4km, 1189m ascent

**Approx Time:** 6-8 hours

**Translation:** field of hard water; hill of the clamshell

**Pronunciation:** byn achalatu; byn a chrech-yin

# THE CRUACHAN HILLS

## The Munros:

## Ben Cruachan    Stob Diamh    Beinn a' Chochuill    Beinn Eunaich

A magnificent group of hills bounded by Loch Etive, Glen Strae and the Pass of Brander with Cruachan in particular offering an impression that it is almost surrounded by great sea lochs. Such is the hill's proximity to the sea that the coastal views, particularly those across to the Isle of Mull, are superb and that, taken together with spectacular rocky ridges, a series of fine peaks, and some high, imposing corries, make this one of the finest hills in the Southern Highlands. The most popular route, and one which probably offers the finest impression of the mountain, is the Dalmally Horseshoe which visits half a dozen tops over the 900m contour.

Partially dwarfed by the huge Cruachan massif, Beinn a' Chochuill and Beinn Eunaich are nevertheless fine hills in their own right. The two summits are the high points in a long 12km ridge which rises between Loch Etive and Glen Strae, a fine expedition in itself although most walkers will take the easier option of the route described. The best base is probably Dalmally which is on the Glasgow to Oban railway.

### Ben Cruachan (31), 1126m/3694ft, Stob Diamh (141), 998m/3274ft

My first visit to Cruachan was on a Trans-Scotland Oban to Montrose walk. Roger Smith and I had left Oban, walked up the length of Glen Lonan and tackled Cruachan in the afternoon. Fed-up and footsore from hard tarmac pounding we followed the tumbling Allt Cruiniche up steep slopes to a boggy bealach between the outlying Meall nan Each and Stob Dearg, Cruachan's western peak which is commonly referred to as the Taynuilt Peak. It was WP Ker, the poet, who, perhaps in a state of homesickness, once referred to the Nordend of Monte Rosa in the Swiss Alps as its Taynuilt Peak.

From Stob Dearg a steepish drop, a long level ridge and a short clamber over boulders took us to the actual summit where the views took our breath away. Below, the Cruachan Reservoir filled the contours of the corrie floor; Loch Awe, the longest loch in Scotland, stretched its long arm south west, and away beyond the island-speckled sea led to the hazy west. Eastwards the ridge opened out in a series of bumps and dips and peaks, more like a small range of mountains than one single hill. To the north the Blackmount and Glencoe tops appeared in a jumble, and further away, beyond the end of Cruachan,

**Route Summary:** Climb steeply up the path beside the Allt Cruachan (Route A) to the Cruachan dam access road. For an E-W round of Cruachan's tops follow the reservoir's E shore before climbing the grassy slopes to Stob Garbh. Continue N, descend slightly then climb to the summit of Stob Diamh. Follow the W ridge over the Drochaid Glas, (slightly N of the main line of the ridge) then along a narrower bouldery crest to the main summit of Cruachan. The ridge continues to a bealach and the 'Taynuilt Peak', Stob Dearg. Return to the bealach, re-ascend the main peak for some distance to avoid the slabby face of Coire a' Bhachaill, then head due S to Meall Cuanail and the grassy slopes back to the Cruachan dam

**Map:** OS Sheet 50: GR069304, GR095308

**Access Point:** Falls of Cruachan, GR078268

*Ben Cruachan from the air*

**Distance:** 14.4km, 1494m ascent

**Approx Time:** 5-8 hours

**Translation:** stacky hill, peak of the stag

**Pronunciation:** kroo-achan; stop dyv

Ben Laoigh rose, unfamiliar from this angle.

From the summit the ridge flows east and then slightly north-east over the uncairned top of Drochaid Glas, 1000m above sea level. This is a narrow and rocky top and in mist or cloud it would be all too easy to carry on down the steep and narrow north ridge into Glen Noe. The ridge to Stob Daimh in fact is best reached by dropping down about 20m short of Drochaid Glas, and on to the north-east ridge which descends, levels out and then climbs again to Cruachan's second Munro.

Pretty bushed by this time we descended Stob Daimh's north ridge into a high corrie where we camped for the night – Beinn a' Chochuill and Beinn Eunaich beckoned across Glen Noe for the morrow.

Most walkers tackle these two Munros via the Cruachan Horseshoe, a high-level circuit which follows the skyline above the Cruachan Reservoir which was created in 1965 as part of a huge hydro-electric scheme. This route begins at the power station beside the A85 and follows an access road up to the Cruachan Reservoir. Easy slopes lead to the Lairig Torran where you can reach the south ridge of Stob Garbh. Continue to this top then follow steeper slopes to Stob Daimh. From Cruachan's summit descend via Meall Cuanail back to the reservoir.

*Ben Cruachan and Beinn a' Chochuill from Beinn Eunaich*

## Beinn a' Chochuill (168), 980m/3215ft, Beinn Eunaich (152), 989m/3245ft

From the bridge over the Allt Mhoille on the B8077 a good track runs up the length of Glen Noe to a bealach which gives access to an obvious rib that leads to the summit of Beinn a' Chochuill. This is the Hill of the Hood and is easily linked to the next Munro by a long bow-shaped ridge which runs in a north-north-east direction. A huge snow cornice often hangs over the north side of the ridge until well into spring, which can make access directly on to the ridge between the two Munros, from the Glen Noe side, quite tricky. There are no difficulties on the ridge to Beinn Eunaich and from the summit descend due south down a broad and easy ridge over Stob Maol and back to the B8077 via Castles.

It is possible to climb Beinn a' Chochuill and Beinn Eunaich along with the Cruachan tops in one long, hard day, but it is difficult to find a good starting point which doesn't involve a long road walk from the finish point.

**Route Summary:** From the road follow the track which runs to the head of Glen Noe (Route B). After 3km bear right, continue up the SE rib of Beinn a' Chochuill to the summit. Walk along the ridge to its E end where it drops to a high bealach which is crossed to the shoulder of Beinn Eunaich. Broad grassy slopes lead back to the start over the subsidiary top of Stob Maol

**Map:** OS Sheet 50: GR110328, GR136328

**Access Point:** Drishaig, GR133283

**Distance:** 12.8km, 1189m ascent

**Approx Time:** 5-8 hours

**Translation:** hill of the hood; fowling hill

**Pronunciation:** byn a' cho-chil; byn ayneech

# THE GLEN ETIVE HILLS

## The Munros:

Ben Starav    Glas Bheinn Mhor    Beinn nan Aighenan
Stob Coir' an Albannaich    Meall nan Eun    Stob Ghabhar
Stob a' Choire Odhair    Creise    Meall a'Bhuiridh
Beinn Sgulaird    Beinn Fhionnlaidh

One of the most popular hillwalking areas of the Highlands, a plethora of fine peaks are joined by high and complex ridge systems to offer many multi-peak extravaganzas. These Etive hills are less craggy than their Glencoe neighbours, but nevertheless make up a number of fine high-level excursions. The traverse from Inveroran to Kingshouse, over Stob Ghabhar and Creise, has become known as something of a classic.

Sgulaird and Fhionlaidh are both big brutes of hills, and since both dip their toes in the waters of Loch Creran hillwalkers have to fully earn their height gain from sea level – Fhionnlaidh in particular is shy and retiring and lies well back from the starting point at Elleric.

## Ben Starav (60), 1078m/3537ft, Glas Bheinn Mhor (142), 997m/3271ft, Beinn nan Aighenan (192), 960m/3150ft

Starav and Glas Bheinn Mhor are impressive looking hills when viewed from Glen Etive, Starav looking particularly imposing as its huge north ridge sweeps majestically up from sea level all the way to the summit. There is some uncertainty as to the translation of the name – some suggest it means big and well built, others believe it could come from starabhan, meaning a rustling noise or even starra, a block of rock.

Big and well built it certainly is and probably the best starting point is at Coileitir where a bridge crosses some big deep pools in the river. A rough path crosses the moorland, then another bridge and once past a fine pine-clad gorge brings you nose to nose with the start of the north ridge. It is, undeniably, a brutal ascent, over 1060m of climbing, but be assured it improves as you gain height with rapidly expanding views and a narrowing, interesting ridge as you come closer to the summit.

A fine summit crest then billows out eastwards and down to a col where you can drop down to another, lower col to make the ascent of the outlying Beinn nan Aighenan. Return to the col and it's a

**Route Summary:** From Glen Coileitir Farm follow a path to a bridge on the Allt Mheuran and a path on its W bank (Route A). After 400m take to the N ridge of Ben Starav. Follow this ridge to the Trig pillar near the summit. The cairn sits a short distance to the SE. From the cairn follow the ridge SE and E to the top of Stob Coire Dheirg and then follow another twist in the ridge to where it turns ESE and drops to an obvious bealach W of Glas Bheinn Mhor. From here head SSE to the broad ridge leading to Beinn nan Aighenan. Retrace your steps to the bealach, turn E and cross the subsidiary top and finish on a rockier ridge to the summit. Return to Glen Etive by Glas Bheinn Mhor's E ridge, then N into the corrie at the head of the Allt Mheuran

**Map:** OS Sheet 50

**Access Point:** Glen Etive, GR136467

**Distance:** 20km, 1710m ascent

*The River Ba and the hills of Black Mount*

**Approx Time:** 5-8hours

**Translation:** unknown; big green/grey hill; hill of the hinds

**Pronunciation:** byn sta-rav; glas vyn voar; byn yan yanan

straightforward ascent of Glas Bheinn Mhor with a twisting descent down to the col beyond from where you can drop down to the head of the Allt Mheuran which is then followed back to Glen Etive by the path on its north-east side.

## Stob Coir' an Albannaich (86), 1044m/3425ft, Meall nan Eun (250), 928m/3045ft

**Route Summary:** Leave Glen Etive but before reaching Coileitir Farm head SE uphill through open woodland (Route B). At the broad NW shoulder of Stob Coir' an Albannaich, follow this ridge to the summit. The continuation to Meall nan Eun involves an awkward switchback ridge and crosses the subsidiary summit of Meall Tarsuinn. The route is obvious in clear conditions but requires careful navigation in bad visibility. From the summit of Meall nan Eun go NW across the plateau and descend in a NW direction towards the waters of the Allt Ceitlein

**Map:** OS Sheet 50

Beinn Chaorach, a westerly outlier of Stob Coir' an Albannaich, presents a rather blunt face to Glen Etive, its lower slopes birch clad while higher up it becomes rocky and craggy. Once you've crossed the River Etive you'll reach a junction in the track, and rather than follow it to Coileitir turn left instead until you reach a gate in the adjoining deer fence. Climb over and start the long, steep climb up to Beinn Chaorach.

Once the shoulder is reached things improve dramatically. Much of the walking is now across great boiler-plate slabs of granite which can ice up and become very slippery in winter! Pass the rim of the rather impressive Coire Glas and climb steadily south-eastwards, first of all on a broad grassy ridge which soon narrows appreciably as you approach the summit cairn of Stob Coir' an Albannaich. The Scotsman's corrie lies immediately below you and the next problem, a rather intricate one, is to reach the connecting col to Meall Tarsuinn and Meall nan Eun without tackling the steep crags of the corrie itself.

On a recent New Year trip some friends and I went down Glen Etive to climb Meall nan Eun and Stob Coir' an Albannaich and started the day in dullish, but not unpleasant weather. It wasn't until we broke from the cover of Albannaich's north ridge that the battering fury of the wind hit us.

*Stob Coir' an Albannaich*

From then it was a struggle against the gusts, avoiding the icy granite slabs and navigating through cloud and spindrift.

The usual exit from Stob Coir' an Albannaich's summit ridge was an awkward one and much of the ridge was corniced. The difficulty of the situation was exacerbated by the low visibility and it was only after some trial and error that we managed to locate a section of the ridge where we could descend. It was a long, hard and testing day which again emphasised the caution with which one should approach the Scottish hills in winter.

The best advice is to descend eastwards for almost a kilometre to where the ridge levels off for a short distance, about the 880m contour. A small cairn indicates the best point but of course won't be seen in snow and remember that much of this ridge cornices in winter conditions. At this point the ground is less steep and rocky and it is possible to descend steeply through rock outcrops in a north-north-east line to reach the lochan-dotted bealach.

The bump of Meall Tarsuinn has to be crossed, or bypassed on its south side and then a long pull up fairly gentle slopes leads to the great dome of Meall nan Eun. Typically, the cairn lies some distance off in the wrong direction – at the far point of the extensive summit plateau.

The descent from Meall nan Eun is an interesting one, down enormous granite pavements to the headwaters of the Allt Ceitlin where a footpath on the north bank of the river takes you back to Glen Etive.

**Access Point:** As for Ben Starav

**Distance:** 15km, 1300m ascent

**Approx Time:** 5-8hours

**Translation:** peak of the corrie of the Scotsman; hill of the birds

**Pronunciation:** stop kor an ala-paneech; myowl nan ayn

# THE GLEN ETIVE HILLS

To Glencoe

Kings House
Hotel

A82

To Bridge
of Orchy

Glen Etive

Route B

Blackrock
Cottage

Sron na
Creise

Creag Dhubh

White Corries
Ski Centre

Allt nan Giubhas

Stob a'
Ghlais Choire
996

Coire Pollach

Creise
1100

Meall a'
Bhuiridh
1108

West Highland Way

Coire Odhar

Clach
Leathad
1099

Creag an
Fhirich
705

Sron nam Forsair

Aonach Mor

Meall
Tionall
582

River Ba

Coireach a' Ba

BLACK MOUNT

Sron na Giubhas

Coirein
Lochain

Stob a'
Choire Odhair
943

Stob
Ghabhar
1087

Beinn Toaig
834

Aonach Eagach

Coire Toaig

Coire
Ghabhar

Coire na Mulc

Allt Toaig

Route A

West Highland Way

N

Forest
Lodge

0                    1 mile

Abhainn Shira

Victoria Bridge

Loch Tulla

0          1 kilometre

Inveroran
Hotel

To Bridge
of Orchy

## Stob a' Choire Odhair (223), 943m/3094ft, Stob Ghabhar (54) 1087m/3566ft,

The Clachlet Traverse is a classic high-level route from Inveroran to Kingshouse and takes in the Munros of Stob a' Choire Odhair, Stob Ghabhar, Meall a' Bhuiridh and Creise over a distance of about 25km. Height ascended is about 1700m. This is fine if you can arrange transport, with a car to collect you at Kingshouse and return you to your own car at Forest Lodge near Inveroran, but most walkers break this ridge down into two distinct outings, Stob Ghabhar and Stob a' Choire Odhair as one round, and Creise and Meall a' Bhuiridh as the other.

For Stob a' Choire Odhair and Stob Ghabhar take the track by Forest Lodge near Loch Tulla. Walk west along the track beside the Linne nam Beathach to the Glasgow University Climbing Club hut at Clashgour. Leave the bulldozed track here and take the footpath northwards beside the Allt Toaig. At GR 252446, the path crosses another burn and west of it a broad ridge rises up to Beinn Toaig and the broad plateau-like ridge which is crowned by the summit of Stob a' Choire Odhair.

Descend west to a wide, knolly bealach, continue west uphill for a few hundred metres then turn south-west and up steep slopes to reach a ridge called the Aonach Eagach.

Several years ago I skied round these two Munros and I recalled a wonderful little arête at the top of this ridge, a thin spine of rock with big drops on either side. On that day it was protected by a double cornice, and I remember tip-toeing very tentatively across it, skis lashed on the pack. Even more recently, at this very spot, I realised the truth behind a statement I saw recently that there is no such thing as winter hillwalking in Scotland – it is mountaineering. From where the Aonach Eagach abuts on to Stob Ghabhar's south-east ridge it's only a short pull to the summit. Descend the south east ridge back to the Allt Toaig.

## Creise (48), 1100m/3609ft, Meall a' Bhuiridh (43), 1108m/3635ft

Gaze across at these hills from the Black Corries on the edge of the Rannoch Moor, and together with the deep defile of Glen Etive and the familiar triangular shape of the Buachaille Etive Mor you have one of the finest mountain panoramas in Scotland. Creise itself is a steep sided hill which offers some superlative scrambling up the steep north nose of Sron na Creise. The rocky ribs which spill down eastwards into the Cam Gleann provide an easier way to the top, although there is still good scrambling to be found here too.

---

**Route Summary:** From Forest Lodge (Route A) follow the track which leads W along the N bank of the Linne nam Beathach. Reach a small corrugated iron hut after about 600m and take the path which runs N from it beside the Allt Toaig. At GR252446, the path crosses another burn and W of it a broad ridge lifts up to Beinn Toaig and the wide plateau-like ridge which is crowned by the summit of Stob a' Choire Odhair. Descend W to a wide knolly bealach, continue W uphill, then turn SW, up steep slopes to reach a ridge called the Aonach Eagach. Follow this ridge, which is narrow and exposed in places, to where it meets the broad SE ridge of Stob Ghabhar. Follow this to the summit. Return by way of the SE ridge

**Map:** OS Sheet 50: GR258461, GR230455

**Access Point:** Forest Lodge GR271423

**Distance:** 20km, 1380m ascent

**Approx Time:** 6-8 hours

**Translation:** peak of the goat; peak of the dun coloured corrie

**Pronunciation:** stob a kora ooer; stop gower

---

**Route Summary:** From the mouth of the Cam Ghleann gain the rocky slopes of Sron na Creise (Route B). Contour W to avoid rocky difficulties and ascend steep slabs to Stob a' Ghlais Choire, the start of the main ridge which runs to Stob Ghabhar. Follow the corrie rim round to a curved crest which rises to Creise. Follow the ridge towards the flat top of Mam Coire Easain. A ridge runs E

*Creise (right) and Meall a' Bhuiridh from the north*

towards a bealach at the foot of Meall a' Bhuiridh. Navigation can be tricky in poor conditions and cornices can pose problems in winter. Climb to summit of Meall a' Bhuiridh then go back to Blackrock Cottage by way of the ski paraphernalia

**Map:** OS Sheet 41

**Access Point:** Blackrock Cottage, GR268531.

**Distance:** 13km, 970m ascent

**Approx Time:** 4-6 hours

**Translation:** unknown; hill of the rutting stags

**Pronunciation:** kraysh, mowl a vooree

**Route Summary:** From Elleric take the track past the house to a bridge on the River Ure near Glenure House (Route A). Beyond the house take the steeply rising ground SSE as the most direct ascent to the summit ridge.

**Map:** OS Sheet 50

**Access Point:** Elleric, GR035489

**Distance:** 6km, 930m ascent

**Approx Time:** 3-5 hours

**Translation:** unknown

**Pronunciation:** byn skoolard

Start at Blackrock Cottage, the Scottish Ladies Climbing Club hut on the road which leads to the White Corries ski grounds. Cross the heather moorland around the top of Creag Dhubh to the mouth of the Cam Ghleann to gain the rocky slopes of Sron na Creise. Contour west to avoid rocky difficulties and ascend steep grass and scree slopes to Stob a' Ghlais Choire, the start of the main ridge which eventually terminates at Stob Ghabhar in the south. Follow the corrie rim round to a curved crest which rises to Creise. Follow the ridge towards the flat top of Mam Coire Easain. An interesting stony rib offers a way of escape from the ridge towards a bealach which leads to Meall a' Bhuiridh. Take care in poor conditions as navigation can be tricky and cornices can pose problems hereabouts. Climb to the summit of Meall a' Bhuiridh and then descend to Blackrock Cottage by way of the ski grounds.

## Beinn Sgulaird (233), 937m/3074ft

Rising from sea level at the head of Loch Creran, Beinn Sgulaird is a fine vantage point for gazing out towards the hills of Mull. It's a big hill, a long ridge of almost three kilometres in length, much of it over the 800-metre mark. Many walkers simply walk up steep slopes from Elleric, bag the summit and return but this does the hill a great injustice for while the ridge certainly doesn't offer the thrill or exposure of an Aonach Eagach it is nevertheless a fine high-level promenade with extensive views.

I would recommend a north to south traverse, simply because the best views are to the west. From Glenure cross the bridge and climb the long and steep slopes to the summit – the higher you climb the rockier is the terrain. A more interesting alternative is to follow the River Ure, on its south bank, above its fine wooded gorge to where it is joined by the Allt Bealach na h-Innsig. Leave the river now, head south through some woods and climb to the small bealach between Sgulaird and its outlier, Stob Goibhre.

The summit itself lies at the north end of the ridge, and the long gently curving ridge is full of little ups and downs and rocky outcrops. Descend the west ridge and just before the little knoll at 480m turn north and make for the farm at Taravocan. From here a footpath runs back to Glenure via Loch Baile Mhic Chailein.

## Beinn Fhionnlaidh (196), 959m/3146ft

Another of those hills described as shy and retiring, Beinn Fhionnlaidh is positively misanthropic! Midway between the head of Glen Creran and Glen Etive, it is defended on its Glen Etive approaches by massive forestry plantations and I must confess that directions which include plodding up forestry fire-breaks leave me cold. The Glen Creran side offers a more benevolent approach, but a long one up Fhionnlaidh's six kilometre ridge – a ridge of multiple false summits. On the positive side the schistose rock is interlaced in places by great bands of limestone which provide the basis for some magnificent Alpine plants. Much of the ridge itself is rocky and is strewn with erratics, and as you climb the view northwards towards Glencoe gradually opens up to provide a rich panorama of the old area of Appin.

Leave Glenure and take the footpath past the woodland and on to the open hill at the foot of the Leac Bharainn. From there it's simply a case of following the narrowing ridge to the summit.

**Route Summary:** Start at Glenure (see access for Beinn Sgulaird), and take the lower grassy slopes in a NE direction towards Leac Bharainn (Route B). Above this the obvious W ridge rises gradually to the summit of Beinn Fhionnlaidh. Descend the same way. An ascent from Glen Etive, once the popular route to the summit, cannot now be recommended because of Forestry Commission activities

**Map:** OS Sheet 41

**Access Point:** Elleric, GR035489

**Distance:** 15km, 950m ascent

**Approx Time:** 5-7 hours

**Translation:** Finlay's Hill

**Pronunciation:** byn yoonly

# GLENCOE

## The Munros:

Sgor na h-Ulaidh    Buachaille Etive Mor (Stob Dearg)
Buachaille Etive Beag (Stob Dubh)    Bidean nam Bian
Aonach Eagach (Meall Dearg, Sgor nam Fiannaidh)
Beinn a' Bheithir (Sgorr Dhearg, Sgorr Dhonuill)

The Glencoe peaks are well known and loved and it's wise to disregard the description of this as the Glen of Weeping, usually given for tourists' benefit. The Massacre of Glencoe was a dreadful betrayal of hospitality, but was no worse than many others which took place throughout Highland history. Despite the tourism it's a wonderful place, introduced by the majestic Buachaille Etive Mor, and dominated by the high Bidean massif in the south and the spectacular wall of the Aonach Eagach ridge to the north. For many, including myself, this is the spiritual home of Scottish mountaineering.

## Sgor na h-Ulaidh (146), 994m/3261ft

The Lost Mountain of Glencoe, Sgor na h-Ulaidh hides its not inconsiderable charms behind the Bidean massif and its long protective ridge, Aonach Dubh a' Ghlinne. The usual way of ascent is to follow the Land Rover track all the way to Gleann-leac-na-muidhe and then follow the Allt na Muidhe halfway up its glen before climbing the west slopes of Aonach Dubh a' Ghlinne to Stob an Fhurain and then the Munro.

A more interesting approach climbs the prominent prow of Aonach Dubh a' Ghlinne, seen clearly from the A82 at Achnacon. It's a steep climb, no doubt about that, but after the initial exertion you can wander happily along the ridge and pour scorn on those climbing the long slopes from the glen below you.

From Stob an Fhurain, a steep descent drops to a high and rocky col, from where very rocky ground leads to the summit of Sgor na h-Ulaidh.

Great care is required in the descent of this hill. Don't try and escape northwards until you have descended west to Corr na Beinne where steep ground takes you to a col from which you can easily walk down to the headwaters of the Allt na Muidhe. If you feel particularly energetic, the Corbett of Meall Ligiche can be easily linked to this

**Route Summary:** Follow the Land Rover track which follows the W bank of the Allt na Muidhe (Route A). Not far before the cottage of Gleann-leac-na-muidhe leave the track and take to the steep prow of Aonach Dubh a' Ghlinne, a fierce ascent which threads through several rocky outcrops. Continue S on the ridge to the top of Stob an Fhuarain. Descend SW to the bealach and follow the remains of an ancient wall and fence along the crest of the ridge up increasingly rocky ground to the summit. From the summit continue W to the spur of Corr na Beinne and carefully descend its steep N slopes to a col. From here easy slopes to the NE take you to the headwaters of the Allt na Muidhe

**Map:** OS Sheet 41

**Access Point:** Achnacon, GR118565

**Distance:** 13km, 1100m ascent

**Approx Time:** 4-6 hours

*The Glencoe mountains from the air, looking north-east from above Beinn Maol Chaluim*

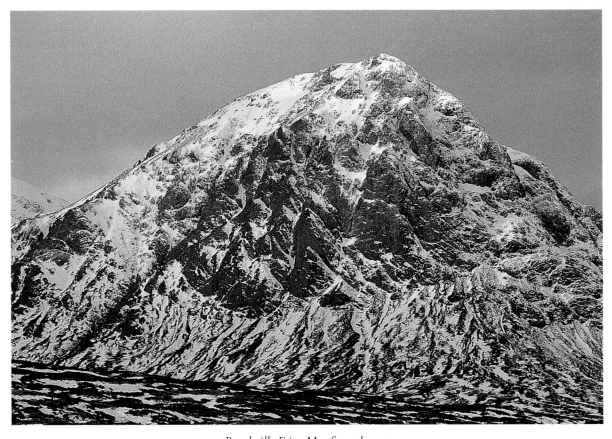

*Buachaille Etive Mor from the east*

**Translation:** peak of the treasure
**Pronunciation:** skor na hoolya

**Route Summary:** Follow the track to the bridge over the River Coupall (Route B) and pass the white-washed climbers' hut called Lagangarbh. Take the right fork in the path and continue into Coire na Tulaich following the path on the W bank of the burn. Follow the path up the corrie to its head where scree slopes offer difficult access to a flat bealach. Turn E and cross red and pink boulders and scree trending E then NE along a ridge which narrows appreciably towards the summit. The complete traverse of the Buachaille Etive Mor ridge is a rewarding walk, from Stob

Munro to make a particularly fine high-level horseshoe round Gleann na Muidhe.

### Buachaille Etive Mor (Stob Dearg) (106), 1022m/3353ft

In the few polls that have been taken to determine the most popular mountains in Scotland, the Buachaille Etive Mor has never failed to reach the top five. This impressive cornerstone between Glen Etive and Glen Coe rises in a resplendent squat pyramid, the epitome of mountain grandeur which throws down its gauntlet to every passer-by. Its great walls, ridges and gullies present an air of impregnability, offering few lines of weakness, although there is one, used mainly by climbers, which is an impressive route for the walker who doesn't mind exposure and is happy to use his or her hands. A curved ridge sneaks its way up from near the base of the mountain following the crest of a broad, solid ridge. It is a scrambling route, but the holds are big, generous and plentiful. The route passes the dramatic Rannoch

Wall and runs out close to the foot of the Crowberry Tower from where an easy gully climb takes you to the Stob Dearg summit.

The walker's breach in the Buachaille's defences is Coire na Tulaich, directly behind the Scottish Mountaineering Club hut at Lagangarbh. A track crosses the River Coupall by a footbridge and makes its steep way up into the depths of the corrie. Beetling crags rise above as the track begins to zigzag onto steep scree slopes and much care is required on the last 100m or so to the ridge.

As you top-out on the ridge you'll see the other tops of Buachaille Etive Mor which is really a long ridge of four summits. The Munro lies to the left, up a rough boulder-strewn path. As you approach the summit cairn the ridge begins to narrow in a rather satisfying way and after one or two false summits you'll reach the large cairn which appears to sit on the very edge of nothing.

The descent follows the same route but the energetic, or Top collectors will go on to climb Stob na Doire, Stob Coire Altruim and Stob na Broige.

Dearg to Stob na Broige, returning to Altnafeath by the Lairig Gartain pass to the NNW

**Map:** OS Sheet 41

**Access Point:** Altnafeath, GR221563

**Distance:** 8km, 790m ascent

**Approx Time:** 3-5 hours

**Translation:** big herdsman of Etive; red peak

**Pronunciation:** booachil etiv moar

## Buachaille Etive Beag (Stob Dubh) (197), 958m/3143ft

The big herdsman's little brother, Buachaille Etive Beag does share a family resemblance but generally lacks all the great features of the bigger hill. Only when viewed from lower Glen Etive do the two hills resemble twins.

Unlike the summit of Buachaille Etive Mor, Stob Dearg, which looks down on the A82 road across the Rannoch Moor, the wee Buachaille reserves its highest point, Stob Dubh, as far from the road as possible, at the end of its four-kilometre ridge. That means you get a good ridge walk for your single Munro top!

The trade route to the wee Buachaille runs from the north, from the A82 Glencoe road, but an alternative, shorter route, begins at Dalness in Glen Etive. This route more or less climbs Stob Dubh directly by its south-west ridge, a long and brutal way of climbing the hill, although you could take the footpath into the Lairig Eilde and climb it from there.

Most folk go in from the Chasm, that narrow part of the Glencoe road which has been gouged from the bare rock. Follow the sign into the Lairig Eilde and take the muddy footpath for about half a kilometre before taking to the hill in a rough southerly direction. Climb steepening slopes to the bealach immediately south-west of Stob Coire Raineach and follow the ridge to a little rocky top at 900m. After a short descent the ridge levels out, narrows considerably, and continues to the final rise of Stob Dubh.

## Bidean nam Bian (23), 1150m/3773ft

This is the highest hill in the old county of Argyll and retires rather shyly behind its outliers. This Peak of the Mountains is well named for its summit is thrown up by four great ridges which give way to no less than nine separate summits and cradle three deep and distinctive corries. A number of alternative routes ascend Bidean nam Bian but one or two have been over-promoted and have suffered accordingly.

The Coire nam Beith route which is described in the Route Summary is probably the most obvious and makes good use of some excellent path renovation work, but I think my favourite route is by Coire nan Lochan below the great crags of the east face of Aonach Dubh. A good path runs all the way to the head of the corrie where three lochans reflect the steep crags above, which lead to the summit of Stob Coire nan Lochan. From there a steep descent and another steep and rocky climb leads directly to the summit of Bidean. As an alternative descent route follow the ridge south east and return to the A82 by the Coire Gabhail or Lairig Eilde. Another alternative is to link Stob Coire nan Lochan and then descend Coire nan Lochan to the A82.

Bidean nam Bian is deservedly one of the most popular hills in the area and the footpaths from the A82 have suffered as a result. However, some sterling footpath work by the National Trust for Scotland seems to have halted the worst of the erosion.

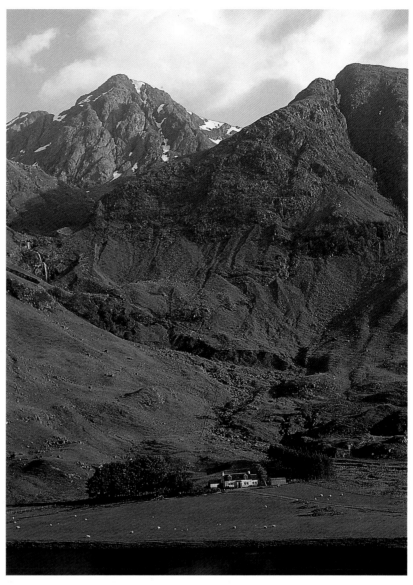

*Bidean nam Bian and Loch Achtriochtan*

## Aonach Eagach Ridge: Meall Dearg (208) 953m/3127ft, Sgorr nam Fiannaidh (183), 967m/3173ft

The huge, broken and gully riven wall that forms the northern barrier of Glen Coe is well named the Notched Ridge. More than three kilometres long and with two Munros it also offers several heart-stopping moments if you're not used to exposure.

A sign-posted path climbs quickly up behind the house at Allt-na-reigh and takes you all the way to the main ridge at the saddle north-east of the Am Bodach summit. From here you get your first view of the sinuous, rocky ridge – a daunting sight. It's a

**Route Summary:** Follow the path behind the house of Allt-na-reigh up the grassy slopes of Am Bodach (Route E). There are a few rocky outcrops but these can be avoided on the E. To reach the crest of the Aonach Eagach ridge follow the edge of the crags to the left of Am Bodach's cairn in a WNW direction. A sudden drop with a 15m scramble on good but polished holds starts the ridge traverse proper. Follow the crest of the

*Aonach Eagach Ridge from the east*

ridge to the grassy hump of Meall Dearg. From Meall Dearg follow the line of fence posts along the crest and then traverse the Crazy Pinnacles. This involves some exposed scrambling on the most sensational section of the ridge. After the Pinnacles more fence posts accompany you on the long pull to Stob Coire Leith, before the ridge levels out towards the second Munro, Sgorr nam Fiannaidh. It is advised to descend due S of this summit, picking a route with care through rocky outcrops and grassy slopes. The alternative descent is further W of the summit and follows a very eroded path on the W side of Clachaig Gully

**Map:** OS Sheet 41

**Access Point:** Allt-na-reigh, GR176566

**Distance:** 6km, 914m ascent

**Approx Time:** 3-5 hours

**Translation:** notched ridge; red hill; peak of the fair haired warriors.

**Pronunciation:** oenoch egoch; myowl d-yerrack; sgor nam feeanee

switchbacked fin of rock and grass, steep-sided and exposed, with occasional pinnacles posing as obstacles at points along the way. Wonderful! Sadly you've little time to ease yourself gently into the difficulties – a sudden drop appears, with about 15m of scrambling on fairly polished rock, but it looks worse than it is. Face inwards, and look for the holds – they're there all right, and soon you'll be traversing on good holds on to the crest of the ridge where an easy gradient takes you on to a top beyond which lie the slopes to the first Munro, Meall Dearg.

The next section, the Crazy Pinnacles, is best. Follow the obvious path and the crampon marks on the rock and enjoy the easy scrambling. The final two pinnacles offer the most exposed scrambles, before a dip in the ridge immediately before Stob Coire Leith indicates the end of the difficulties. It's now an easy walk on a broad ridge to the second of the Munros, Sgorr nam Fiannaidh. Descend due south of this summit, picking your way with care through some rocky outcrops and down for a well-earned pint in the Clachaig Inn. The path, on the west side of Clachaig Gully has a lot of loose stones and rock on it and there is a danger of knocking scree into the gully, putting other climbers at risk. There is also the danger of actually falling into the gully; there have been several fatalities at this point in recent years.

# Beinn a' Bheithir (Sgorr Dhearg (104), 1024m/3360ft, Sgorr Dhonuill (132), 1001m/3284ft)

This dramatically named Hill of the Thunderbolt rises gracefully above the narrows of Loch Leven at Ballachulish, a fine mountain in every sense, made up of two peaks on a long, curving ridge forming magnificent north-facing corries.

Forestation has caused considerable access problems to these peaks and you're as well to use the forest tracks to their best advantage. A forest road rises steadily into the Gleann a' Chaolais and after a kilometre or so it begins to zigzag up some steeper ground. Just past an old quarry you'll reach a crossroads – cross over until you reach a concrete bridge over a burn and just east of the stream you'll find a small cairn which marks the start of a boggy path through the trees.

Eventually you'll break clear of the conifers and the path continues up to the high col between the two peaks. Take your choice of which peak to go for first, both offer a good rocky climb and you'll have to return to the col from both of them.

A good alternative descent is to climb Sgorr Dhonuill first, return to the col and climb Sgorr Dhearg, continue round the head of the corrie to descend down Dhearg's north ridge. A good footpath eventually twists its way down the blunt nose of the ridge and deposits you in the forest above the old manse and church east of the Ballachulish Bridge.

**Route Summary:** Leave the road about 800m W of the Ballachulish Bridge on a minor road which leads you to some houses at the foot of Gleann a' Chaolais. Cars can be left here. Follow Forestry Commission road S and after a while it zigzags up steeper ground, passes an old quarry and comes to a cross roads. Go straight across, round another bend, over a bridge and cross a burn at GR 047569. A cairn by the track indicates the path which climbs SE through the forest and on to the open hillside above the trees. Climb S to the obvious bealach between the two peaks of Beinn a 'Bheithir, Sgorr Dhonuill on your right and Sgorr Dhearg on your left. Both peaks are easily reached from the bealach

**Map:** OS Sheet 41

**Access Point:** A828, GR044595

**Distance:** 16km, 1210m ascent

**Approx Time:** 5-8hours

**Translation:** hill of the thunderbolt; red peak; Donald's peak

**Pronunciation:** byn vair; sgor d-yerrack; sgor ghawil

# THE MAMORES

## The Munros:

Binnein Beag    Binnein Mor    Na Gruagaichean    Sgurr Eilde Mor
An Gearanach    Stob Coire a' Chairn    Am Bodach
Sgor an Iubhair    Sgurr a' Mhaim    Stob Ban    Mullach nan Coirean

Stretching on for fully 15km the ridge of the Mamores creates a high, corrie-bitten wall between Glen Nevis in the north and Loch Leven in the south. As a complete traverse it is a long and airy walk along a narrow and curving ridge with very few difficulties to hold up progress. The only real scramble in the entire ridge is the dramatically named Devil's Ridge between Sgor an Iubhair and Stob Choire a' Mhail, and even that poses little problem in good conditions. In winter snows it demands a little more respect!

Most hillwalkers will satisfy their hunger with bite-sized Mamore chunks and the formation of the ridge lends itself well to that simpler approach, breaking down nicely into three superb outings of different character.

Another fine characteristic of the Mamores is that they are well served by a fine network of stalker's paths which can be used to access the main ridge. To make the best use of these, base yourself at Kinlochleven. Alternatively, the big car park at Polldubh in Glen Nevis gives access through the Nevis Gorge to Steall and upper Glen Nevis, north of the Mamore ridge.

*Na Gruagaichean from Binnein Mor*

## Binnein Beag (228), 940m/3084ft, Binnein Mor (30), 1128m/3701ft, Na Gruagaichean (71), 1055m/3461ft, Sgurr Eilde Mor (120), 1008m/3307ft

Binnein Mor is arguably the finest of the Mamores, its tent-like shape the product of the culmination of high, sweeping ridges. Many walkers will climb the two Binneins together, leaving Gruagaichean and Eilde Mor for another day, but the inclusion of all four gives a good day out, particularly in the long days of summer.

I've suggested in the route summary that you tackle these hills from Glen Nevis, first climbing little Binnein Beag, before tackling the fine north-east ridge of Binnein Mor. I climbed this ridge a few years ago in conditions of deep snow and it really was a challenging climb, but the technical difficulties were a relief from the heavy plodding through knee-deep snow to reach the bealach below.

From Binnein Mor the beauty of the Mamores ridge becomes apparent and it's an easy high-level stride southwards to a subsidiary top before turning south west to the twin summits of Na Gruagaichean. The first summit is the highest. Retrace your footsteps now to the subsidiary top just south of Binnein Mor, pass it and continue in a south-east direction to drop steeply off the ridge and pick up the stalker's path from Kinlochleven. Follow this northwards into Coire an Lochain. Sgurr Eilde Mor provides a real test of stamina at this stage in the day and the loose bouldery slopes don't help the temper. However, from the top it's a long, but easy descent down the long north-east ridge to Tom an Eite, the watershed which has to be the wettest place in Scotland, and back down Glen Nevis to Polldubh. A long day but very worthwhile.

**Route Summary:** Leave the car park at the head of Glen Nevis and follow the track through to Steall and along the N bank of the Water of Nevis (Route A) to GR 215690. Cross the river here and climb the NE slopes of Binnein Beag. From the summit head SSW, past a lochan and climb the narrow and interesting NE ridge of Binnein Mor. Continue S on a narrow ridge from the summit to a subsidiary top and then SW to the twin summits of Na Gruagaichean. The first summit reached, the SE summit, is the highest. Retrace your steps to the subsidiary top S of Binnein Mor and continue on a narrowing ridge to the SE to Coire an Lochain. Climb the SW slopes of Sgurr Eilde Mor over fairly unpleasant scree and boulder fields. Descend by NE ridge to Tom an Eite, and return to Glen Nevis by the Water of Nevis path

**Map:** OS Sheet 41

**Access Point:** Glen Nevis, Polldubh car park

**Distance:** 25.6km, 1372m ascent

Approx Time: 7-10 hours

**Translation:** small peak; big peak; the maidens; big peak of the hind

**Pronunciation:** beenyan beck; beenyan mor; na grooakeechan; skoor ailta moar

You can climb these hills from Kinlochleven using the forementioned stalker's path but such a route does involve a lot of retracing your steps if you want to climb all four Munros. Sgurr Eilde Mor can be climbed on its own from this path, returning another day to climb the three others, making use of another stalker's path which descends Coire na Ba just west of Na Gruagaichean.

## An Gearanach (162), 982m/3222ft, Stob Coire a' Chairn (165), 981m/3218ft, Am Bodach (96), 1032m/3386ft, Sgor an Iubhair (133), 1001m/3284ft, Sgurr a' Mhaim (49), 1099m/3606ft

**Route Summary:** As route above but cross the Water of Nevis by the wire bridge at the Steall climbing hut (Route B). Go E past the hut, past the waterfall and a wooded buttress until the path turns S up a small glen. Continue on the path which eventually takes long zigzags and in time takes you on to the NNE spur of An Gearanach (unmarked on the OS map). Continue S from the summit along the short ridge to An Garbhanach. From this top continue SW for a short distance and climb to the summit of Stob Coire a' Chairn. From here the (obvious) ridge links SW to Am Bodach, then WNW to Sgor an Iubhair. N of Sgor an Iubhair, the Devil's Ridge links with Stob Choire a' Mhail. From here the slopes open on to the wide quartzy summit slopes of Sgurr a' Mhaim and then a long descent N to Glen Nevis

**Map:** OS Sheet 41

**Access Point:** Glen Nevis, Polldubh Car park

**Distance:** 8km, 1219m ascent

**Approx Time:** 6-8 hours

**Translation:** the complainer; peak of the corrie of the cairn; the old man; peak of the yew; peak of the large rounded hill

**Pronunciation:** an gyeranach; stob corrie a cairn; am podach; skor an yooar; skor a vaim

Collectively known as the Ring of Steall, these Munros form a great horseshoe around Coire a' Mhail from which issues the very impressive Steall Waterfall. Seven tops over 900m make up this superb round, all linked by high, narrow ridges – Scottish mountain walking at its very best.

Strangely enough one of the best parts of this route is the walk-in! From the car park at Polldubh a track weaves through the trees above the deep and noisy Nevis Gorge, a place which WH Murray once described as the 'best half mile in Scotland.' It is truly splendid, of Himalayan character if not scale, made even more impressive by your sudden arrival at Steall meadows. In a total contrast to the confines of the gorge, the green grass of Steall opens out in a wide plain, backed by the 900-m white slash of the Grey Mare's Tail above the old cottage.

Many commentators suggest that the Ring of Steall is best walked in an anti-clockwise direction but I would disagree. It's a long and unpleasant haul up from Steall to gain the north-east ridge of Sgurr a' Mhaim. Far better to cross the wire bridge at Steall and follow the river eastwards to where it is joined by the Allt Coire na Gabhalach. Follow the path up the glen, a good path which begins to zigzag in its higher reaches to attain the An Gearanach ridge. From here you start some of the finest ridge walking in the land, a long and high level promenade with some fabulous views of the Ben, the Aonachs and the Grey Corries and southwards across Loch Leven to the Glencoe hills and beyond.

Fine narrow ridges connect with Stob Coire a' Chairn, Am Bodach, Sgor an Iubhair, the tight and exposed Devil's Ridge (no great difficulties in good conditions, it can be tricky in winter) to Stob Coire a'Mhail and then the wide quartz-covered slopes of Sgurr a' Mhaim and the long descent back to Polldubh by the north-north-east slopes.

## Stob Ban (138), 999m/3278ft,
## Mullach nan Coirean (231), 939m/3081ft

These two Munros are rich in contrast – one is craggy and rugged, the other whalebacked and smooth topped. Stob Ban offers magnificent views along the tortuous switchback of the Mamore Ridge while Mullach nan Coirean lifts you high above Loch Linnhe with the huge impressive bulk of Ben Nevis just across the glen.

A good footpath carries you high above Achriabhach and into the tight confines of Coire a' Mhusgain. Higher up the corrie opens out and you begin to feel the presence of Stob Ban. Towering from its gradual northern ridge it begins to dominate the scene, great scree runnels splitting the steep slopes into a complete system of buttresses and crags, the topmost ones sparkling white in the sun – not the effect of snow but of quartzite.

Soon the path begins to zigzag up the western slopes of Sgurr a' Mhaim and into the head of Coire a' Mhusgain, a wonderful spot complete with a lochan which nestles into the contours below the red screes of Sgor an Iubhair, the Peak of the Eagle. The footpath crosses the stream well below the lochan and joins up with a stalker's path which soon dwindles out on the southern slopes of Stob Ban. Continue up the north-east ridge to where a short walk takes you to the summit.

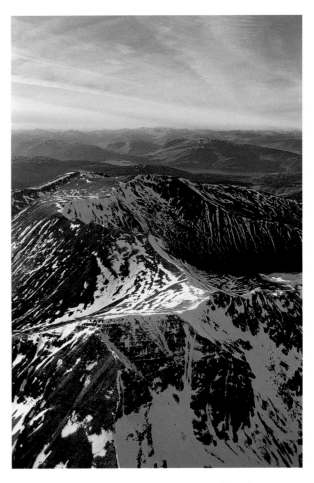

*Stob Ban and Mullach nan Coirean from the air*

As you descend from the summit of Stob Ban you'll notice a change below your feet as the white quartz is replaced by red granite. Follow the rim of the north-facing corries, cross a subsidiary top and then climb the final few metres to the flat-topped Mullach. When you descend check that you take the east ridge – many walkers head directly down the north ridge to reach impenetrable forest far down Glen Nevis. The east ridge eventually swings northwards and gives you a further choice of descent. You can drop down the steep eastern slopes of this ridge to the Allt a' Choire Dheirg and back to Achriabrach, or follow the ridge down to the edge of the forest where a small cairn indicates a route through the trees to a forest drive.

**Route Summary:** Reach the NNE ridge of Mullach and follow this to the summit (Route C). Descend slopes to the SE and follow the undulating ridge which goes SE then S to the Mullach's SE top. Soon the ridge drops E to the col between the two mountains. Climb E then S up angular boulders and screes to the summit of Stob Ban

**Map:** OS Sheet 41

**Access Point:** Achriabhach in Glen Nevis

**Distance:** 14.4km, 1219m ascent

**Approx Time:** 4-7 hours

**Translation:** light-coloured peak; summit of the corries

**Pronunciation:** stob baan; mullach nan kooran

# BEN NEVIS, THE AONACHS AND THE GREY CORRIES

## The Munros:

Ben Nevis    Carn Mor Dearg    Aonach Beag
Aonach Mor    Stob Ban    Stob Choire Claurigh
Stob Coire an Laoigh    Sgurr Choinnich Mor

Together with the Mamores, these hills make up the Round of Glen Nevis, one of the great challenges for marathon walkers, but most people will be more than happy to break them down into three or even four outings.

Ben Nevis, Britain's highest hill, can be one of two things: a long, dull plod up the tourist route which in itself is more of a facility than an amenity, or an exciting expedition via Carn Mor Dearg and its superb scythe-like arête, taking the walker high above the Allt a' Mhuillin to gaze upon the incredible north-east faces of this majestic mountain. Really, there's no comparison.

The two Aonachs have been tamed a little by the creation of the Aonach Mor ski development but it's easy to enjoy a day on these hills without coming into contact with any of the paraphernalia at all, and the Grey Corries, like the Mamores, form a long switch-backed ridge of remote and classic proportions.

Fort William makes the best base for these hills, although Spean Bridge or Roy Bridge are best for the Grey Corries.

## Ben Nevis (1), 1344m/4409ft, Carn Mor Dearg (7), 1223m/4012ft

There are several routes to the summit of Ben Nevis and all of them are infinitely preferable to the Tourist Route via the Half-Way Lochan. Sadly, the vast majority of folk who climb Ben Nevis never see the real guts of the mountain, but perhaps they wouldn't want to. The north-east crags, buttresses and spires reflect a totally different impression of the mountain, an aspect that is mean and demanding, a gaunt face of, to quote one writer, 'loveless loveliness'.

I can empathise with that quote – there is a sometimes fatal attraction in such places – it is a cold, mean and bare mountain face and all the more attractive for it. Here man realises his own stature, his own insignificance, his mortality – he may come and climb the long buttresses, the big ridges, the steep faces, but he is never the

Route Summary: Leave Achintee and follow the obvious Ben Nevis track (Route A) as far as Lochan Meall an t-Suidhe. The track to Ben Nevis continues on a series of broad zigzags above but to reach Carn Mor Dearg continue past the loch around the flanks of Carn Dearg to drop down into the valley of the Allt a' Mhuilin. Cross the river near point GR154739 and climb E up rough bouldery slopes to Carn Beag Dearg. Continue SSE on ridge over Carn Dearg Meadhonach to Carn Mor Dearg. To continue to Ben Nevis follow the ridge S and cross the Carn Mor Dearg

*Ben Nevis from the air, looking south-west from above Aonach Mor*

Arête. Where the arête abuts on to the bulk of Ben Nevis, climb W over blocks and boulders to the summit. Take care in this area in conditions of snow cover: many walkers have slipped from this point into Coire Leis below

**Map:** OS Sheet 41

**Access Point:** Achintee

**Distance:** 20.8km, 1769m ascent

**Approx Time:** 7-10 hours :

**Translation:** possibly venomous mountain; big red hill

**Pronunciation:** byn nevis; caarn more jerrack

**Stalking Information:** British Aluminium Company. Tel: Fort William 2411

conqueror. Not on Ben Nevis.

To climb the Ben without experiencing even a hint of what the north-east face is like, is like going to the beach and never seeing the sea. To far too many walkers Ben Nevis is the sum experience of a long trudge up a stony, artificial track in the company of hundreds of others. For too many the summit means piles of human graffiti in the shape of cairns, ruins, a rusting shelter and a misplaced memento of war.

Far better to leave the tourist track at the Half-Way Lochan, Lochan Meall an t-Suidhe, and continue due north into the glen of the Allt a' Mhuillin. Already you'll be aware of the great cliffs to your right. Don't follow the footpath to the right, up the glen, but instead drop down rough heathery slopes, cross the burn and clamber steeply up the red granite slopes of Carn Beag Dearg. Carn Mor Dearg is another 800m or so along the ridge, which also crosses Carn Dearg Meadhonach.

*Ben Nevis from the west*

This crest provides a wonderful high-level walk with superb views across Coire Leis to the frowning crags of the Ben's north-east face.

From Carn Mor Dearg descend south on a rough path to the start of the arête, a high-level exposed ridge which connects the summit with the north-east ridge of Ben Nevis. The great feature of the ridge is its beautifully curved sweep, perfect in its balance and symmetry.

Where the arête eventually merges with the north-east ridge of the Ben a faint track picks its way upwards through a maze of giant boulders to the summit plateau. Pass the huge cairn, the rescue shelter and the ruins of the old weather observatory and make your way carefully across the plateau, especially in wintry weather. Many climbers have mistakenly marched across the plateau and fallen through the cornice into Five Fingers Gully. It's wise to remember that this so-called plateau is really just a wide ridge – accurate navigation is crucial to find the top of the tourist track, back down to Lochan Meall an t-Suidhe and the start at Achintee.

*Aonach Beag and An Cul Choire from Stob an Cul Choire*

## Aonach Beag (6), 1234m/4049ft, Aonach Mor (8), 1221m/4006ft

The Little Ridge is higher (in terms of height) than the Big Ridge but
these names only go to prove that the people who named these hills
did so by describing their bulk, not their height. Aonach Beag, as
though to confirm its standing as the higher of the two, is also the
more interesting mountain.

You can reach these hills by gondola to the Snow Goose gully on the
north side of Aonach Mor, from where it is only a short walk to the
summit, but I wouldn't recommend it, although the ski uplift is fine in
winter, when easy access allows you time to explore, on skis, the great
plateau of Aonach Mor, or enjoy an easy trip to Aonach Beag.

Another route to these hills leaves Torlundy on the A82, follows the
old British Aluminium Company railway eastwards for about 5km and
then takes to the hill to Tom na Sroine, Stob Coire an Fhir Dhuibh,
Stob an Cul Choire and a final steepish rib to Aonach Mor itself.

Probably one of the most popular routes starts at Polldubh, follows
the wonderful Steall path to the old ruins at the Allt Coire

Giubhsachan, and then follows the burn all the way to the 822m bealach between Carn Mor Dearg and the great wall formed by the western slopes of Aonach Mor. From the bealach a steep climb south-eastwards, then due east, brings you out on the col between the two Aonachs from where it's an easy walk to Aonach Mor. Return to the col, climb Aonach Beag and return to Glen Nevis via the south-west ridge.

**Distance:** 22.4km, 1488m ascent

**Approx Time:** 7-10 hours

**Translation:** little ridge; big (broad) ridge

**Pronunciation:** oenach bayk; oenach more

## Stob Ban (173), 977m/3205ft, Stob Choire Claurigh (14), 1177m/3861ft, Stob Coire an Laoigh (37), 1115m/3658ft, Sgurr Choinnich Mor (50), 1095m/3592ft

These hills, the Grey Corries, make up part of the superb panorama that holds the eye as you drive along the road from Spean Bridge to Roy Bridge in Nether Lochaber, the quartzite summits appearing like the new snows of autumn.

The walk into the Lairig Leacach is an enjoyable one, leaving the forest for the narrow pass with the steep slopes of Stob Coire na Ceannain on one side and the twin Corbetts, Cruach Innse and Sgurr Innse, on the other. Stop for a brew at the bothy and consider the route ahead, a long but easy climb up beside the Allt a' Chuil Choirean into a magnificent upper corrie and the short east-north-east ridge of Stob Ban, a 977m Munro, but dwarfed by its neighbouring Grey Corries.

The descent from Stob Ban to the bealach below Stob Choire Claurigh is very awkward, on moving screes and very loose rock. However it's not a long descent and soon you'll be striding over granite slabs, past a small lochan and on up the rocky slopes of Claurigh.

From here the ridge stretches ahead towards the unmistakable bulk of Ben Nevis, a narrow switchbacked ridge, the whiteness of its quartz illuminating the gloom on dark days. Nowhere is the ridge difficult, there is very little scrambling involved, and it rarely drops below the 1000m contour. Probably the narrowest point is above the Castle, An Caisteil, between Stob Coire Cath na Sine and Stob Coire an Laoigh.

Stob Coire Easain is your departure point from the ridge, but you'll probably want to climb the ridge leading out to Sgurr Choinnich Mor. Unfortunately it's a big drop in height and you have to retrace your steps to Stob Coire Easain, thereby doubling the ascent. Descend by Easain's north ridge, down to the forest and the old railway line which leads you all the way back to Coirechoille.

**Route Summary:** Take the track past Corriechoille farm and through the forest to the Lairig Leacach (Route C). Follow the track to the hut beside the Allt a' Chuil Choirean. Strike uphill in a SW direction up the ENE ridge of Stob Ban. Follow this ridge to the summit. Take care on the descent to the bealach between Stob Ban and Stob Choire Claurigh as the N slopes are precipitous and very loose. Descend slightly to the W. Above the bealach, there is a sharp pull up to Claurigh on loose scree and blocks. From the summit follow the broad crest W to Stob a' Choire Leith and Stob Coire Cath na Sine, where the ridge narrows considerably, over Caisteil to Stob Coire an Laoigh. The next top on the ridge is Stob Coire Easain, the N ridge of which takes you back to Coirechoille, but first continue on the Grey Corries ridge to Sgurr Choinnich Mor. Return to Easain and follow its N ridge over Beinn na Sachaich and back to Coirechoille

**Map:** OS Sheet 41

**Access Point:** Corriechoille, GR252807

**Distance:** 32km, 2012m ascent

**Approx Time:** 10-12 hours

**Translation:** light coloured peak; peak of the corrie of clamouring; peak of the corrie of the calf; big peak of the moss

**Pronunciation:** stop baan; stop corrie clowree; stop corrie an looee; skoor choanyeech more

# LOCH TREIG AND LOCH OSSIAN

## The Munros:

### Stob a' Choire Mheadhoin    Stob Coire Easain
### Stob Coire Sgriodain   Chno Dearg   Beinn na Lap
### Sgor Gaibhre   Carn Dearg

These hills border the edges of one of the true wilderness areas of Scotland, the ochreous acres of the vast Rannoch Moor. Loch Treig bites deep into the area, like a long fjord, with the Stob a' Choire Mheadhoin and Stob Coire Easain pair on one side and Stob Coire Sgriodain forming a huge wall on the other. These hills, along with the big rounded hump of Chno Dearg and the vast corrie it shares with Sgriodain, can be easily seen from the Laggan/Spean Bridge road at Tulloch.

More retiring are Beinn na Lap, Sgor Gaibhre and Carn Dearg, true hills of the Rannoch Moor. These can be reached by the marvellous West Highland Railway line, leaving the train at Rannoch or Corrour. The ascent of these hills can make the subject of a marvellous weekend away, in beautiful, remote country with bunkhouse accommodation at Corrour (Morgan's Den), or the Scottish Youth Hostel Association hostel at lovely Loch Ossian. An area for the Munro connoisseur.

## Stob a' Choire Mheadhoin (44), 1106m/3629ft,
## Stob Coire Easain (36), 1116m/3661ft

Hamish Brown, in his marvellous book *Hamish's Mountain Walk*, nicknamed these hills 'This Yin' and 'That Yin'. There's an Oriental ring to that and perhaps it is no surprise that these two Munros, lying like Siamese twins to the immediate west of Loch Treig, are joined at the hip by a high bealach.

The minor road from the Laggan/Spean Bridge road at Tulloch to Fersit is a delight, passing the old house where Rudolf Hess was held captive during the war, and the little lochan nearby which always seems to be rippling with rising trout. Near the head of the loch leave the easy walking of the Land Rover track and take to the hill, following easy contours towards the long prominent north-east ridge of Stob a' Choire Mheadhoin. This long ridge rises very sharply in a couple of steep steps, the first over Meall Cian Dearg requiring a bit of easy scrambling. Continue south-south-west to the stony summit of Mheadhoin. Descend south-west down rocky slopes to the

**Route Summary:** From the dam at the head of Loch Treig climb steep slopes in a SW direction (Route A) to the 760m contour and the open ridge. Climb two small rises and continue SSW to Stob a' Choire Mheadhoin. Descend SW down rocky slopes to the bealach and climb a rock-strewn ridge SSW to Stob Coire Easain. Descend the NW ridge to the open moorland of Coire Laire. Follow the river to the old British Aluminium Company railway track which leads back to Fersit

**Map:** OS Sheet 41

**Access Point:** Fersit, GR350782. Tulloch Station is on the Glasgow/Fort William Railway

**Distance:** 15km, 1006m ascent

**Approx Time:** 5-7 hours

*Stob Coire Easain from above Glen Spean*

Translation: peak of the middle corrie; peak of the corrie of the little waterfall

Pronunciation: stop kora vane; stop kora esan

bealach and then ascend a rough and rocky ridge west-south-west to Stob Coire Easain. From the summit cairn follow the steep north-west ridge which drops down to the open moors of Coire Laire. Follow the Allt Laire until you reach another bulldozed track. This leads through a forest plantation and at the far side drop down easy slopes to pick up the old British Aluminium Company railway track which leads leisurely back to your starting point.

Route Summary: Take the forestry track E from Fersit (Route B) then take rough ground via various sheep fanks to the S. Climb open slopes then craggy ridge to Stron

## Stob Coire Sgriodain (174), 976m/3202ft, Chno Dearg (82), 1047m/3435ft

The circuit of these two Munros makes a marvellous ski touring outing, with the big, open corrie between them usually offering great downhill running until well into the spring. From the summit of Chno Dearg there is a run of some 5km with about 750m of descent and even if the snow cover is incomplete, many of the stream beds hold snow well, so by linking these together you can still ski most of the way down.

For the walker, the circuit of the two hills makes a fairly easy day out. Many Munro-baggers are happy to lengthen it by adding Beinn na Lap, although that adds a big descent from the subsidiary top of Meall Garbh southwards and a climb of some 450m to the summit of Beinn na Lap before turning round and having to repeat it to regain the

*Stob Coire Easain from the western slopes of Stob a' Choire Mheadhoin*

original Chno Dearg route. Alternatively, drop down to Corrour Station from Beinn na Lap and return to Tulloch Station by train.

From the end of the Fersit road follow a forestry road east for about 500m then take rough ground to the south. Climb the rough, open slopes to beyond a small craggy top where the ridge begins to narrow appreciably. Beyond Sron na Garbh-bheinne the ridge flattens and then narrows again before rising to the summit of Stob Coire Sgriodain, with its superb views of Loch Treig and the steep east faces of Stob a' Choire Mheadhoin and Stob Coire Easain. From the summit cairn descend south to an obvious bealach and then south-east to the south top of Sgriodain. Cross bumps and knolls in a east-south-east direction, over a double top and down to another wide bealach with scattered lochans. This all sounds rather confusing but on a clear day the route is quite obvious. In mist it isn't so easy and care should be taken. From the wide bealach easy slopes lead to the subsidiary top of Meall Garbh and from there follow the ridge north-east to the big hump of Chno Dearg. Descend back to Fersit by the obvious north-north-west slopes.

na Garbh-bheinne. Follow ridge to Stob Coire Sgriodain. Descend S to bealach and then SE to S top of Sgriodain. Cross more open ground in an ESE direction over a double top and down to another bealach. Climb Meall Garbh. Follow ridge NE to Chno Dearg. Descend easy slopes NNW to Fersit track

**Map:** OS Sheet 41

**Access Point:** Fersit, GR350782

**Distance:** 12km, 914m ascent

**Translation:** peak of the scree corrie; red nut or red hill

**Pronunciation:** stop kora sgreeadan; knaw jerrack

## Beinn na Lap (232), 937m/3074ft

**Route Summary:** Follow the track E from the station and take the left fork at the loch (Route C). Continue on track along N side of loch. Leave the track and climb N on easy angled slopes to broad ridge. Follow ridge ENE to the summit

**Map:** OS Sheet 41

**Access Point:** Corrour Station

**Distance:** 8km, 530m ascent

**Approx Time:** 2-4 hours

**Translation:** possibly mottled hill

**Pronunciation:** byn na lap

You can make this hill as easy or as difficult as you like – easy by taking the train to Corrour Station and following the track east from the station to Loch Ossian from where you should take the left fork of the track where it splits at the loch and follow it along the north shore. At almost any point before you reach the forestry leave the track and climb the hill's easy angled slopes to the summit ridge.

For a longer, and much more interesting, day take a mountain bike from Fersit and follow the various forestry tracks through the Loch Laggan Forest to reach Strath Ossian above Loch Ghuilbinn. Leave your bike at the bridge over the Allt Feith Thuill and climb the Sron na Cloiche Sgoilte and then head south-west to the summit of Beinn na Lap.

## Sgor Gaibhre (203), 955m/3133ft, Carn Dearg (225), 941m/3087ft

**Route Summary:** Follow the Road to the Isles track to the footbridge over the Allt Eigheach. Climb slopes of Sron Leachd a' Chaorainn and continue on ridge to Carn Dearg.

These two Munros can be climbed from either Corrour Station on the West Highland Line, or from Rannoch Station further to the south. The advantage of Rannoch is that you're not solely dependent on train times – you can drive there. Park to the north of Loch Eigheach and take the Road to the Isles footpath to the footbridge over the Allt Eigheach. Half a kilometre from here, at a bifurcation in the footpath, take to the lower slopes of Sron Leachd a' Chaorainn which gradually steepen and become narrower until you reach the start of a 3km ridge which leads to the summit of Carn Dearg. All the way along this ridge you can enjoy great views to the west, across the great expanse of the Rannoch Moor towards the distant hills of the Blackmount Deer Forest, or eastwards into Coire Eigheach, the great corrie around which this route forms a great horseshoe.

From the summit take the north-east ridge which drops in a series of steps to the Mam Ban, the White Pass. Continue in an east-north-east direction up easy slopes to Sgor Gaibhre.

A number of years ago I enjoyed a longer

*Sgor Gaibhre from Sgor Choinnich*

trip following this route to Sgor Gaibhre but instead of completing the horseshoe back to Rannoch I continued north to enjoy the long high-level ridge which leads to Meall a' Bhealaich and Beinn a' Chumhainn. The views from here to the Aonach Beag group in the north and down into the jaws of the Bealach Dubh were magnificent. The parish boundary can then be followed down into the lower reaches of the Bealach Cumhainn and on to Ben Alder Cottage on the shore of Loch Ericht. Next day I made my way back to Rannoch by a series of stalker's paths and rough slopes.

But back to the original horseshoe route. From Sgor Gaibhre follow its south ridge to the Corbett of Meall na Meoig of Beinn Pharlagain, then follow the twisting, undulating ridge to the footbridge over the Allt Eigheach and back to the road.

The route from Corrour takes about 6-8 hours so if you think you can squeeze it in between train times have a go, but in my opinion it's not as fine a route as the one just described. From Corrour, head along the south shore of Loch Ossian to the cottages at the end of the loch. Follow the Uisge Labhair for a short distance before turning south to climb the long, rough slopes of Meall Nathrach Mor. From its summit cross the shallow bealach and climb Sgor Choinnich. Sgor Gaibhre can be easily reached now from the bealach immediately south. Descend west-south-west across the Mam Ban, continue to Carn Dearg and then descend virtually due west to pick up the Road to the Isles footpath back to Corrour.

Follow NE ridge to the Mam Ban and climb to Sgor Gaibhre. Follow S ridge over Meall na Meoig of Beinn Pharlagain and continue to the Allt Eigheach

**Map:** OS Sheet 42 and 41

**Translation:** goat's peak; red hill

**Pronunciation:** skor gyra; kaarn jarrack

**Access Point:** Loch Eigheach on the B846 Rannoch Station road

**Distance:** 25km, 1100m ascent

**Approx Time:** 7-9 hours

# LOCH ERICHT TO LOCH LAGGAN

## The Munros:

Carn Dearg    Geal-Charn    Aonach Beag    Beinn Eibhinn
Ben Alder    Beinn Bheoil    Beinn a' Chlachair
Geal Charn    Creag Pitridh

These are amongst the remotest mountains in the Central Highlands and, with the exception of Beinn a' Chlachair, Geal Charn and Creag Pitridh, are best tackled from Loch Pattack/ Culra, a good 16 km by Land Rover track from Dalwhinnie.

These hills form the high points in a great tract of land between Loch Laggan and Loch Ericht and although much of it is heavily forested there are no roads and few tracks. Access can be gained by the revigorated West Highland Railway, from the station and bunkhouse at Corrour and there is a Youth Hostel at Loch Ossian. This can be the start of a fabulous multi-day expedition taking in the Aonach Beag ridge, the Beinn a' Chlachair trio and Ben Alder and Beinn Bheoil, walking out to Dalwhinnie to return home by train. However you tackle them, you are assured of fine hills making the most of their central position to offer majestic views in all directions.

## Carn Dearg (95), 1034m/3392ft, Geal-Charn (25), 1132m/3714ft, Aonach Beag (38), 1114m/3655ft, Beinn Eibhinn (47), 1100m/3609ft

These are remote mountains which come together to provide a worthy ridge walk, full of interest and variety. Many kilometres from the nearest public road these are indeed hills for the connoisseur of isolation and are a good advertisement for the concept of 'the long walk-in'. When George Oswald was keeper of the Ben Alder estate he would happily allow walkers to drive down Loch Ericht-side as far as Loch Pattack, although he did warn drivers that his white garrons which grazed on the Loch Pattack flats had a liking for chewing wing mirrors. I personally hope that the track down Loch Ericht-side is never open to the public for the 'long walk-in' has a lot going for it. Too many of our hills are being made easy of access, with the resulting loss

**Route Summary:** From Culra Bothy climb W and NW on the S flanks of Carn Dearg (Route A) to the summit. Another cairn, slightly S, leads to a ridge which drops to a flat bealach and then rises to Diollaid a' Chairn. Beyond, the ridge narrows and leads to a steep and terraced slope which fronts the plateau of Geal-Charn. Choose a route through the terraces to the plateau and the summit cairn. Beyond, a long slope leads WSW to a grassy bealach. Descend to the bealach and climb to Aonach Beag. At the cairn, turn SW to descend to a narrow bealach above Lochan a'

*Ben Alder from the air*

*Beinn Bheoil and Ben Alder from Carn Dearg*

Charra Mhoir. The ascent of Beinn Eibhinn involves a steep pull to the curve of a broad ridge, which in turn rises to the cairn. To return to Culra descend S and E to the Bealach Dubh path and follow it through the Bealach back to the bothy

**Map:** OS Sheets 41 and 42

**Access Point:** Culra Bothy, GR355664

**Distance:** 22.4km, 1372m ascent

**Approx Time:** 6-10 hours

**Translation:** red hill; white hill; small ridge; delightful hill

**Pronunciation:** caarn jerrack; gyal chaarn; oenach byek; byn ayveen

of remoteness and wilderness flavour. What's wrong with riding a mountain bike down the long kilometres?

Using Culra Bothy, 16km from Dalwhinnie, as an access point is the best of many choices. From there climb west and then north-west on the southern flanks of Carn Dearg to the summit. Another cairn, slightly south, leads to the ridge which drops to a flat bealach and then rises to Diollaid a' Chairn. Beyond here the ridge narrows and leads to a steep and terraced buttress-like slope which fronts the plateau of Geal-Charn. Pick a route through the grassy terraces and on to the extensive summit plateau. You may well experience some difficulty locating the summit cairn, even in clear weather. Beyond the cairn a long slope leads west-south-west down to a grassy bealach. Descend to the bealach and climb a short sharp rise to Aonach Beag. At the cairn, turn sharply south-west to descend rough terraces to a narrow bealach above Lochan a' Charra Mhoir. The ascent of Beinn Eibhinn involves a steep pull to the curve of a broad ridge, which in turn rises to the cairn. To return to Culra descend south and east to the Bealach Dubh path and follow it through the Bealach back to the bothy.

To Spean Bridge

To Kingussie

A86

Moy

River Spean

Binnein Shuas
746 ▲

Meall Buidhe
863 ▲

Coire a' Mhaigh

Lochan na Hearba

Abhainn Ghulbinn

Lochan An Tuirc

Allt Meall Ardruighe

Creag Pitridh
924 ▲

Geal Charn
1049 ▲

Allt Coire Pitridh

Loch a' Bhealaich Leambain

Route C

Allt an Reidh Choire

Beinn a' Chlachair
1088 ▲

Allt Cam

An Lairig

Coire Sron an Nid

Garbh Bhruthach

Dubh Lochan

Carn Dearg
1034 ▲

Bothy

Culra Lodge

Ⓐ

Diollaid a' Chairn
925 ▲

Loch Coire Cheap

Route A

Loch an Sgoir

Meall Nathrach
835 ▲

Geal -Charn
1132 ▲

Sgor Iutharn

Allt a' Chaoil-reidhe

Sron Dreineach

Aonach Beag
1114 ▲

Bealach Dubh

Lochan a' Charra Mhoir

Sron Ruadh

Beithe

Beinn Eibhinn
1100 ▲

Meall an t- Slugain

Garbh-choire Beag

Bealach

Beinn Bheoil
1019 ▲

Uisge Labhair

Lochan Bhealaich Bheithe

Beinn a' Chumhainn
903 ▲

Ben Alder
1148 ▲

Lochan a' Garbh Choire

Garbh Choire

Ston Coire na-h-Iolaire
955 ▲

Coire Chomhlain

Bealach Breabag

Route B

Alder Burn

0          1 mile
0          1 kilometre

N

Benalder Cottage
Ⓑ

## Ben Alder (24), 1148m/3766ft, Beinn Bheoil (110), 1019m/3343ft

**Route Summary:** Follow the path on the E bank of the stream behind the cottage to the Bealach Breabag (Route B). Just short of the summit of the bealach climb the broken and craggy slopes W to a ridge high above the Garbh Coire of Ben Alder. After 800m cross the expansive plateau to a high level lochan and the summit cairn. Return to the Bealach Breabag and climb the short and easy slope to Sron Coire na h-Iolaire. This is a short spur with cairns at either end. To the N of the W cairn a ridge drops to a stony bealach which then rises to the slabby summit slopes of Beinn Bheoil

**Map:** OS Sheet 42

**Access Point:** Ben Alder Cottage, GR499680. Walk-in to Ben Alder Cottage from Rannoch Mill (GR506576) is 12.8km

**Distance:** 12.8km, 1067m ascent

**Approx Time:** 4-6 hours

**Translation:** hill of the rock water; hill of the mouth

**Pronunciation:** byn awlder; byn vyawl

I've often driven south on the A9 past Dalwhinnie and gazed down the great geological fault that holds Loch Ericht to the vast buttressed form of Ben Alder. In winter raiment the mountain appears closer than its 19 km, often fooling visitors into thinking they can 'knock it off' fairly quickly. No so. This hill stands proud, aloof and distant, and it's all the better for it!

Ben Alder is a vast, high plateau containing about 160 hectares of ground above the 1066m contour. Cairngorm-like, it's surrounded by fine corries, particularly those which show their sculptured faces to the east. These fall into the high-level Loch a' Bhealaich Bheithe, beyond which, like a cradling arm, lies the ridge of Beinn Bheoil.

A short distance from Culra, a stream runs down from the high corrie that holds Loch a' Bhealaich Bheithe and joins up with the Allt Chaoil-reidhe which pours down from the Bealach Dubh between Ben Alder and the Lancet Edge. Follow the burn up to the loch, beyond it and on to the craggy Bealach Breabag. Don't cross the bealach but just short of its summit climb the broken ground westwards to reach the prominent ridge which skirts the rim of the impressive Garbh Coire. After 800m or so you find a high level lochan, the Lochan a' Garbh Choire and at this point leave the corrie edge and cross the huge, flat plateau, to the summit cairn and trig point. In misty weather accurate navigation is essential.

Make your way back down to the Bealach Breabag and from a point south of the bealach summit turn north-east and climb heather and boulder slopes to the summit of Sron Coire na h-Iolaire, a magnificently airy perch high above Loch Ericht. Northwards the ridge stretches out for some distance and after a short descent climbs steadily to the summit of Beinn Bheoil. Follow the ridge for another couple of kilometres then drop down north-westwards to pick up the footpath which leads back to Loch Pattack.

Alternative ascent, or descent, routes involve the two Leachas ridges, the Short Leachas, which drops down just north of Loch a'Bhealaich Bheithe, and the Long Leachas, which forms the southern boundary of the Bealach Dubh. The Short Leachas is steeper and involves some good scrambling while the Long Leachas is technically easier.

*Geal Charn from the east*

## Beinn a' Chlachair (53), 1088m/3570ft, Geal Charn (78), 1049m/3442ft, Creag Pitridh (260), 924m/3031ft

Not as remote as their neighbours, these hills lack the grandeur and ruggedness of Ben Alder and the Aonach Beag ridge. Beinn a' Chlachair is probably the finest of the three with its big north-facing corrie holding snow well into the spring. It's been suggested to me more than once that it would be ideal for ski development – God forbid!

From the head of Lochan na h-Earba a rough footpath climbs up to a high bealach beside the Allt Coire Pitridh. This pass gives access across to Loch Pattack, provided you can cross the Allt Cam – in times of spate the ford marked on the OS map becomes a raging torrent. Just north of the summit of the pass, the footpath turns south east. Follow it for a short distance and then take to the broad north-east flank of Beinn a' Chlachair. Follow this to the summit. Return to the footpath and pick up another stalker's path which runs northwards to reach the shallow col between Geal Charn and Creag Pitridh. Don't follow the path as far as the bealach but almost immediately climb easy slopes to the flat summit of Geal Charn. Return to the bealach west of Geal Charn and climb the easy slopes to Craig Pitridh. From the summit descend SW to regain the stalker's path alongside the Allt Coire Pitridh.

**Route Summary:** Follow the Abhainn Ghuilbinn for about 1km (Route C). Turn left and follow the track to the head of Lochan na h-Earba. Take a stalker's path up the hillside beside the Allt Coire Pitridh. After about 1.5km bear S on open hillside towards the NE flank of Beinn a' Chlachair. Climb to the summit. Return ENE along a broad ridge which stops above a large crag. Descend N to a stalker's path with another path a few metres lower. Follow this lower path on to the W flank of Geal Charn. Go E and climb easy slopes to the flat summit. Return to the bealach W of Geal Charn and climb the easy slopes to Craig Pitridh

**Map:** OS Sheet 42

**Access Point:** Luiblea, GR432830

**Distance:** 24km, 1219m ascent

**Approx Time:** 7-9 hours

**Translation:** stonemason's hill; white hill; possibly Petrie's hill

**Pronunciation:** byn a' claachar; geel kaarn; craig peetrie

# THE DRUMOCHTER HILLS

## The Munros:

### A' Bhuidheanach Bheag    Carn na Caim    Meall Chuaich    Geal Charn
### A' Mharconaich    Beinn Udlamain    Sgairneach Mhor

In the past few years I sometimes feel that I've set myself up as a lone defender of these rounded Grampians, a voice speaking in a wilderness of sharp Sgurrs and pointed Stobs and Stucs. But the most wonderful aspect of hillwalking in Scotland is the variety that is on offer and these rounded hills are a definite contrast to the craggier peaks of the west and herald their own fine characteristics in a way that is neither overpowering nor lacking in inspiration.

Geal Charn, A' Mharconaich, Beinn Udlamain and Sgairneach Mhor make up a fine round, especially on skis, and from a starting point of over 450m! Carn na Caim and A' Bhuidheanach Bheag are also ski tourers' hills, but in summer offer an experience of these high Grampians with their wide, sweeping skies and gentle curving slopes which can be dominated by plover and skylark song. Meall Chuaich makes an ideal afteroon or evening stroll in summer conditions and offers wide views of Badenoch and Strathspey. Kingussie, Newtonmore and Laggan make the best bases and there is a railway station at Dalwhinnie.

## A' Bhuidheanach Bheag (235), 936m/3071ft,
## Carn na Caim (226), 941m/3087ft

I'm always surprised to see so many hillwalkers coming down from the hills which form the east side of the Drumochter Pass. I would guess that the majority of them are counting Munros, for Carn na Caim and A' Bhuidheaneach Bheag, the two Munros in the area, have, in the eyes of most walkers, little going for them other than their height above sea level.

In several books I've read these hills are described as dull, but a hill is only dull when seen through dull eyes. Having said that, I too would probably have avoided them if I weren't trying to get round the Munros for a second time. My first visit, a good 12-15 years ago, was on a grey misty day and I skied over both hills on wet, slushy snow. I was concentrating so much on my skis that I singularly failed to take in anything about the hills, other than the fact that the descent back down to the A9 was promising in better snow conditions.

**Route Summary:** Leave the A9 S of Balsporran (Route A) and climb steep heathery slopes raked with shallow gullies to Meall a' Chaorainn. Continue E and follow a fence to the summit of A' Bhuidheanach Bheag. N of the summit the fence crosses an area of peat at the head of Coire Chuirn. Follow the fence to Carn na Caim, two rounded tops on either side of a shallow depression. Follow open and obvious slopes SW back to the A9 in Drumochter Pass.

**Map:** OS Sheet 42

**Access Point:** Balsporran Cottages

**Distance:** 12.8km, 610m ascent

**Approx Time:** 4-6 hours

*A' Mharconaich from the north-east*

**Translation:** the little yellow place; cairn of the curve

**Pronunciation:** a vooanach vek; caarn a kym

A track leads up the hill from the A9 to an old quarry which is gouged out of the hillside and as I made my way uphill I recalled some comments of a friend of mine, comments that were made as we walked on the Glencoe peaks a week earlier. He had suggested that the Cairngorms and the hills of the Eastern Highlands had little to offer, and the real thrills were to be found on the sharper peaks of the West.

As I reached the high rounded ridge which joins A' Bhuidheanach Bheag and Carn na Caim the views around me put a perspective on my thoughts. While I love the peaks and pinnacles of the west I also appreciate these big, rounded hills which seem to roll on forever in all directions. Here the skies are huge and dominant, and at virtually 950m, it's good to be able to walk freely for long distances without losing height and having to regain it.

Up here you become aware of the shapes around you, not so much the shape of the hills themselves, but the smooth flowing contours of the corries which bite their way into these high uplands. Here are curves which are sensuous in form, smooth, gradual and majestic, the gracefulness of the high Grampians. There is nothing sharp, or jagged, or jarring to the eye, nothing scabrous nor irregular.

In summer the song of skylarks, with the possible exception of the spring song of the cock snow bunting, the finest of all mountain melodies, fills the air, and watch for snipe darting out from below a peat hag. Now and again you might pick out the plaintive whistle of the golden plover, a

*The eastern Drumochter Hills from the air*

melancholy sound which is nevertheless appealing, the sound of these high, rounded places, the song of the Grampians.

## Meall Chuaich (209), 951m/3120 ft

Rising high above the loch of the same name, Meall Chuaich is an isolated top which, because of its position in the clench of Glen Truim and Strathspey offers superb views of Badenoch towards the high Cairngorms and along the length of Loch Ericht towards the Ben Alder group. It's a straightforward ascent and makes a great afternoon jaunt on a winter's day.

A private road leads from the A9 to Loch Cuaich and just to the south of it a footpath runs past a bothy and crosses the Allt Coire Chuaich which runs down from the big, rounded hills of Gaick. On the north side of the stream a path has been worn through the heather straight up the hill's south-west ridge to a flatter, stony area by Stac Meall Chuaich. From there it's a straightforward walk up the stony ridge to the big summit cairn.

**Route Summary:** Leave the A9 just S of the Cuaich cottages (Route B) and follow a private road through a locked gate. In a short distance reach a track beside an aqueduct and follow it to the Loch Cuaich dam. Open heather slopes lead to the summit of the hill

**Map:** OS Sheet 42

**Access Point:** Cuaich, GR654876

**Distance:** 11.2km 610m ascent

**Approx Time:** 3-5 hours

**Translation:** hill of the quaich

**Pronunciation:** myowl chooeech

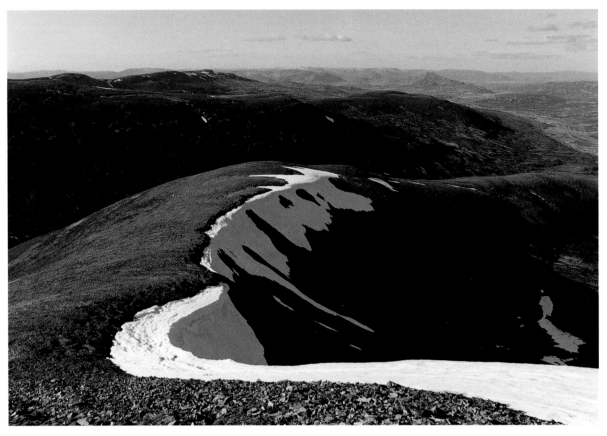

*Looking north from the summit of A' Mharconaich*

## Geal Charn (272), 917m/3008ft, A' Mharconaich (178), 975m/3199ft, Beinn Udlamain (119), 1010m/3314ft, Sgairneach Mhor (151), 991m/3251ft

**Route Summary:** Leave Balsporran Cottages, cross the railway and follow the track up Coire Fhar. A sketchy path leaves the track and runs up the hillside to the NE ridge of Geal Charn. Pass the cairns at 840m and continue W to the rocky summit. Continue S on a broad ridge to a height of 970m where a ridge appears to run off NE. The summit of A' Mharconaich lies 800m along this ridge. Return to the 970m point, cross a wide bealach to the SW and continue SW on a broad ridge, over an unamed top and across a featureless plateau to the summit of Beinn Udlamain. Descend S to a boggy bealach. On the far side take an E bearing to locate the summit cairn on the most W top of the hill. Descend to Coire Dhomhain via the E spur,

The Pass of Drumochter separates the rounded hills of Carn na Caim and A' Bhuidheanach Bheag from these more distinctive mountains, an area once known as the Druim Uachdair, the ridge of the upper ground. Gathered nicely together in one corner of this old area these four Munros make a good expedition and offer some of the best views possible of the Ben Alder hills across the long trench of Loch Ericht, particularly from Geal Charn.

This hill can be reached easily from Balsporran Cottages on the A9 by a footpath through the deep heather and on up to the northeast ridge. Higher up the ridge there were once a series of high, slender cairns which looked like a row of marching men when seen from below. For some reason someone has knocked them down but they seem to be growing again. It seems that few hillwalkers can resist putting stones on cairns – any cairns!

From the summit of Geal Charn, with its long views down the length of Loch Ericht, drop down the very rocky slopes to a col and then climb south-east up grassy slopes to reach A' Mharconaich's long, broad ridge – the summit cairn is at the north-east end, perched high above a big corrie. A long and twisting ridge leads to the next Munro, Beinn Udlamain, the Gloomy Hill, and a line of fence posts marking the boundary between Perthshire and Inverness-shire make a useful navigational aid. You can follow them all the way on to the wide and fairly featureless plateau and the summit itself.

Continue past the big summit cairn in a southerly direction, still keeping company with the fence posts until they suddenly vanish westwards in a tight right-angle. At this point, marked on the map as Carn 'Ic Loumhaidh, drop down over very rocky ground to the bealach which is in fact the head of Coire Dhomhain, take an easterly bearing and climb grassy slopes to reach the south-west ridge of Sgairneach Mhor which can then be followed to the broad summit and the trig point. Leave the summit in an easterly direction to gain a ridge which gradually swings round to north east. Take care hereabouts in winter for the lip of Coire Creagach cornices quite severely. A friend of mine once skied over the cornice in misty conditions – fortunately he missed the steep, rocky part and eventually managed to stop himself on very steep snow with his ski poles.

Once you reach the footpath in Coire Dhomhain it's an easy walk back to the A9 and a road walk back to Balsporran.

then follow the footpath to the railway and the A9 about 4km S of Balsporran

**Map:** OS Sheet 42

**Access Point:** Balsporran Cottage GR628792

**Distance:** 25km, 1143m ascent

**Approx Time:** 6-8 hours

**Translation:** white hill; the horse place; gloomy mountain; big stony hillside

**Pronunciation:** gyal chaarn; a varkaneech; byn ootlaman; skaarnyatch vore

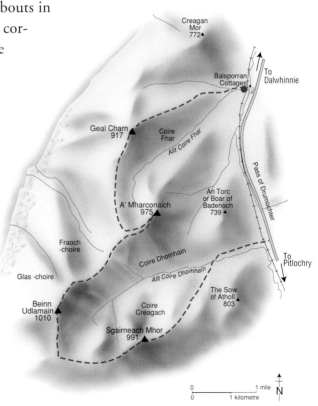

# THE TARF AND TILT HILLS

## The Munros:

## Beinn a' Ghlo (Carn Liath, Braigh Coire Chruinn-bhalgain, Carn nan Gabhar)
## Beinn Dearg   Carn a' Chlamain   Carn an Fhidleir   An Sgarsoch

Between Glen Bruar and the Cairnwell lies a great wilderness of high tops and deep glens, split right through the middle by the long, deep cleft of Glen Tilt. The high peaty area to the west of Tilt is dominated by Beinn Dearg, Carn a' Chlamain, An Sgarsoch and Carn an Fhidleir, a quartet known as the Ring of Tarf, a long and arduous expedition involving many kilometres of tough, remote walking. To the east of Tilt, the Beinn a' Ghlo massif rises to its four tops, the highest of which is Carn nan Gabhar.

Adam Watson, the ecologist and author has described Beinn a' Ghlo as 'one of the most beautiful and mysterious hills of Scotland', an odd description for a scientist to offer. Perhaps he is referring to the old legend which suggests that the hill has 19 corries, in any of which a rifle could be fired without being heard in another.

**Route Summary:** Behind Balaneasie Cottage on the S bank of the River Tilt climb grassy slopes to the headwaters of the Fender Burn (Route A, p.99). Traverse the hillside SE, past Craig-choinnich Lodge and then east up steep slopes to the summit ridge of Carn Liath. Follow the twisting ridge N over Beinn Mhaol. It soon broadens out as it approaches Braigh Coire Chruinn-bhalgain. Continue NE along the ridge for 1km before dropping down grassy slopes to cross the Bealach na Fhiodha. Continue E to the slopes which lead to another bealach between Airgiod Bheinn and Carn nan Gabhar and finally NE along a broad and easy ridge to the twin cairns of Carn nan Gabhar down Glen Tilt

**Map:** OS Sheet 43

**Access Point:** Balaneasie Cottage in Glen Tilt

**Distance:** 20km, 1220m ascent

## Beinn a'Ghlo (Carn Liath (175), 975m/3199ft, Braigh Coire Chruinn-bhalgain (63), 1070m/3510ft, Carn nan Gabhar (29), 1129m/3704ft)

The walk up Glen Tilt from Blair Atholl is a long one at the start and finish of what is a fairly strenuous hill day. Probably a mountain bike is the answer.

WH Murray has suggested that the walker will never find his interest flagging in Glen Tilt – the river is continually lively, the woods are mature and varied and there is a continuous, gradual change from the lower fertility to an upper desolation.

About 8km up the glen, just beyond Marble Lodge, a bridge crosses the River Tilt at Balaneasie Cottage. Beyond the cottage grassy slopes cross a low ridge below which runs the Fender Burn. On the hillside opposite some pines denote Creag-choinnich Lodge, a good indicator for the route, which follows a burn up to the north-north-west ridge of Carn Liath. Once you've visited the summit retrace your steps and follow the curving ridge over Beinn Mhaol and on to the broader ridge of Braigh Coire Chruinn-bhalgain, one of the most wonderful-sounding names of all the Munros.

North-east of here you have to find a high level bealach, like a mighty drawbridge between the tops – this leads to a short scramble

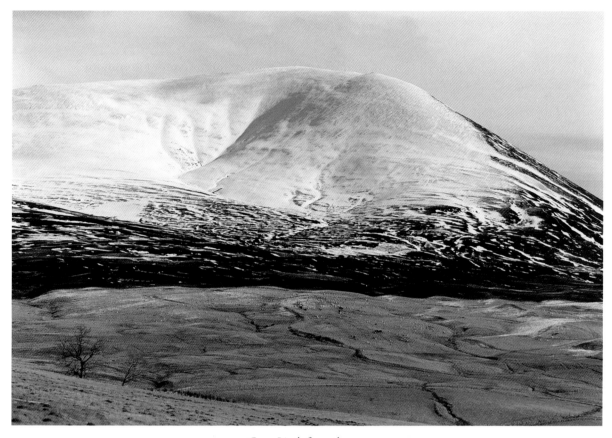

*Carn Liath from the west*

on grassy slopes which leads to yet another high bealach, this time between Airgiod Bheinn and the Munro top of Carn nan Gabhar. Climb the Munro by broad ridge and descend back to Glen Tilt the north ridge – cross the river by the bridge below the Allt Fheannach.

## Beinn Dearg (121), 1008m/3307ft

Blair Castle in Blair Atholl, now a popular tourist destination, has a chequered history which goes back to the 12th century when John Comyn of Badenoch built his Cummings Tower.

Behind the Castle, Diana's Grove marks the start of the Minigaig, an ancient 48km route between here and Kingussie. This track climbs gently through dense woods of birch, larch and pine, keeping in sight of the chuckling burn which passes through a series of cascades, pools and deep-set ravines, all darkly shaded in bottle green. After a short time, the Rumbling Bridge is reached, a stone, hump-back of a bridge which was built in 1762 and bears witness to the fact that the chuckling Banvie Burn can, in spate, turn into

**Approx Time:** 6-8 hours

**Translation:** grey hill; upland of the corrie of round blisters; hill of the goats.

**Pronunciation:** kaarn lee-a; bray corrie kroon vaalakan; kaarn nan gower

**Route Summary:** From Old Blair walk up the private road in Glen Banvie (Route B) and continue up E side of the Allt an t-Seapail to a bothy beside the Allt Sheicheachan. A track continues along the NW side of this stream to the 800m contour. From there follow the broad and easy ridge N to the summit

**Map:** OS Sheet 43

**Access Point:** Old Blair, GR867667

**Distance:** 25km, 833m ascent

**Approx Time:** 6-8 hours

*Beinn Dearg from the south-west across Glen Garry*

**Translation:** red hill
**Pronunciation:** byn jerrack

such a vociferous stream that it actually 'rumbles' the stones and rocks in its riverbed.

The Minigaig doesn't actually cross this bridge, but marches forward through a gate into the Whim Plantation before splitting at another gate which marks the end of the woods and where the Minigaig drops down to the burnside where it crosses the Quarry Bridge, built eight years after the Rumbling Bridge from stones taken from the quarry a few hundred metres upstream.

Walk out of the gloominess of the woods and on to the Banvie moors. Clear of the trees, the landscape changes dramatically – above the track a series of zigzags on the slope indicate the old path once used by peat cutters fetching their turf from Tom nan Cruach, the Hillock of Peat Stacks. Soon the track, known locally as the West Hand Road, begins to incline as it pulls away from Glen Banvie up the glen of the Allt na Moine Baine towards a tall pile of stones, the Lady March Cairn. Apparently, in the 19th century Lady March built a small cairn during a picnic lunch, and, as is the way with indiscriminate cairn building, some workmen, supposed to be repairing the West Hand Road nearby, later added to the cairn until it was over two metres high. Like a dog leaving its scent, it seems that man also has a desire to leave his mark, however inappropriate, a precursor of modern graffiti I suppose!

Beyond the cairn the road crosses the Allt na Moine Baine and skirts around the long open slopes of Carn Dearg Beag to drop into the shallow valley of the Allt an t-Seapail, the stream of the chapel. Just after the old trackside milestone there is a fine ancient circular well by the name of Fuaran Bhadenoch, another indication of this road's antiquity and its ultimate destination.

Pass another large cairn, the Carn Mhic Shimidh, this one a memorial to a battle between the Murrays of Atholl and a raiding party of Frasers led by Simon Lovat. The cairn marks the spot where Lovat was slain and also the final stretch to the bothy beside the Allt Sheicheachain. From here, follow the track along the north-west side of the Allt Sheicheachan to where it runs out and then simply follow the broad ridge all the way to the stony summit.

*Carn a' Chlamain from the south*

Route Summary: Just beyond Forest Lodge (Route C) a zigzag stalker's path makes its way up the steep hillside. It then crosses easier open slopes running parallel for a distance with the Allt na Maraig before climbing on to the summit of Carn a' Chlamain. Descend the hill's SW ridge back to Glen Tilt and return by track to Forest Lodge

Map: OS Sheet 43

Access Point: Forest Lodge, Glen Tilt

Distance: 10km, 730m ascent

Approx Time: 3-4hours

Translation: hill of the kite or buzzard

Pronunciation: kaarn a klaavan

## Carn a' Chlamain (188), 963m/3159ft

One of the easiest Munros, Carn a' Chlamain makes a good afternoon walk from Forest Lodge in Glen Tilt. Alternatively, you can walk up Glen Tilt from Old Blair and make a day of it. The hill itself lifts its head shyly above the extensive Tarf plateau and offers good views of the Beinn a' Ghlo massif across the deep trench of Glen Tilt.

Follow the Glen Tilt track past Forest Lodge and through the woodland until you reach a gate. Don't go through the gate but turn left, climb up through the trees and on to the open hillside where you'll find an old stalker's path which eventually zigzags its way up the steep heather-covered hillside and on to the plateau itself.

From here the views are extensive north and north-east towards the Cairngorms and the Glenshee hills and westwards towards the hills of Perthshire. The path continues over the undulating plateau and eventually passes close to the summit cairn.

To make a circuit of the walk, descend the hill's long and curving south-west ridge back to Glen Tilt.

## Carn an Fhidhleir (145), 994m/3261ft,
## An Sgarsoch (124), 1006m/3301ft

These big heather-covered domes may lack the visual features of the western hills, but, situated as they are close to the headwaters of the Geldie, the Feshie and the Tarf, they have an air of remoteness which challenges most walkers. My first ascent of these hills was via a long, rough mountain bike ride from Glen Feshie, following the infant Feshie to the watershed with the Geldie. Subsequently, I climbed the hills from Linn of Dee, again by mountain bike, but this time on a much better surfaced track.

It's a long route from Linn o' Dee, some 40km for the return trip, so a mountain bike makes good sense if you want to climb these hills in one day. The best alternative, of course, is to backpack round the four Munros of the Ring of Tarf.

From Linn of Dee follow the north bank of the River Dee to White Bridge, cross it and continue on the track beside the forest plantation to where the Geldie turns westwards. Continue on this track, past the Red House, for another 5km to where it crosses the river and continues to the ruins of Geldie Lodge. Prepare to get your feet wet.

At Geldie Lodge walk up the bulldozed track to its highest point, just above the Allt a' Chaorainn burn. Leave the track, cross over the burn, and climb the heather covered slopes of the corrie south-westwards to the north ridge and the summit of Carn an Fhidhleir.

This summit is the meeting place of Perthshire, Inverness-shire and Aberdeenshire and its neighbouring summit, An Sgarsoch, was in years gone by a market place, where cattle and horses were bought and sold. The event was known as the Feill Sgarsaich.

To reach the summit we have to drop the long, wide and easy slopes of the Fiddler's south-east ridge to an obvious bump in the ridge. From the top of this bump, turn due east and drop down to the col at 710m.

From here it's a long pull to the summit. Descend to the north to Scarsoch Bheag and then north-east to pick up the bulldozed track which leads back to Geldie Lodge.

**Route Summary:** Follow N bank of the River Dee to White Bridge and then along the Geldie Burn to Geldie Lodge. A mountain bike would be useful. Follow a bulldozed track WSW to its highest point. Continue SW over peat hags and climb the NE slopes of Carn an Fhidhleir to reach the N ridge close to the summit. Drop SSE along a broad ridge and then down the E side of the ridge to reach the bealach at 700m. From there climb NE to the flat summit of An Sgarsoch. Return to Geldie Lodge by following the N ridge and then E of Sgarsoch Bheag over peaty ground to reach the bulldozed track again.

**Map:** OS Sheet 43

**Access Point:** Linn of Dee.

**Distance:** 40km, 914m ascent

**Approx Time:** 10-12 hours

**Translation:** hill of the fiddler; the place of sharp rocks,

**Pronunciation:** kaarn an yeelar, an skaarsoch

101

# THE CAIRNWELL HILLS

## The Munros:

An Socach    Glas Tulaichean    Carn an Righ    Beinn Iutharn Mhor
Carn Bhac    The Cairnwell    Carn a' Gheoidh    Carn Aosda

Bounded by the Dee in the north, the Tilt in the west and the A93 in the east, this large sprawling upland area boasts eight Munros. Unfortunately, two of them represent the most depressing aspect of man's commercial development in the mountains – the Cairnwell ski area is probably the worst, in terms of planning and landscaping, of Scotland's four ski areas. To be frank the whole area is a mess – and the two Munros in whose arms much of the development has taken place, The Cairnwell and Carn Aosda, have been hideously scarred. Walkers have little incentive to visit these hills.

In contrast, the other hills in this area share the same quality of isolation as the hills west of Glen Tilt. This is typical rolling Grampian country – heather-covered hills which echo to the guttural call of the red grouse.

## An Socach (221), 944m/3097ft, Glas Tulaichean (77), 1051m/3448ft, Carn an Righ (98) 1029m/3376ft, Beinn Iutharn Mhor (85), 1045m/3428ft, Carn Bhac (216), 946m/3104ft

This is a big round, another where a mountain bike can be used to advantage by cycling up the 8km from Inverey to Altanour Lodge. South-east of the lodge ruins An Socach presents its curved ridge and the most direct approach is best, due south to climb straight to the summit cairn by the hill's north ridge. The OS map mistakenly name the east top An Socach.

From the summit drop down steep slopes in a southerly direction and traverse easy angled slopes to the lonely waters of Loch nan Eun, set in its natural bowl among these big, rounded hills. South-west of the loch, above the great glacier-scoured Glas Choire Bheag, a long ridge, narrow for these parts, climbs to the summit of Glas Tulaichean, the highest hill of the round. While there is a temptation to return all the way back down the ridge, leave it about halfway down and traverse northwards to the head of Gleann Mor where a track runs west below the scree-covered slopes of Mam nan Carn. Where the track suddenly turns to the north, leave it and immediately climb westwards to the

Route Summary: Walk, or take a bike up the 8km of Glen Ey to the remains of Altanour Lodge (Route A). Head due S from the ruins and climb the N ridge of An Socach to the summit cairn. Continue past the cairn and descend S before climbing easy slopes to Loch nan Eun. Climb the NNE ridge of Glas Tulaichean before dropping down N to the head of Gleann Mor to where a track runs round the slopes of Mam nan Carn. Follow the track W for 1km and continue W to climb the slopes of Carn an Righ. Return to the track, climb the SW ridge of Mam nan Carn to its summit then NNW to Beinn Iutharn Mhor. From here follow the summit ridge E then N before leaving the ridge in a NNE direction to cross high undulating ground to the brroad, featureless W summit of Carn Bhac. Follow the broad

*Beinn Iutharn Mhor from above Glen Ey*

103

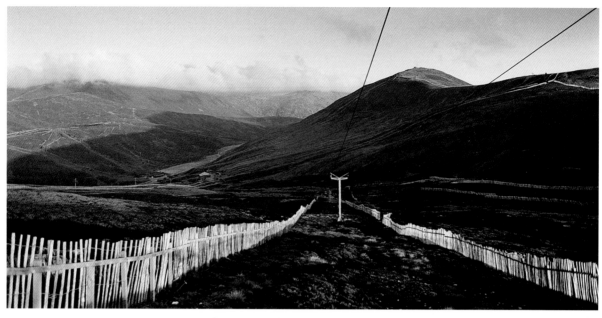

*The Cairnwell from the adjacent ski area*

ridge NE for a kilometre to the summit cairn. From the summit descend S then SE by the Allt an Odhar back to Altanour Lodge.

**Map:** OS Sheet 43

**Access Point:** Inverey

**Distance:** 40km, 2000m ascent.

**Approx Time:** 10-16 hours

**Translation:** the projecting place; green hills; hill of the king; big hill of the edge; hill of peat hags

**Pronunciation:** an sochkach; glas tooleechan; kaarn an ree; byn yooarn vore; kaarn vachk

summit of Carn an Righ. Return to the track, climb the obvious south-west ridge of Mam nan Carn to its summit then turn north, for a long undulating and often boggy walk over Beinn Iutharn Mhor and on to the western top of Carn Bhac. This long section can be tricky in misty weather and is a good test of navigational skills.

Once again the OS have put the spot height on the lower top, the west one, but the true summit is at the north-east end of Carn Bhac's long and broad summit ridge.

From the cairn, the quickest descent is to drop down due south, picking up the Allt an Odhar – this can then be followed all the way back to Altanour Lodge.

An Socach can be climbed on its own from Baddach in Glen Clunie, Carn Bhac and Beinn Iutharn Mhor in a shorter day from Altanour, while Glas Tulaichean and Carn an Righ can be reached in a long day out from the Cairnwell.

**Route Summary:** Start just south of the ski area (Route B) and climb heather slopes to the summit. Descend NNW past the top chairlift point and continue on a broad ridge with snow fences. Just before the Cairnwell-Aosda col turn west and drop to another col, the

## The Cairnwell (242), 933m/3061ft, Carn a' Gheoidh (177), 975m/3199ft, Carn Aosda (270) 917m/3008ft

The Cairnwell and Carn Aosda are probably the most accessible Munros in the country – they are also the most depressing. It's hard to believe that man can cause so much damage in such a small area and even harder to believe that, in these days of environmental concern, that particular ski development is still being increased in size.

The visit to Carn a' Gheoidh, beyond Loch Vrotachan, helps add a touch of reality to this outing, but first of all we must climb The Cairnwell. Leave the road just south of the ski centre buildings, avoiding the worst of the paraphernalia and bulldozed roads. Short, clipped heather and scree offers fairly easy going despite the steepness of the road and there is some consolation in the fact that you don't have to climb far from the road, one of the highest in the country, to reach the 933m summit cairn and ski lift hut. You probably won't want to spend too much time here so descend to the north-north-west, first of all past the top chairlift pylon and then along a broad ridge decorated by large snow fences.

After 800m or so, just before you reach the Cairnwell/Aosda col, turn westwards and descend again to the lowest point between The Cairnwell and Carn a' Gheoidh.

From here, with the metalwork and rubble behind you, it's a pleasant walk along gentle moss-covered slopes, along the lip above the steep and rocky Coire Direach, past Carn nan Sac and across a flat heath to Carn a' Gheoidh.

Return to the Cairnwell/Aosda col, follow the bulldozed track north-east and then east passing the Butchart's ski tow to reach the summit of Carn Aosda. Follow the bulldozed roads south back to the Cairnwell road.

lowest point between The Cairnwell and Carn a' Gheoidh. Continue SW past Carn nan Sac and west over a small plateau to Carn a' Gheoidh. Return the way you came to the Cairnwell-Aosda col. From there ascend NE then east along a broad ridge to the flat summit of Carn Aosda. Descend S by bulldozed tracks and roads to the Cairnwell road

**Map:** OS Sheet 43: GR135773, GR107767, GR134792

**Access Point:** Devil's Elbow, GR140780

**Distance:** 8km, 579m ascent

**Approx Time:** 3-5 hours

**Translation:** From Carn Bhalg, hill of bags; hill of the goose; hill of age

**Pronunciation:** cairn-well; kaarn a yowee; kaarn oesh

# GLENSHEE AND LOCHNAGAR HILLS

## The Munros:

Creag Leacach    Glas Maol    Cairn of Claise    Tom Buidhe
Tolmount    Carn an Tuirc    Lochnagar    Carn a' Coire Boidheach
(White Mounth)    Carn an t-Sagairt Mor    Cairn Bannoch
Broad Cairn    Driesh    Mayar    Mount Keen

Bounded by the Cairnwell Pass in the west and Deeside in the north, this corner of the Mounth is epitomised by rounded green hills, vast rolling plateaux and features some wild open glens. At least two of them, Glen Callater and Caenlochan, are glacial trenches with steep-sided corries at their top.

Glen Muick is probably the most dramatic of the glens with its mountain-bound loch and upper glen overlooked by the precipitous Creag an Dubh-Loch. The rock of the area is mainly schist with patches of quartzite but here and there fertile areas of limestone are found – Caenlochan, for example, is rich in uncommon arctic-alpine plants, rivalling Ben Lawers in the south.

The plateau of grass, sedge and moss offers unsurpassed high-level walking and big distances can be covered with a minimum of effort. Sadly, the south side of Loch Muick has been spoiled by the creation of crudely bulldozed tracks, for sporting purposes, but the greater part of the area is still very rewarding for the hillwalker and even more so for the ski tourer.

Because of the nature of the high, rolling terrain, the main chunk of these hills can be easily climbed in a couple of longish expeditions, or broken down into smaller groups. However, apart from Glas Maol and Creag Leacach which can both be climbed from the Cairnwell in a fairly easy afternoon, there is little real advantage in climbing these hills in two or threes. Their relative remoteness requires a big walk-in, from almost any direction, and once you have gained the altitude you are as well to make the most of it and stay high. The judicious use of a mountain bike can also make a huge difference.

Lochnagar is of course the main attraction in the area – the royal mountain ever since Queen Victoria and Prince Albert chose to purchase Balmoral Estate rather than Ardverikie in the west. Celebrated in Byron's 'Lachin y Gair', thousands have come to visit the '…crags that are wild and majestic, the steep frowning glories of dark Lochnagar.'

*Lochnagar from the north across Glen Dee*

**Route Summary:** From the Devil's Elbow on the A93 (Route A, p.108) climb the N ridge of Meall Gorm and follow the ridge round to the stony tops of Creag Leacach. Follow the broad ridge N beside a stone wall to the summit of Glas Maol. Continue N and NE on the undulating ridge to Cairn of Claise, then E over the Ca Whims to Tom Buidhe. Return to the Ca Whims, and climb the stony S slopes of the Tolmount. Descend to the W, skirting the head of Glen Callater and Coire Kander to the summit of Carn an Tuirc. Drop down W to the glen and follow the footpath to the old bridge beside the A93

**Map:** OS Sheets 43, 44

**Access Point:** A93 at the Devil's Elbow

**Distance:** 22km, 1017m ascent (5km on the A93 between starting and finishing points.)

**Approx Time:** 6-8 hours

**Translation:** slabby rock; green/grey bare hill; hill of the hollow; yellow hill; hill of the valley; hill of the boar

**Pronunciation:** krayk lyechach; glas moel; kaarn an claes; tom booee; tolmount; kaarn an toork

# Creag Leacach (157), 987m/3238ft, Glas Maol (67), 1068m/3504ft, Cairn of Claise (68), 1064m/3491ft, Tom Buidhe (200), 957m/3140ft, Tolmount (199), 958m/3143ft, Carn an Tuirc (112), 1019m/3343ft

Creag Leacach and Glas Maol can easily be climbed in a short day, linking the two by a fine, gently winding ridge, but there are few areas where you can walk over six Munros in such a relatively short distance – about 22km, with only 1017m of climbing. This is possible by using either two cars, or a car and a bicycle.

Drive to where the A93 Cairnwell road crosses over the Allt a' Garbh-choire, just immediately west of Carn an Tuirc. Just south of this point, a footbridge crosses the stream leading to a path which runs up the glen in an eastwards direction. The bridge here stands at the site of An Seann-spideal, the old spital that carried an early military road. Either leave a car, or hide a bicycle in the heather, to be collected at the end of the walk. Now drive southwards over the Cairnwell road to a car park at GR128757, at the Devil's Elbow, drop down heather-covered slopes from the car park, cross the infant Allt a' Ghlinne Bhig and climb the north ridge of Meall Gorm, a fairly steep climb over deep heather. From the summit descend south-eastwards to a wide bealach and continue in much the same direction up the scree-covered slopes of Creag Leacach's south-west top. From there the obvious scree- and boulder-covered ridge swings to the north-east, to the summit of Creag Leacach, and winds its way for about 2.5km to the big dome of Glas Maol. An old wall also runs the entire distance.

With most of the hard work behind you now you can begin to appreciate this high-level promenade. Most of the tops in front of you are mere rises in the mossy plateau and the whole area is typified by rounded smooth slopes, heathery hollows and an air of spaciousness.

Leaving Glas Maol, cross the route of the old Monega Pass which runs from Glen Isla to Glen Clunie, the highest of the rights of way which cross the Mounth, and follow the broad, undulating ridge with the steep hollow of Garbh-choire to your left, to the summit of Cairn of Claise.

It's a pleasant stroll from the summit cairn, across the boggy Ca Whims, towards the unlikely Munro of Tom Buidhe – a mere rise in the centre of a great tableland. It was Sir Hugh Munro himself who said of this area, 'So elevated and flat is the range that a straight line of 10 miles could be drawn from Creag Leacach to the Meikle Pap of Lochnagar.' He went on to suggest that there was some relief for about half a mile, or 1km, on each side of the Tolmount and, indeed, it's from that summit that we get the best view of this particular outing.

Return to Ca Whims and from there it's an easy stroll to the summit of the Tolmount. Perched on the edge of the upper corrie of Glen Callater, the view down the crag-girt glen is a particularly fine one. Descend from the Tolmount around the heads of Glen Callater and Coire Kander and follow the broad grassy ridge between Coire Kander and the Cul Riabhach to the flat stony summit of Carn an Tuirc and views down Glen Clunie. The footpath in the corrie below follows the burn back to your awaiting car or bike, passing the fine rocky gorge of the Allt a' Garbh Choire on the way.

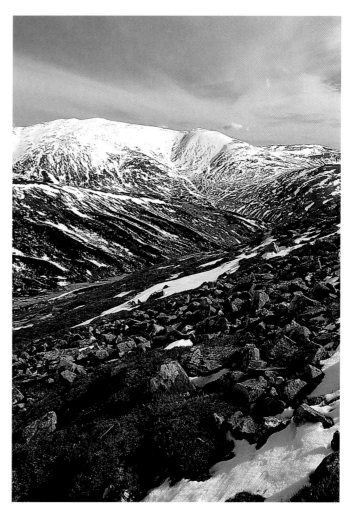

*Glas Maol from the north-west*

## Lochnagar (19), 1155m/3789ft, Carn a' Coire Boidheach (White Mounth) (33), 1118m/3668ft, Carn an t-Sagairt Mor (81), 1047m/3435ft, Cairn Bannoch (114), 1012m/3320ft, Broad Cairn (139), 998m/3274ft

These hills can also be broken down into shorter expeditions, but a fine horseshoe traverse around the great glaciated trench of Loch Muick and its neighbouring Dubh Loch carries you over all these Munros in one long outing.

There are a number of routes to the summit of Lochnagar, a mountain well appreciated by climbers, walkers, poets and royalty. Contained within the Queen's Balmoral Estate, members of the royal family have enjoyed the mountain since Victoria and Albert bought the estate last century.

**Route Summary:** Take the path which runs along the edge of the plantation to cross to the other side of the glen at Allt-na-giubhsaich (Route B) and continue along the S bank of the burn through the pinewoods to reach a track. Follow it W for about 3km to the bealach which leads through to Gelder Shiel. At this point take an obvious path WSW across a slight hollow and then more steeply to the Foxes' Well on the left of the path. Soon the slope steepens again before 'The Ladder' and the top of the summit ridge. A short descent across a wide col and another climb leads to the flat summit ridge of Lochnagar. Walk along the rim of the corrie, past Cac Carn Mor and the deep chasm of the Black Spout to the summit cone of Cac Carn Beag where you'll find the trig point. Return to Cac Carn Mor and take another footpath in a SW direction to a shallow col. Leave the path and climb Carn a' Coire Boidheach. Continue over the summit to regain the footpath and where it crosses the Allt an Dubh-loch climb W to the summit of Carn an t-Sagairt Mor. Walk SE from the summit onto a flat plateau and ascend the slight rise to Cairn Bannoch. Continue SE over Cairn of Gowal, ENE to a col and E to the summit of Broad Cairn. From there descend E to pick up a footpath which soon becomes a bulldozed track. Pass a wooden shelter, drop down a footpath into Corrie Chash to the head of Loch Muick and follow the footpath and bulldozed tracks alongside the loch to Spittal of Glenmuick

**Map:** OS Sheet 44

**Access Point:** Spittal of Glenmuick car park

**Distance:** 32km, 1100m ascent

**Approx Time:** 8-10hours

**Translation:** named after Lochan na Gaire in Lochnagar's NE Corrie. Little loch of the noisy sound; hill of the beautiful corrie; big hill of the priest; possibly peaked hill; broad cairn

**Pronunciation:** loch-na-gar; kaarn a corrie vawyach; kaarn an takarsht moar; kaarn bannoch; broad kaarn

Probably the finest approach to Lochnagar is from the Invercauld Bridge through the Ballochbuie Forest, the oldest stand of ancient Caledonian pines in Scotland. Another route from the north is via the estate cottage and adjacent hut at Gelder Shiel, while walkers staying in Braemar frequently take the footpath from Glen Callater via the stalker's path up Carn an t-Sagairt Mor. By far the most popular, and the most eroded, route is from the Spittal of Glenmuick at the end of the public road which runs up Glen Muick from Ballater.

The tracks from Gelder Shiel and the Spittal of Glenmuick meet at the foot of the slopes east of Meikle Pap where a badly eroded footpath runs roughly westwards up towards the col between Meikle Pap and the Cuidhe Crom passing the Foxes' Well, or the Fox Well Cairn to give it its proper name. Just before the col is reached the path starts to zigzag its way leftwards up a steeper slope known as The Ladder, to reach the plateau above. It's well worth a little divergence below The Ladder to catch a glimpse down into the Corrie of Lochnagar, a great cirque of granite cliffs rising sheer from the dark lochan away below.

From the north-west shoulder of Cuidhe Crom above The Ladder, the path makes its way across the plateau, close to the corrie rim. Just before the cairn of Cac Carn Mor, the path splits, with one branch dropping downhill in a south-westwards direction and another continuing northwards. This latter path carries you past the deepset gully of the Black Spout, to the rocky summit, Cac Carn Beag, about 400m away across the plateau, complete with cairn, trig point and view indicator. Return on the same path to the junction below Cac Carn Mor, and follow the south-west path around the head of the cliffs of The Stuic, which rise from Loch nan Eun below. Just as the path begins to ascend again, bear slightly left from the footpath and climb the easy tundra-like slopes to the summit of Carn a' Coire Boidheach, sometimes known as the White Mounth.

Beyond the summit, wide stony slopes lead you back to the footpath which skirts the slopes of Carn an t-Sagairt Beag and crosses the infant Allt an Dubh-loch. Just at this point leave the path again to climb westwards to Carn an-Sagairt Mor where some rocks form a rude cairn around some crashed aircraft debris.

The route between Carn an-Sagairt Mor and Cairn Bannoch is a easy stroll over springy turf, but don't be fooled — in misty weather many walkers pass Cairn Bannoch without realising it. It is an imperceptible rise to Cairn Bannoch, but a couple of kilometres further on, passing the crags of Creag an Dubh Loch on your left, Broad Cairn offers greater character, with its rocky, granite summit. Descend eastwards across fields of broken granite to reach a path which soon becomes a rudely gouged-out track – the work of the uncaring bulldozer. Pass the wooden hut and continue east for a short distance to where another path drops down Corrie Chash to the head of Loch Muick, follows the south shore through some scattered birch woods and meets up with the bulldozed track again at the Black Burn. Follow the track all the way to Spittal of Glenmuick.

Cac Carn Beag 1155
Lochnagar Burn
Meikle Pap 980
Clais Rathadan
Allt na giubhsaich
To Ballater
Carn an t-Sagairt Beag 1044
Loch nan Eun
LOCHNAGAR
Route B
Spittal of Glenmuick
Visitor Centre
Carn an t-Sagairt Mor 1047
The Stuic
Cuidhe Crom 1083
Carn a' Coire Boidheach 1118
Coire Boidheach
White Mounth
Glen Callater
Allt an Dubh-loch
Eagles Rock
Dubh Loch
Loch Muick
Carn Dubh 822
Cairn Bannoch 1012
Fafernie 1000
Creag an Dubh-loch
Broad Cairn 998
Corrie Chash
Carn an Tuirc 1019
Loch Kander
Knaps of Fafernie
Cairn of Gowal 983
To Braemar
Sron na Gaoithe 814
Tolmount 958
Crow Craggies
Loch Esk
Cairn of Claise 1064
Allt a' Garbh-choire
Garbh-choire
Ca Whims
Tom Buidhe 957
Jock's Road
Glenshee Ski Centre
Route A
Glen Doll
Glendoll Lodge
To Kirriemuir
Glas Maol 1068
A93
Devil's Elbow
Caenlochan Glen
White Water
Route C
To Perth
Little Glas Maol 973
Monega Hill 908
Glendoll Forest
Fee Burn
The Scorrie
Meall Gorm 759
Creag Leacach 987
Caenlochan Forest
River Isla
Shank of Drumfollow
Winter Corrie
Mayar 928
Driesh 947

0    1 mile
0    1 kilometre
N

*Driesh from the summit of Mayar*

**Route Summary:** Start at the
Forestry Commission car park
400m past Braedownie Farm
(Route C). A track from Acharn,
near the Youth Hostel in Glen
Doll, crosses the White Water to
a forestry fence which runs up
the hill for just under 300m.
Where the fence contours off to
the W continue directly upwards
to the top of The Scorrie, where
the slopes ease off. Continue to
the summit. From Driesh follow
the long and obvious ridge W for
about 3km to Mayar. To descend
follow grassy slopes NNE to the
edge of Corrie Fee. Continue on
the SE side of the Fee Burn to a
path at the foot of one of the
steeper sections. Follow this ENE
down the lower corrie, over a
stile and into the forest. The path
soon becomes a forest road
which eventually runs past the
Youth Hostel to the car park

**Map:** OS Sheet 44

**Access Point:** Braedownie,
GR288757

**Distance:** 12.8km, 823m ascent

**Approx Time:** 4-6 hours

**Translation:** From Gaelic dris;
bramble or thorn bush; possibly
from m' aighear; my delight, or
from magh, a plain

**Pronunciation:** dreesh; may-yer

## Driesh (213), 947m/3107ft, Mayar (248), 928m/3045ft

The lovely Glen Clova and Glen Doll are heavily coniferised which
inevitably means that there can often be some confusion over forestry
tracks and footpaths. The most popular route to the summit of
Driesh climbs for a distance up through the Glendoll Forest, following the old Kilbo hill path. Shortly after leaving the forest at a deer
fence the path rises uphill above the deep Shank of Drumfollow to
the high col between Driesh and Mayar where Driesh is easily
reached in about 1.5km of easy walking. Mayar is reached by returning to the col and following an old fence west over grassy slopes.
From the summit, steepening slopes drop away northwards to the
head of Corrie Fee, where a steep section to the south east of the
burn leads you down past some waterfalls to a footpath which
continues to follow the Fee Burn into the forest where the footpath
becomes a forestry road leading all the way back to Glen Doll past
the Youth Hostel.

An alternative route of ascent, which is steeper but does have the
advantage of cutting out a bit of forestry walking, climbs The Scorrie,
a bold prow which climbs steeply up the west side of Winter Corrie,
known locally as Corrie Winter! Cross the White Water by the bridge
at Acharn, just east of the Youth Hostel, follow the forestry fence for
a short distance and then climb the obvious steep ridge. At the top of
the Scorrie you're well rewarded for your efforts by superb views into
the cliffs of Corrie Winter, the redeeming feature of what is otherwise
a rather dull hill. From the top of Corrie Winter it's an easy walk to
the summit of Driesh.

## Mount Keen (229), 939m/3081ft

Glen Tanar is magnificent, Mount Keen less so! The hill's chief claim to fame is that it is the most easterly of all the Munros and the fact that it is also one of the most solitary means that you can't just hinge it on to a round of other Munros. Lying mid-way between Glen Tanar and Glen Esk the summit of Mount Keen lies immediately adjacent to the eastern-most of the Mounth roads, the Mounth Keen, so access can be easily gained from the south, in Glen Esk, or Glen Tanar on Deeside in the north.

My own preference is for the Glen Tanar approach, largely because of the lovely walk-in to the mountain through the Glen Tanar pine woods, a fine remnant of the Great Forest of Caledon. Glen Tanar lies south-west of Aboyne where a public road runs to a car park beside Glen Tanar House. From there a track follows the lovely Water of Tanar through the woods and out on to open moorland beyond the Half Way Hut. The track continues in a more southerly direction beyond Etnach to the Shiel of Glentanar which was burned down in 1992. Just before the track sweeps round to the remains of the Shiel, a crude bulldozed track crosses the river and makes its way up the north-west ridge of Mount Keen. Just beyond, above the rocky hollow known as the 'korlach' (the OS call it Corrach for some reason), another path forks to the left, up to Mount Keen's stony granite summit.

The southern route starts from a car park where Glen Esk splits into Glen Lee and Glen Mark. The path then follows the Water of Mark in a north westerly direction for just over 2km where it passes a monument known as the Queen's Well where, apparently, Queen Victoria stopped for refreshment during one of her excursions over the Mounth Keen in 1861. From the monument, the track splits and the Mounth road follows the right-hand branch, climbing quite steeply up beside the Ladder Burn to where a series of zigzags climb the southern shoulder of Mount Keen. Higher up the ridge, the track bifurcates again, the left-hand one being the Mounth road, while the right-hand branch takes you directly to the summit.

**Route Summary:** Start at the end of the public road which runs up Glen Tanar. Walk past a sawmill and through a gate which leads to an estate road. Follow this through pinewoods for about 5km and on up the open glen, crossing the river twice. At the third crossing (GR 407896) ascend the Mounth road S by a bulldozed track through heathery slopes. Diverge SE up the path to Mount Keen's summit

**Map:** OS Sheet 44

**Access Point:** Glen Tanar House, GR473957

**Distance:** 24km, 762m ascent

**Approx Time:** 6-10 hours

**Translation:** from monadh caoin, smooth or pleasant hill

**Pronunciation:** mount keen

# Northern Cairngorms

## The Munros:

### Mullach Clach a' Bhlair    Sgor Gaoith    Braeriach    Cairngorm
### Beinn Mheadhoin    Bynack More

The Cairngorms, for practical purposes, can be broken up into two groups of hills – those that are normally climbed from Speyside in the north, and those climbed from Deeside in the south. Needless to say, many of the hills can be climbed in groupings other than these listed here, for example Braeriach and Cairn Toul can be climbed together and all the hills of the Moine Mhor, Mullach Clach a' Bhlair, Sgor Gaoith, Monadh Mor and Beinn Bhrotain can be climbed in one round.

From Speyside, particularly around Aviemore, the Cairngorms appear almost as a high escarpment rising above the Queen's and Rothiemurchus Forests with the deep defile of the Lairig Ghru separating the main Cairngorm massif from the corrie sculptured dome of Braeriach. From Loch Morlich at the foot of Glen More, Cairngorm and its corries form one of the finest views in Scotland.

The Cairngorms are broken into three major massifs. The Ben Avon/Beinn a' Bhuird group is separated from the Cairngorm/Macdui group by the long Lairig an Laoigh, while the Braeriach/Cairn Toul group is separated from the central group by the Lairig Ghru. On the fringes lie the hills of the Moine Mhor and Bynack More/A' Choinnich.

It is probably true that the name 'Cairngorms' is a modern misnomer. These hills were once known as Am Monadh Ruadh, the red hills, distinguishing them from Am Monadh Liath, or the grey hills west of the Spey. Last century, visitors began referring to the hills collectively as the Cairngorms, using the name of the hill most obviously visible from Strathspey.

Geologically, the Cairngorms are very uniform, rough weathered granite forming high plateaux, the largest tracts of land over 600m, 900m and 1200m in the British Isles. Because of their height and exposure, these hills have the most Arctic-type climate of all the British hills, and the landforms, soils, vegetation, invertebrates and birds all have a greater similarity to those of Arctic Canada, Iceland or Greenland than to the southern European ranges of the Alps, Pyrenees or Caucasus.

The wonders of the Cairngorms can't be experienced by gazing up at the hills from below. They are too big and rounded for that. The Cairngorms demand that you climb to the high summits and vast plateaux and gaze down into the deep trenches and chasms, and the plethora of wind-scoured craggy corries.

These are the most important mountains, ecologically, in Britain, and have been

*The northern corries of the Cairngorms from the air, looking south-west from above Coire na Ciste*

*The Cairngorms from the north (Bynack More on the left, Cairngorm right of centre)*

subjected to a whole host of potentially detrimental developments. The ski development on Cairngorm is generally reckoned to have been an ecological mistake and subsequent proposals to extend the ski-ing facilities into the northern corries and Lurcher's Gully area were the subject of a public enquiry before the Secretary of State for Scotland finally decided against them.

Bulldozed tracks on to the Moine Mhor and Beinn a' Bhuird have also been heavily criticised and the threat of coniferisation on the fringes of the Cairngorms is always there. In the past decade conservation bodies have bought large chunks of the Cairngorms and it is disappointing that they have never been made Scotland's first National Park.

**Route Summary:** Leave Achlean in Glen Feshie by the Foxhunter's Path which climbs Carn Ban Mor E above the Allt Fhearnagan. Continue over the shoulder S of Carn Ban Mor until the footpath joins up with a bulldozed track. Follow this track SW and S over the Moine Mhor and past the head of Coire Garbhlach. Beyond this point another track joins from the W but continue S and where the track begins to bend due E leave it and climb the easy stony slopes of Mullach Clach a' Bhlair. Return to Carn Ban Mor and from there

## Mullach Clach a' Bhlair (111), 1019m/3343ft, Sgor Gaoith (34), 1118m/3668ft

The Moine Mhor, the Great Moss, is a vast expanse of stony ridge, green hollows of turf and moss, with a profusion of sparkling clear streams. A high tableland, it is a favourite feeding place for red deer and a haunt of ptarmigan and dotterel and although it's not much lower in height than the great plateaux of Braeriach and Cairngorm it doesn't share the harshness and bite of these lofty areas. Instead it offers a lonely solitude, green rather than grey, tending to the softer end of harsh, a pearl in a crown of diamonds.

In winter, under a mantle of snow, the character of the place changes. The Great Moss is often a desert of driving wind and blinding snow and even when the sun shines from a deep blue, almost black, sky, there is an ominous feel to these vast, white, endless morraines. I have seen it when not a rock, blade of grass, nor clump of heather protuded from the snow – a never-ending blanket of white, offering no relief to sun-strained eyes.

Most walkers approach the Moine Mhor from Glen Feshie where the public road stops at the little farm of Achlean. From behind the farmhouse, the Foxhunter's Path (the name of the path recalls a family of celebrated foxhunters who once lived at Achlean) skirts the Scottish Natural Heritage woods of Baden Mosach and climbs to Carn Ban Mor by way of Coire Fhearnagan. Once over the crest of the broad Carn Ban Mor ridge the vast sweep of the Great Moss becomes apparent.

If you follow the contours due south the great gouge of Coire Garblach appears, biting its way into the tableland. This is a long winding corridor housing the Allt Garblach and it is possible to gain access to the Moine Mhor via a steep climb up one of the corries' headwalls.

Unfortunately man has blighted the superb feeling of wilderness on the Moine Mhor in the form of bulldozed roads. The track can be put to advantage to reach the most southerly of the Moine Mhor Munros, Mullach Clach a' Bhlair. Despite its 1019m elevation Mullach is a mere swell in the rolling terrain although a series of rocky outcrops in the vicinity gives promise of better things.

To the north of Carn Ban Mor, broad slopes lead to a shallow col before rising again to Sgor Gaoith. This, the Peak of the Wind, is one of the finest summits of the Cairngorms. It rises gracefully in a long sweep from Sgoran Dubh Mor and ends abruptly at its cairn. Far below shimmer the waters of Loch Einich. Long ridges of granite blocks, seemingly thrown together

descend NNE to the broad bealach above the Fuaran Diotach then climb the easy slopes of Sgor Gaoith. Return to Achlean via Carn Ban Mor

**Map:** OS Sheet 43

**Access Point:** Achlean in Glen Feshie

**Distance:** 25.6km, 823m ascent

**Approx Time:** 6-8 hours

**Translation:** summit of the stone of the plain; peak of the wind

**Pronunciation:** moolach clach a vaar; skor goo-ee

in haphazard fashion lead down towards the loch, offering some good scrambling routes.

Sgur Gaoith can also be climbed via Sgoran Dubh Mor from Rothiemurchus, or indeed can be included in a fine traverse from the Foxhunter's Path to Carn Ban Mor, over Sgur Gaoith, Sgoran Dubh Mor and Sgoran Dubh Beag and down to Rothiemurchus near Loch Gamhna or Loch an Eilean.

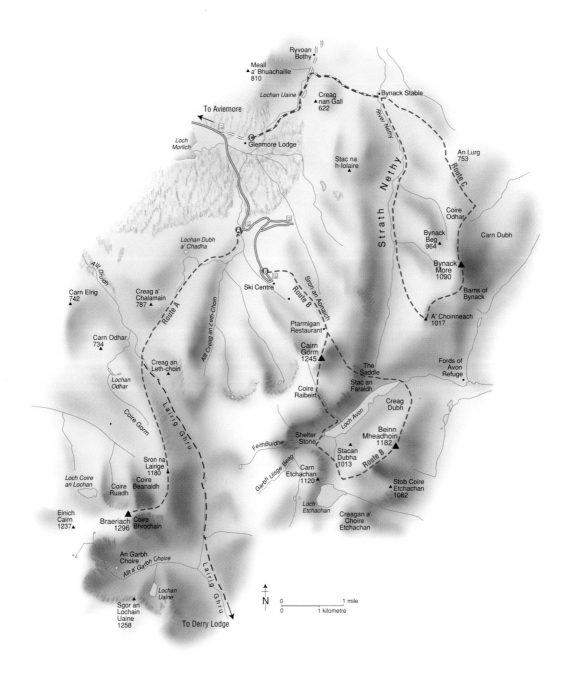

# Braeriach (3), 1296m/4252ft

Braeriach is the Brindled Upland and it's an airy place. If you stand by the summit cairn and gaze down the long empty kilometres of Glen Dee, past the bulk of Ben Macdui and the long arm of Carn a' Mhaim you'll see great cliffs of red granite thrust up out of the rough corrie below you in pinnacles and buttresses and spires and the snow wreaths which circle the upper corries until late in summer. The summit of Braeriach is actually made up from the apexes of no less than five corries and in the depth of winter it becomes a complex system of snow cornices.

Most folk climb Braeriach from the car park known as the Sugar Bowl. This lies just below the first steep bend on the road from Glenmore up to the Cairngorm Chairlift car park. From there a good footpath runs through the impressivly rocky Chalamain Gap and down into the Lairig Ghru (where the Sinclair Memorial Hut stood before its demolition.) From there an obvious path climbs on to the long ridge of Sron na Lairige, over a high col between Coire Beanaidh and Coire Ruadh and up the narrowing eastern ridge of Braeriach to the summit, perched precariously above the pinnacles and buttresses of Coire Bhrochain.

A much longer expedition follows this route to Braeriach, and then proceeds to Sgurr an Lochain Uaine and Cairn Toul around the rim of the An Garbh Coire, the huge corrie which separates Braeriach from Cairn Toul. This latter Munro can also be climbed along with Braeriach from the Moine Mhor via Loch nan Stuirteag, returning via Einch Cairn.

Braeriach, on its own, can also be climbed from the Moine Mhor, arguably a route of greater variety than the others. From the top of the Foxhunter's Path from Achlean the route to Braeriach takes an uncompromising line across the high plateau following the Allt Sgairnich to Loch nan Cnapan. From here a north-easterly line follows the broad south west shoulder of Einch Cairn to its flat, gravelly plateau, with views to your left down into the great trench of Gleann Einich. The loch lies deep in this glen below the steep ribs and buttresses of the Sgorans and Sgor Gaoith on one side and the great scoop of Coire Dhondail on the other. It's an easy walk across the plateau from Einch Cairn to Braeriach but you'll have to navigate fairly precisely in misty weather. In winter conditions this is a long and demanding route.

**Route Summary:** Leave the Sugar Bowl car park, cross the ski road and follow the footpath over the Allt Mor bridge (Route A). Continue on this path to the Chalamain Gap. Go through the gap and descend to the Lairig Ghru. Climb the hillside opposite by way of the obvious footpath and reach the Sron na Lairige ridge which is then followed S to the edge of Coire Ruadh. Here the ridge swings to the right to meet the E ridge of Braeriach. Follow this ridge to the edge of Coire Bhrochain and then follow the corrie lip to the summit

**Map:** OS Sheets 36 and 43

**Access Point:** Car park in Coire Cas of Cairngorm

**Distance:** 20.8km, 838m ascent

**Approx Time:** 8-10 hours

**Translation:** brindled upland

**Pronunciation:** brae-reeach

**Route Summary:** Leave the car park and climb Cairngorm by way of the Sron an Aonaich and the 'Ptarmigan Bowl' (Route B). A dubious alternative is to climb up through the ski paraphernalia in Coire Cas by way of bull-dozed tracks. From the summit of Cairngorm descend S into Coire Raibert and down the steep and loose path beside the burn to Loch Avon. Follow the path round the W head of the loch, past the Shelter Stone, and up into Coire Etchachan. From Loch Etchachan climb stony slopes NE to the granite tors of Beinn Mheadhoin. The largest of these is the summit and can be climbed by an easy scramble from its N side. Descend steep slopes, avoiding Creag Dubh, to the foot of Loch Avon. Cross the stream at its outlet from the loch and follow the footpath W to the Saddle at the head of Strath Nethy. Climb the SE slopes of Cairngorm to Ciste Mhearaid which is just below the col between Cairngorm and Cnap Coire na Spreidhe. Return to car park

**Map:** OS Sheet 36

**Access Point:** Coire Cas car park

**Distance:** 17.6km, 1676m ascent

**Approx Time:** 6-10 hours

**Translation:** blue hill; middle hill

**Pronunciation:** cairngorom; byn vee-an

**Stalking Information:** No restrictions

# Cairngorm (5), 1245m/4085ft, Beinn Mheadhoin (12), 1182m/3878ft

Cairngorm is, of course, home to Scotland's major ski development where two of its corries, Coire na Ciste and Coire Cas have largely been developed into pistes. A chairlift and system of ski tows operate in both corries and it is possible to be carried by lift to within 160m of the summit.

A long route to the summit of Cairngorm which largely avoids the ski paraphernalia runs from Ryvoan Pass just south of An Lochan Uaine, the Green Lochan. A rough path climbs up on to heather moorland north of Carn Lochan na Beinne and then follows the lovely ridge of Sron a' Cha-no high above the steep slopes which drop down into Strath Nethy. It then skirts the rocky tor of Cnap Coire na Spreidhe and climbs the final slopes of Cairngorm above Ciste Mhearad, Margaret's Coffin.

Another route leaves the chairlift car park in Coire Cas, climbs steeply north-east to reach the path which follows the Sron an Aonaich between Coire Cas and Coire na Ciste, and then proceeds to the dome of the Ptarmigan Restaurant beside the top station of the chairlift. The summit lies about 1km to the south via a horrendous, cairned, fenced-in tourist path.

From the summit of Cairngorm, leave the grossly enlarged cairn and weather station behind you and drop down rocky slopes in a southerly direction into the flushes of Coire Raibert. Even here, a few minutes from the crowds, you can begin to feel something of the splendour of the Cairngorms. Ahead of you, across the great gulf that contains Loch Avon, the tor-studded whaleback of Beinn Mheadhoin is obvious, rising beside the glittering waters of Loch Etchachan, whose shoreline caresses the 914m contour. This is big country, an area of deep-cut chasms, high craggy cliffs and great rounded prows.

A well-maintained path follows the burn down Coire Raibeirt to the lovely Loch Avon where another path follows the shoreline to the head of the loch. A great jumble of massive boulders lies below the frowning precipices of the Sticil (sometimes referred to as the Shelterstone Crag) and Carn Etchachan. The old howff below the Shelter Stone is in the middle of this great boulder field.

Continue south-eastwards up the slanting path that very quickly lifts you high above the loch and into the great glaciated hollow that houses Loch Etchachan, one of the most atmospheric parts of the Cairngorms.

Just before you reach the loch leave the path and climb eastwards up to the first of Beinn Mheadhoin's granite tops. Follow the broad crest

*Beinn Mheadhoin and Loch Avon*

along the line of tors to the highest which forms the summit. It can be climbed in a simple scramble from its north side.

You can return to Cairngorm either by retracing your footsteps to the Shelter Stone and climbing on to the Cairngorm plateau via Coire Dhomhain, completely retracing your steps via Coire Raibeirt, or by dropping down steep slopes north-north-east of the summit of Beinn Mheadhoin, avoiding the crags of Creag Dhubh to your left, to the foot of Loch Avon. Cross the outflow of the loch and follow the foot-path on to The Saddle at the head of Strath Nethy. From there, climb steeply in a north-north-west direction to the shallow scoop of Ciste Mhearad and across the Ptarmigan Bowl to Sron an Aonaich. Alternatively, follow Strath Nethy to Bynack Stable where a bulldozed track continues to the Pass of Ryvoan.

Beinn Mheadhoin can also be climbed from the south. From the Linn of Dee take the track to Derry Lodge and through Glen Derry to Coire Etchachan. Follow the path up through the corrie past the Hutchison Memorial Hut to Loch Etchachan. From there climb north-east to reach the first of Beinn Mheadhoin's summits.

# Bynack More (52), 1090m/3576ft

**Route Summary:** Leave parking area just beyond Glenmore Lodge and follow the forestry track into the Pass of Ryvoan (Route C). Continue through the Pass, past Lochan Uaine. About 400m beyond the lochan take another path E to Bynack Stable and the River Nethy. Cross the river and follow the footpath SE over the lower shoulder of Bynack More. Follow this path to its highest point then leave it to bear S up the N ridge to the summit. Return the same way or by Strath Nethy

**Map:** OS Sheet 36

**Access Point:** Glenmore Lodge, GR992097

**Distance:** 19.2km, 762m ascent

**Approx Time:** 5-8hours

**Translation:** big cap

**Pronunciation:** bie-nack moar

Rising from the flattish hills to the north-east of the main Cairngorm group, Bynack More is a peak of some individuality and character and shows its finest aspect to the north above the Forest of Abernethy. From here it forms a fine conical peak, unusual in the rounded Cairngorms, although it must be said that it is dominated by the massive shoulders of Cairngorm.

The Lairig an Laoigh path from Glenmore to Braemar skirts Bynack More's northern and eastern slopes and offers a good approach to the hill, but first, enjoy the delights of Ryvoan.

Just beyond Glenmore Lodge, the National Mountaineering Centre, there is a small parking area. From there a Forestry track enters the Scottish Wildlife Trust Reserve of Ryvoan, a beautiful stretch of Caledonian pine, juniper and birch. A little further on, An Lochan Uaine, or the Green Lochan, lies in a hollow below the scree-girt slopes of Creag nan Gall, the Crag of the Stranger. The waters of the lochan are an unusual translucent greenish-blue colour the local legend claiming that the tint comes from the fairies washing their green clothes in it!

Sadly, the bank leading down to An Lochan Uaine has been severely eroded which has led to the building of a fence round the loch and wooden steps down to the shore.

About half a kilometre beyond the lochan another path leads off to the right and crosses the heather moorland past the old estate shelter of Bynack Stable, across the River Nethy by footbridge and up on to the long, broad northern ridge of Bynack More. This footpath, the Lairig and Laoigh path, climbs gradually on to a high plateau north of Bynack More and swings gently to the left of the mountain. As it begins to drop down into Coire Odhar, leave the path and head for the prominent north nose of Bynack More where another path climbs up the rocky ridge to the summit. Further on, on the south-east slopes of the mountain, the amazing granite tors of the Barns of Bynack are well worth a visit.

Return to Glenmore by the outward route or for an alternative continue from the summit south westwards to the flat topped A' Choinnich with its fine views up Loch Avon to the Sticil and Carn Etchachan, returning to Glenmore by Strath Nethy.

*The Cairngorm plateau from the north in winter*

# SOUTHERN CAIRNGORMS

## The Munros:

Devil's Point   Cairn Toul   Monadh Mor   Beinn Bhrotain   Carn a' Mhaim
Ben Macdui   Derry Cairngorm   Beinn Bhreac   Beinn a' Chaorainn
Ben Avon (Leabaidh an daimh Bhuidhe)   Beinn a' Bhuird

In 1995 the National Trust for Scotland bought the Mar Lodge Estate in the Cairngorms, an estate which contains the vast majority of the Munros in this section. The importance of that purchase highlights the significance of this area, arguably the most important mountain landscape in Britain. The plethora of corries and the high arctic-like plateaux are the two most important landscape features of the Cairngorms and the associated flora, fauna and birds of these high wind scoured quarters unite to make the Cairngorms unique.

In the first edition of the Scottish Mountaineering Club *District Guide to the Cairngorms* (1928), Sir Henry Alexander suggested that for many, first acquaintance with these hills was occasionally accompanied by a sense of disappointment. But, he goes on to say, 'as one explores them and wanders among them, the magnitude of everything begins to reveal itself, and one realises the immensity of the scale upon which the scene is set, and the greatness and dignity and calm of the Cairngorms cast their spell over the spirit.'

## The Devil's Point (Bod an Deamhain) (127), 1004m/3294ft, Cairn Toul (4), 1293m/4242ft

There is an apocryphal story which suggests that Queen Victoria once asked her ghillie John Brown the name of a rather fine mountain just south of Cairn Toul. Knowing that if he told her the Gaelic name she would immediately ask for a translation he thought it best to offer her a euphemistic translation. The literal translation of Bod an Deamhain (pronounced pot-in-john), the penis of the demon, could have caused some embarrassment. Sadly the translation he offered, The Devil's Point, has stuck and now we even have an Angel's Peak (Sgor an Lochain Uaine) above An Garbh Choire to help balance out the religious analogy.

I'd love to see a campaign mounted which encouraged the Ordnance Survey to revert to the original name – surely there should be no place

**Route Summary:** Take the private road from Linn of Dee to Derry Lodge (Route A, p.127). Follow the track up Glen Luibeg to the Lairig Ghru. Take the path which skirts the S slopes of Carn a' Mhaim and drops to Glen Dee. Cross the river to Corrour Bothy. A worn path leads W behind the bothy up steep zigzags above the Allt a' Choire Odhair. From the col at the head of the corrie head S then bear E to the summit of the Devil's Point. Return to the col. Follow the broad grassy ridge which rises N. Follow the ridge to Coire an t-Saighdeir and then to Cairn Toul

**Map:** OS Sheets 36 and 43

*The Devil's Point and Glen Dee from the air*

*Cairn Toul and Sgor an Lochain Uaine from the south*

**Access Point:** Linn of Dee

**Distance:** 36.8km, 1128m ascent

**Approx Time:** 8-12 hours

**Translation:** from the Gaelic Bod an Deamhain, penis of the devil; from Carn an t-Sabhail, hill of the barn.

**Pronunciation:** devil's point; kaarn towal

in these Highland mountains for such woolly translations, even if it does come from a good story.

Cairn Toul comes from Carn an t-Sabhail, the hill of the barn, a name which seems unlikely when the hill is viewed from the east. This aspect presents a shapely and attractive form, a wedge of a summit formed by the apex of three great scalloped corries. But from the west, particularly from the Moine Mhor, it does appear square shaped and uninspiring, and probably deserving of the name.

Cairn Toul is often climbed with Braeriach in a traverse around the rim of An Garbh Choire, one of the finest corries in the highlands. This expedition, most often attempted from the north, is a big day out and should only be tackled in the long days of summer. However, since Cairn Toul is only some 11km from Derry Lodge, it and its near neighbour, The Devil's Point, can be climbed quite comfortably in a day, especially if you use a bike as far as Derry Lodge or Glen Luibeg.

The Lairig Ghru path from Glen Luibeg meets another path from White Bridge just opposite Corrour Bothy which is named after the corrie which lies behind it, Coire Odhar, or Dun Corrie. This great scoop stretches from the black glistening slabs of The Devil's Point all the way round to the containing ridge of Coire an t-Saighdeir of Cairn Toul and a stalker's path climbs its steep slopes from behind the bothy.

The final zigzags of this path thrust you on to one of the most delightful spots in the Cairngorms, An Diolland, the mossy saddle which connects our two mountains. Head north along the edge of the precipitous Coire an t-Saighdeir, the soldier's corrie, to a small dip in the ridge. A final climb over angular granite blocks brings you to the narrow summit. If you didn't want to climb The Devil's Point, you can enjoy a fine descent into Glen Geusachan by dropping west to the saddle before Sgor an Lochain Uaine and following the valley of the Allt Clais an t-Sabhail all the way to the head of Glen Geusachan, claimed by some to be the finest glen in the Cairngorms.

Return to An Diolland the way you came and simply follow gently rising slopes in an east-south-east direction to the summit. The view is spectacular down Glen Dee and into Glen Geusachan. Return to An Diolland and the stalker's path to Corrour.

## Monadh Mor (39), 1113m/3652ft, Beinn Bhrotain (18), 1157m/3796ft

Loch nan Stuirteag makes a fine destination for a day on the Great Moss, nestling snugly as it does into a fold in the hills between Monadh Mor and the long slopes of Cairn Toul and the Einich Cairn massif. It's a place of desolate beauty, this Loch of the Gulls, the reed-edged waters lapping gently on the tiny sand beaches. To my mind, little gems like this are the real Cairngorms, too remote for day trippers and far removed from the busy trade routes of Cairngorm and Macdui.

You can reach Loch nan Stuirteag from either Glen Geusachan in the east, or Glen Feshie in the west. Although I've described the eastern approach in the Route Summary, the western approach is equally fine, offering an opportunity to wander over the Moine Mhor towards the Loch, high above the head of Loch Einich. Probably the best way of visiting these high hills is to make a camp by Loch nan Stuirteag, explore the hills of the Moine Mhor on one day and then climb Cairn Toul and the Devil's Point the next, allowing yourself to be seduced by the remoteness and scale of this massive massif.

Behind the loch, Monadh Mor lies with its long ridge leading south, a sore temptation for Munro folk. To bag Monadh Mor and then cross the steep bealach and grab Beinn Bhrotain fills a summer evening well from a high camp, but in winter an expedition to these two hills is a major undertaking. It's a long way for the short days of November, but if there is time it's good to sit for a while between these two big hills, just above the screes of Coire Cath nam Fionn, the Corrie of the Battle of the Fingalians.

As the breeze sighs coldly up from Glen Geusachan, let your imagination wander back through the mists of time, back to a time as old as these hills themselves. Who fought in the Battle of the Fingalians? Who won? Only the remaining rocks can tell of the deeds of that once proud race. The distant voice of Ossian, Fingal's bardic son, casts little light on the matter:

'Though the plains of our battles are dark and silent, our fame is in the four grey stones. The voice of Ossian has been heard. The harp has been strung in Selma. Come Ossian, come away, come fly with thy father on clouds. I come, I come, thou king of men.'

*Ben Macdui from the north*

## Carn a' Mhaim (93), 1037m/3402ft, Ben Macdui (2), 1309m/4295ft, Derry Cairngorm (20), 1155m/3789ft

This big horseshoe walk takes you into the very heart of the central massif of the Cairngorms and touches on some of the real splendours of this area – the beauty of Glen Luibeg, the long ridge of Carn a' Mhaim, an unusual feature for the Cairngorms, the wide and spacious tundra of Macdui, the crags and cliffs of Coire Sputain Dearg and the spectacular situation of Loch Etchachan.

Ben Macdui, Britain's second highest mountain and for many years thought to be the highest (Cairngorm enthusiasts from Speyside were determined to build a huge cairn on the summit when it was discovered that Ben Nevis was just over 300m higher. Thankfully their plans never succeeded), is most often climbed either from Cairngorm, across the plateau via Lochan Bhuidhe, or via the lovely Sron Riach ridge in Glen Luibeg. Carn a' Mhaim is occasionally climbed from the north but it's a long way from Ben Macdui when you have to retrace your steps back over Macdui's stony dome.

Derry Cairngorm can be climbed in another long day from the north

**Route Summary:** Take the private road from Linn of Dee to Derry Lodge. Cross the Derry Burn by the bridge W of Derry Lodge. Follow the track to the SNH deer fences S of Luibeg Bridge and then leave the track to climb the SE ridge of Carn a' Mhaim (Route C, p.127). The NW top is the summit. From here follow the narrowing ridge in a NNW direction to a wide col at 800m. Climb the steep and stony slopes due N to the summit of Ben Macdui. Descend E over wide bouldery and featureless slopes to the edge of Coire Sputain Dearg and follow the ridge NE to a col just W of Creagan a Choire Etchachan. Skirting the SW slopes of Creagan a Choire Etchachan descend S to the bealach N of Derry Cairngorm. Climb bouldery slopes S to the summit.

Return to Derry Lodge by Carn Crom

**Map:** OS Sheets 36 and 43

**Access Point:** Linn of Dee

**Distance:** 30.4km, 1372m ascent

**Approx Time:** 8-12 hours

**Translation:** cairn of the large round hill; hill of the black pig; blue hill of Derry (from doire, a thicket)

**Pronunciation:** kaarn a vame; byn macdooee; derry cairn-gorom

and some even combine it with Beinn Mheadhoin in a big day from Cairngorm via the head of Loch Avon. A shorter round can be enjoyed by approaching from Glen Derry, climbing Coire Etchachan to the loch and then heading south over a stony ridge to the summit. The descent is then via the long south ridge before heading south-west over heathery slopes into Glen Luibeg.

Long walk-ins tend to be a feature of the Braemar side of the Cairngorms and regular Cairngormers become very, very familiar with the track from Linn of Dee to Derry Lodge – mountain bikes are now regularly used to speed up access and it is well worth while using a bike on this route as far as the Scottish Natural Heritage enclosures just south of the Luibeg Bridge.

This plethora of deer fencing has undoubtedly spoiled what was once a lovely area and it could be that it will be there for many years until the pine woods recover from the ravages of too many hungry deer. If you can find your way through the fencing stay on the westbound Lairig Ghru track as it climbs on to the south-east ridge of Carn a' Mhaim. The popularity of the Lairig Ghru is revealed hereabouts by massive erosion and that, if nothing else, is a good excuse to leave the path and take to the heather in a north-west direction, climbing increasingly stony slopes to the 1014m south top of Carn a' Mhaim.

From here it's only a short distance to the summit, then the long bumpy ridge which becomes increasingly narrow towards the Ceann Crionn, or thin end. From the high bealach between Carn a' Mhaim and Macdui it's a long pull over boulders and scree to the summit of Britain's second highest hill, but the views west to The Devil's Point, Cairn Toul and Braeriach are justly rewarding. The line of the Allt Clach nan Taillear, the Tailors' Burn, is a good one to follow and takes you on to the broad stony expanse just east of Macdui's summit – it's an easy walk on a gravelly path to the huge summit cairn and view indicator.

From the summit return to the top of the Tailors' Burn and follow the Loch Etchachan path round the head of Coire Sputain Dearg for about a kilometre. Leave the path and climb to the 1108m top of Creagan a' Choire Etchachan and follow its broad stony ridge southwards to a shallow col at 1014m. From here Derry Cairngorm lifts its head in rocky dominance and it's a straightforward walk to its bouldery summit. Descend south to the col between it and its southern top, Carn Crom and follow the more open, heather-covered slopes in a west-south-west direction towards the Luibeg Burn, where a footpath takes you back to the enclosures in Glen Luibeg.

*The Cairngorms from the south (Glen Derry on the left and Glen Quoich on the right)*

## Beinn Bhreac (245), 931m/3054ft,
## Beinn a' Chaorainn (58), 1082m/3550ft

These two hills form the northern and southern limit of a vast upland plateau the slopes of which pour down from the north top of Beinn a' Bhuird. Forming the eastern boundary to Glen Derry, this huge area, the Moine Bhealaidh, the peat moss of the broom, is a lumpy expanse of peat hags, bog, turf and countless pools of water.

Both Munros can be climbed independently, Beinn Bhreac from Glen Derry and Beinn a Chaorainn from the Fords of Avon Bothy by the River Avon in the north, but a good route combines both summits with a fine walk down the length of Glen Derry making use of the ancient Lairig an Laoigh path. Just past Derry Lodge a bulldozed track forces its ugly way through the trees on the east bank of the river and rises to a high point of about 500m. From here, about two kilometres from Derry Lodge, leave the track and work your way between the trees and up heathery slopes in a north-east direction to the obvious col between Meall an Lundain and the scree-speckled Beinn Bhreac. From the col it's an easy walk to the summit from where the lochan-splattered Moine Bhealaidh lies at your feet. Beyond it the conical shape of Beinn a' Chaorainn gives way to steep crags which pour down westwards into the defile of the Lairig an Laoigh pass.

You can treat the Moine Bhealaidh two ways – curse it for its boggy, peat hag ridden nature, or enjoy the plover-haunted atmosphere of it. It helps to follow the high ground of it as much as possible and in good weather you'll be delighted by the westward views over Glen Derry to the tops of the central massif.

**Route Summary:** Take the private road to Derry Lodge. Continue on the bulldozed track on the E side of Glen Derry for 1.6km or so (Route D, p.127) then strike uphill over heathery slopes and through trees to the col between Meall an Lundain and Beinn Bhreac. From here climb NNE to the summit. Continue NW then N across the Moine Bhealaidh to Beinn a' Chaorainn. Return to Derry Lodge by the Lairig an Laoigh

**Map:** OS Sheets 36 and 43

**Access Point:** Linn of Dee

**Distance:** 28.8km, 823m ascent

**Approx Time:** 7-10 hours

**Translation:** speckled hill; hill of the rowan

**Pronunciation:** byn vrechk; byn a choeran

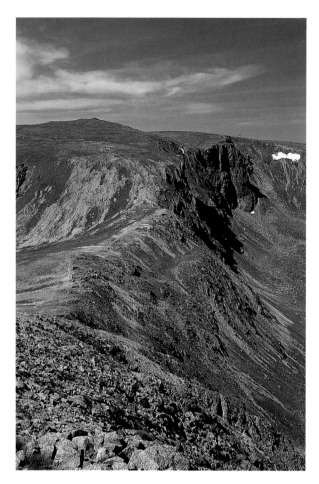

*Beinn a' Bhuird from the slopes of Ben Avon*

The closer you come to Beinn a' Chaorainn the easier is the terrain, eventually climbing the mountain's broad south ridge over gravel and scree to the summit.

Descend in a south-west direction then westwards steeply down into the Lairig an Laoigh with direct views up the length of Coire Etchachan towards Ben Macdui. From the summit of the pass walk south into Glen Derry and over the flats to the pines of Derry Lodge.

### Ben Avon (Leabaidh an daimh Bhuidhe) (16), 1171m/3842ft, Beinn a' Bhuird (10), 1196m/3924ft

These easterly Cairngorms don't compare with anything else. No soaring pinnacles here, no serrated peaked horizons. These are rounded hills, but big hills, on a scale that takes a while to grasp.

Ben Avon is a hill that is almost a mountain range in itself. It's a big, complex mass of muscley shoulders which bulge out in every direction, throwing up a series of tor-studded tops. The name of the hill, Avon, is thought to be taken from the river which scours its northern flanks and Celtic scholars believe the name to be a derivative of Ath-fhionn, the bright or fair-haired one. Local legend claims that the wife of Fionn MacCumhail, or Fingal, slipped when crossing the river and was swept to her death. The name has absolutely no connection with Shakespeare's Stratford, and it is correctly pronounced A'an.

Beinn a' Bhuird has two personalities. Its western slopes fall away gently into the anonymity of the Moine Bhealaidh between Beinn a' Chaorainn and Beinn Bhreac while its eastern side is torn and rent by a series of dramatic corries. Coire na Ciche, with its great tor of A'Chioch, and the superb Coire an Dubh Lochain are well worth visiting in their own right.

There are a number of routes to these hills and all are long and strenuous. Ben Avon can be reached from Tomintoul in the north and from the Lecht road in the east but on balance routes from the south can more easily accommodate visits to both hills in one expedition.

**Route Summary:** Leave your car at Keiloch and take the private road to Glen Quoich. Continue past the ruins of Slugain Lodge to the end of the path beyond the boulder of Clach a' Chleirich. From there climb NNE to the obvious saddle at 970m called The Sneck. From here climb E on to the plateau and the summit tor of Beinn Avon, Leabaidh an Daimh Bhuidhe. Return to The Sneck, cross it and continue ESE over the plateau to the N top of Beinn a' Bhuird. Return to Glen Quoich by the S top and Carn Fiaclach where a stalker's path takes you back to just N of Slugain Lodge

**Map:** OS Sheets 36 and 43

**Access Point:** Invercauld Bridge

From any direction a mountain bike is invaluable.

Gleann an t-Slugain probably offers the best approach and you can reach it from Invercauld, a few kilometres east of Braemar.

Beyond the ruins of Slugain Lodge a footpath continues up the east side of Glen Quoich and past the huge erratic known as the Clach a' Chleirich, the Stone of the Clergyman. From the end of the footpath it's an easy climb up grassy slopes to reach The Sneck (from the Gaelic snaig, or notch), the narrow saddle between our two hills. From here, with the dramatic corrie of Slochd Mor falling away steeply to the north, climb eastwards up the gravelly slopes on to Ben Avon's plateau. The summit tor, Leabaidh an Daimh Bhuidhe, lies about 1.5km away to the north-east.

Return to the Sneck; with corries falling away on either side it's a superb position with rock buttresses soaring up to the green slopes of Cnap a' Chleirich to the south west. From where the Sneck abuts onto the vast Beinn a' Bhuird plateau, continue east-south-east to the North Top. This is the summit of Beinn a' Bhuird. It lies some 1196m above sea level, but clouds often drench these high parts and visibility is limited to a few rock-strewn-metres. A good descent continues southwards to the South Top, skirting the lip of the dramatic Coire an Dubh Lochain, and then south-east to Carn Fiaclach where a stalker's path leads down into Glen Quoich just to the north of Slugain Lodge.

**Distance:** 40km, 1372m ascent

**Approx Time:** 11-15 hours

**Translation:** bed of the yellow stag; hill of the table

**Pronunciation:** lyepay an dyv vooee; byn a voord

# LAGGAN AND THE MONADH LIATH

## The Munros:

A' Chailleach   Carn Sgulain   Carn Dearg   Geal Charn
Carn Liath   Stob Poite Coire Ardair   Creag Meagaidh
Beinn a' Chaorainn   Beinn Teallach

The Monadh Liath have suffered a bad press. Several writers on the outdoors have written off these hills as dull and uninspiring but while the summits may be rounded and bald, they nevertheless rise above a clutch of interesting side glens running off the main one, Glen Banchor. Indeed the whole area is rather like the back of a hand, with several long fingers running on from a great central plateau. There may not be any great pinnacles here, rocky spires and sheer rock faces are non-existent, but there are other attributes – a wide open aspect, a feeling of vast skyscapes and spaciousness, and you'll see more wildlife here in a day than you'll see in the Skye Cuillin in a week.

Further west, Creag Meagaidh has gained a little more respect – this is a big mountain with a huge character, a mastiff of a mountain and every winter climbers enjoy the snow- and ice-covered crags of the huge Coire Ardair. In summer these same crags are slippery and vegetated but the scale never changes – it is a fine walk around the summits that enclose the long Coire Ardair.

Beinn Teallach is the newest Munro, promoted to 3000ft status in 1984, after a re-survey by the Ordnance Survey, and while it keeps its best attributes hidden for most of the ascent, it's well worth combining with neighbouring Beinn a' Chaorainn to experience its finer aspects.

## A' Chailleach (247), 930m/3051ft, Carn Sgulain (263), 920m/3018ft, Carn Dearg (219), 945m/3100ft

The Allt a' Chaorainn runs down from Coire a' Chaorainn and into the River Calder in Glen Banchor, a broad and lovely glen to the north of Creag Dhubh. A motorable road runs up to the glen from Newtonmore as far as a parking space above the Shepherd's Bridge. In front of you the flat glen floor gives rise to the birch-covered slopes of Creag Dhubh on the left, while to the right, the north, several long ridges run down from a high plateau. A' Chailleach is the high point of the first of those fingers, while Carn Dearg is several fingers up the glen. Carn Sgulain is the high point of the plateau from which these long fingers run.

A' Chailleach offers its best profile from the footpath which runs north from Shepherd's Bridge. Its north-east facing corrie, which is the hill's finest feature, is hardly spectacular but when snow swathes the steep, rocky flanks of its north-east buttress there's fun, if not a little challenge, to be had by following the line of least resistance up through the rock-bands and steep terraces.

The usual route of ascent is from the end of the footpath which runs north from Shepherd's Bridge. At the turning point in the track drop down to the left to where a footbridge across the stream is partly hidden by some trees. For years I crossed the burn here, usually getting very wet feet, before I noticed there was a bridge!

Long heathery slopes roll down from A' Chailleach's summit ridge in a southerly direction and from the crossing of the Allt a' Chaorainn it's a long relentless pull up these slopes to the summit. Things improve as you climb higher – once over a series of peat hags the going becomes easier over stony ground.

Carn Sgulain lies less than two kilometres north of A' Chailleach, and easy slopes drop down to the narrow defile which contains the Allt Cuil na Caillich. Beyond it, steeper grassy slopes climb to the broad summit of Sgulain, complete with fence posts leading past the summit. These same fence posts make navigation easy almost all the way to Carn Dearg for 8km over a series of minor tops and bumps. The going is not difficult, although it's quite featureless, over grass and heather and a couple of small lochans. The fence posts can be followed as far as Carn Mor just to the south of Lochan Uisge, where you must leave them behind and climb the north-north-east ridge of Carn Dearg. This is probably the finest of the Monadh Liath hills, a long two-and-a-half kilometre ridge with steep craggy slopes dropping to the east. On the other side grassy slopes drop down to secretive Loch Dubh and lonely Coire nan Laogh.

**Route Summary:** Drive up Glen Banchor to the parking area above Shepherd's Bridge. Follow the footpath N beside the Allt a' Chaorainn till it ends in a turning point. Drop down to the stream and cross by a footbridge which is hidden from the path. Climb heathery slopes NNE to the rounded summit of A' Chailleach. Descend N into a deep glen and then continue N on steep and tussocky grass to the summit of Carn Sgulain. From the summit follow a line of fence posts W then SW over undulating plateau crossing several minor tops. At Carn Ban, leave the fence posts and go S to a short and steep climb to the summit of Carn Dearg. Continue on the narrow ridge S to a bealach and drop E into Gleann Balloch down broad heathery slopes. A narrow footpath follows the stream back into Glen Banchor from where a track beside the River Calder takes you back to Shepherd's Bridge

**Map:** OS Sheet 35

**Access Point:** Glen Banchor, GR693998

**Distance:** 24.1km, 838m ascent

**Approx Time:** 6-8 hours

**Translation:** red hill; the old woman; hill of the basket or of the old man

**Pronunciation:** a kaalyach; kaarn skoolin; kaarn jerrack

To return to Shepherd's Bridge, follow the ridge south of the summit cairn over a subsidiary top and down to the bealach below Carn Macoul. From the bealach descend eastwards to the Allt Ballach, cross the burn and follow the footpath past Dalballoch into Glen Banchor where a path on the north side of the River Calder takes you back to your starting point.

## Geal Charn (256), 926m/3038ft

**Route Summary:** From the bridge follow the path which runs up the SE side of the Feith Talagain. At the end of the path cross the Allt Coire nan Dearcag and climb the heather-covered SW ridge of Geal Charn direct to the summit. Return by Beinn Sgiath and the SW ridge

**Map:** OS Sheet 35

**Access Point:** Garva Bridge

**Distance:** 14.4km, 610m ascent

**Approx Time:** 4-6 hours

**Translation:** white hill

**Pronunciation:** gyal kaarn

The most westerly of the Monadh Liath Munros, Geal Charn rears up its rounded shoulders above lonely Glen Markie north-west of Laggan. Twin spurs emanate from the hill's twin summits and drop down grassy slopes south westwards to Garva Bridge while the north-east of the mountain shows a very different face. A craggy corrie wall is split by a steep-sided col, the result of glaciation, separating Geal Charn from its subsidiary top, Beinn Sgiath. Lochan a' Choire lies in the deep grasp of the corrie.

Two alternatives offer straightforward routes to the summit. A sketchy path follows the east bank of the Feith Talagain from near Garva Bridge, ten kilometres west of Laggan Bridge. At the termination of this path cross the Allt Coire nan Dearcag and climb the heathery south west spur of Geal Charn to the wide grassy summit and finely built cairn. A good descent is by the southern top, Beinn Sgiath and down its spur to Meall an Domhnaich and Garvabeg.

Probably the most popular route is by Glen Markie. A track runs for three and a half kilometres beside the Markie Burn from Spey Dam before turning into a footpath. A short distance beyond this, Piper's Burn runs down the hillside from Geal Charn's north-east corrie. Cross the Markie Burn and follow the Piper's Burn to where it flows out from Lochan a' Choire. Continue climbing easy slopes north of the lochan, avoiding the crags, to crest the summit ridge. Go south west now on to the grassy summit plateau and the cairn.

*Coire Ardair, Creag Meagaidh*

## Carn Liath (123), 1006m/3301ft, Stob Poite Coire Ardair (75), 1053m/3455ft, Creag Meagaidh (26), 1130m/3707ft,

Lying midway between Fort William and Aviemore, just east of the Lochaber/Badenoch boundary, the great whaleback of Creag Meagaidh has been popular with walkers and climbers for generations. In many ways she's a contrary mountain – straddling the historic Druim Alban, the watershed of Scotland, she can offer delights when others cannot, and conversely, she can be a miserable huddle of cloud and rain when other hills are bathing in sunshine. But when Creah Meagaidh smiles she smiles in a thoroughly hospitable way and shows off her great and cavernous Coire Ardair to best possible advantage.

And it's this great array of vegetated cliffs which makes Creag Meagaidh so special. Laid out for almost two kilometres and in places reaching higher than 450m above the waters of Lochan a' Choire, the cliffs are breached only by a high 'window', a glaciated gap in the curtain which offers access from the corrie floor to the high plateau-like summit.

There is little decent rock climbing in Coire Ardair although the

**Route Summary:** Behind the Scottish Natural Heritage buildings at Aberarder Farm a good path crosses the lower moorland (Route A, p.139). After 1.5km or so, as the track climbs through birch trees strike uphill NNE on the heather-clad slopes of Carn Liath. From the summit head NW to follow the edge of Coire Ardair over Meall an t-Snaim, Sron Garbh Choire and the E top of Stob Poite Coire Ardair. Continue W to the summit. From the cairn continue W then S as the slopes fall away to 'The Window', a deep col. Climb the steep slopes on to the plateau, past Mad Meg's Cairn to the true summit. Walk E to the edge of the corrie and follow the ridge SE and E over Puist Coire Ardair, and Creag Mhor. Drop down open slopes to Aberarder.

Map: OS Sheets 34 and 42

Access Point: Aberarder Farm

Distance: 16miles/4500ft;
25.6km/1372m ascent

Approx Time: 8-12 hours

Translation: grey hill; peak of
the pot of the high corrie; bog-
land rock

Pronunciation: kaarn leea; stop
potya kor aardar; crayk meggie

winter climber can have a thoroughly grand time when the cliffs are plastered with snow and ice and the vegetated cliffs freeze up. For mountain walkers, the round of Carn Liath, Stob Poite Coire Ardair and Creag Meagaidh itself makes a marvellous high-level walk.

Carn Liath is reached after a long climb over heather covered slopes from the Coire Ardair footpath and the walker is rewarded for his efforts by a tremendous direct view up into the corrie and its huge headwall. From the stony summit head west and follow the mossy ridge along the edge of Coire Ardair over Meall an t-Snaim to where it narrows above Coire a' Chriochairein. The next steeper rise leads to the crest of Stob Poite Coire Ardair, the highest point of which is at the west end. From the summit continue west than south as the slopes fall away to The Window, a narrow pass which cuts over the ridge from Coire Ardair to the headwaters of the River Roy.

From this narrow pass climb up steep grassy slopes on to the vast summit plateau. Pass Mad Meg's cairn and continue over the plateau beyond it to the true summit cairn which lies at the west end of the plateau. Either descend back to The Window and down into Coire Ardair to return to Aberarder, or cross the plateau eastwards to the corrie rim and continue round the edge of the cliffs. A well defined ridge runs south east then east over Puist Coire Ardair and Creag Mhor from where open slopes can be followed back to Aberarder.

## Beinn a' Chaorainn (76), 1052m/3451ft, Beinn Teallach (276), 915m/3002ft

Route Summary: Follow the forestry road NW for 800m to the slopes below Meall Clachaig (Route B). Follow a firebreak N to reach a deer fence and a gate near the road junction. Climb N and then bear NE up easy slopes to the S top and then along the broad ridge to the summit of Beinn a' Chaorainn. Continue on the ridge to the N top and then drop NNW, then W to the col at the head of the Allt a' Chaorainn. Climb the slopes W to reach the NE ridge of Beinn Teallach. Follow the ridge to the summit

Map: OS Sheets 34 and 41
GR337813

Distance: 17.6km, 1143m ascent

Approx Time: 4-7 hours

While these two hills are separated by the long glen containing the Allt a' Chaorainn, the high bealach at its head, at a height of just under 600m, links the two hills quite nicely. Beinn a' Chaorainn's summit ridge runs in a north/south direction over three tops the highest of which is the middle one. It's a ridge on which considerable snow cornices build up in winter and several walkers have fallen through this cornice, so beware!

The western and southern slopes of the hill are steep but not rocky other than one or two small outcrops although dense forestry does skirt the lower southern slopes and can make access difficult.

Beinn Teallach, on the other hand, rises from wide easy angled slopes, although the eastern and northern slopes are much steeper and rockier. Sitting a good 5km back from the Laggan-Spean Bridge road it has a rather shy and retiring air. The old Ordnance Survey one inch to the mile maps gave it a height of 2994ft while the Second Series of their

1:50,000 maps confirmed that with 913m/2995ft. However, the later 1:25000 series gave Beinn Teallach a height of 915m, which, at 3002ft, took it over the 3000ft Plimsoll line.

Forestry roads lead into the forest from a lay-by across the road from the cottages at Roughburn. The main track runs in a north-west direction for about 800m before turning sharply right and climbing across the lower slopes of Coire Clachaig. Some distance after this turning a firebreak gives access to the open corrie by the Allt Clachaig. Climb the slopes past Meall Clachaig in Coire Clachaig to reach the broad south-west shoulder of Beinn a' Chaorainn which can be followed to the south summit.

Continue north on the summit ridge, being careful to avoid any cornices, over the main summit and on to the north summit. Long heather slopes now lead down to a cairn at Tom Mor at the top of the Allt a' Chaorainn glen. Climb the rocky slopes immediately to the west of the cairn to reach the north-east ridge which leads to the summit.

Descend the long southern ridge and drop down into the Allt a' Chaorainn glen as soon as possible to cross the burn before it becomes too wide. Follow the footpath back down the glen to the start.

**Translation:** hill of the rowan; forge hill

**Pronunciation:** byn a choerin; byn tyellach

# LOCH LOCHY, LOCH ARKAIG AND LOCH EIL

## The Munros:

### Meall na Teanga   Sron a' Choire Ghairbh   Gulvain
### Sgurr Thuilm   Sgurr nan Coireachan

This is Jacobite country, rich in historic association, legend and romance. At the head of Loch Shiel, Charles Edward Stuart raised his Standard at the spot where the clans gathered to begin their long, and subsequently tragic, 1745 campaign – a Rising which gave way to the destruction of a highland way of life, the death of the clan system and a culture which some would suggest led to the highland clearances and a vastly different land use – sheep instead of people. Months later, after the fateful Battle of Culloden, Charles returned to this area but this time as a fugitive, spending a night out on Sgurr Thuilm itself.

There is a danger in writing a book about the Munros that you ignore the other, smaller hills, and here I would put in a plea for the Corbetts, those mountains between 2500ft (762m) and 2999ft (914m). While your attention may be taken up with Sgurr Thuilm and Sgurr nan Coireachan, south of the A830 Mallaig road lie no fewer than 16 Corbetts some of which, like the Rois-bheinn horseshoe or Sgurr Ghuibhsachain or Garbh-Bheinn of Ardgour, compare favourably with most Munros.

## Meall na Teanga (271), 9I7m/3008ft
## Sron a' Choire Ghairbh (237), 935m/3068ft,

Easily seen from the A82 road north of Spean Bridge, these two hills dominate the north-western side of Loch Lochy, rising up on bulging shoulders from their green skirt of forestry plantations. For some years the Forestry Commission has been busy clear-felling in this area and access to these two hills via the connecting Cam Bhealach has been tricky, unless you've been willing to wade through the forestry debris of broken branches and felled trees. I tried it once and swore I'd never do it again. However, the little footpath which runs up from the forest road on the north-west shore of Loch Lochy is clear, once again offering the best approach to these two hills.

From Kilfillan, just beyond the Laggan Locks, a forest road runs

**Route Summary:** At the N end of Loch Lochy cross by the Laggan Locks to Kilfillan. Follow the Forestry Commission track SW above the loch. After about 3.2km follow a track which climbs from the forest track uphill NW then W to the obvious pass between the two hills. From the top of the pass, climb Meall na Teanga first, return to the head of the pass then climb Sron a' Choire Ghairbh. Descend by the latter's long E spur to Kilfillan.

**Map:** OS Sheet 34

**Access Point:** North end of Loch Lochy

**Distance:** 20.8km, 1295m ascent

*Meall na Teanga from the air above Loch Lochy*

**Approx Time:** 6-9 hours

**Translation:** hill of the tongue; nose of the rough corrie

**Pronunciation:** myowl na tyenga; srawn a corrie ghirav

in a south-west direction. After a kilometre the road splits – keep to the higher one for just over another two kilometres, beside the Allt Glas-Dhoire, which has given its name to a ruin just below on the shore of the loch, Glas-dhoire. There is a small cairn at the side of the road which indicates the start of a footpath which runs north-west and then steeply west between craggy mountain walls to the summit of the Cam Bhealach.

It's best to climb Meall na Teanga first – steeply south up on to the spur of Meall Dubh, across a shallow bealach and onto the north ridge of Teanga. The summit cairn is a few hundred metres to the south. Return to the Cam Bhealach and climb the zigzags of an old stalker's path which leads almost all the way to the south-east ridge of Sron a' Choire Ghairbh. An easy walk along the mossy ridge leads to the summit. You can either return to the Cam Bhealach the way you came or, alternatively, follow the east ridge of Sron a' Choire Ghairbh over Sean Mheall and Meall nan Dearcag and down to the Kilfinnan Burn. Take some time to view the Kilfinnan Fall, a dramatic waterfall which hurtles down into a craggy gorge. It's well worth a visit and makes a great finale to a grand hill day.

*Looking south-west along the summit of Gulvain*

## Gulvain (156), 987m/3238ft

Gulvain is a shy hill, hiding itself well back from the road and even throwing up a high top between its summit and the route from the south. The ridge between these two tops dips only slightly but gives the hill a remarkable linear feel – it runs in a rough north/south direction between the long trenches of Gleann Fionnlighe and Glen Mallie and when you stand by the summit cairn there is a distinct awareness of remoteness. Long steep slopes drop away on either side and the long ridge you have just climbed reminds you that you have to return along it, together with a steep climb back onto the south top. Gulvain, as much as any other Munro, makes you work for your tick in the book!

  A good footpath runs up Gleann Fionnlighe from Drumsallie on the A830 Mallaig road and a bike would be useful to ride along the 5-6km to the footbridge over the Allt a' Choire Reidh. Beyond the bridge the path continues but soon fades out on Gulvain's south-south-east ridge. Some guidebooks describe this ridge as 'relentless', and it is, but underfoot conditions are good and it's just a question of plodding upwards with ever widening views all around you as consolation. Pass a craggy knoll on to the south summit, complete with trig point and continue down steep and rocky slopes to the broad ridge. Once past the low point of the ridge it narrows considerably and is quite entertaining for its final few metres to the summit and large cairn. Return to the start by re-tracing your steps – the west slopes of the hill are steep and craggy.

**Route Summary:** Start from Drumsallie on the A830 Fort William to Mallaig road and follow the track up the E side of the Fionn Lighe river (Route A, p.145). Continue up the glen for about 6km to the foot of the SSE ridge of Gulvain. Climb the ridge, past a craggy knoll and the S top (trig point) and climb the narrowing ridge to the summit

**Map:** OS Sheets 40 and 41

**Access Point:** Drumsallie, GR960794

**Distance:** 119.2km, 1128m ascent

**Approx Time:** 6-8 hours .

**Translation:** from Gaor Bheinn, possibly filthy hill

**Pronunciation:** goolvan

*Sgurr nan Coireachan from Sgurr Thuilm*

Route Summary: Follow the
private road up the right side of
the River Finnan below the railway viaduct (Route B). Just over
3km up the glen pass the
Corryhully Bothy and continue
on the track until it crosses the
stream that drains Coire
Thollaidh and Coire a' Bheithe.
Cross the stream and head for
the obvious spur that leads to
Druim Coire a' Bheithe and the
summit of Sgurr Thuilm. From
the cairn return S for a short
distance to join the main ridge
which runs W over the ups and
downs of Beinn Gharbh and
Meal an Tarmachain to the final
climb to Sgurr nan Coireachan.
From the summit descend SE
and then climb to Sgurr a'
Choire Riabhaich where the
ridge becomes very steep sided
and care should be taken.
Follow the ridge to the track
NE of the Corryhully Bothy

Map: OS Sheet 40

Access Point: Glenfinnan

Distance: 19.2km, 1219m ascent

Approx Time: 6-9 hours

Translation: peak of the round
hillock; peak of the corries

Pronunciation: skoor hoolim;
skoor nam korachan

## Sgurr Thuilm (189), 963m/3159 ft,
## Sgurr nan Coireachan (202), 956m/3136ft

The round of these hills, the Glenfinnan Horseshoe, as well as being
a superb outing in its own right, gives a taste of the rough conditions
found slightly north in the Knoydart area. Leave your car at the
small car park on the A830 on the west side of the River Finnan and
walk up the private road, below the West Highland Railway viaduct,
an impressive feat of engineering which was completed in 1899. It
was claimed that during the construction a horse and cart fell into
one of the hollow pillars.

After a kilometre or so, a road branches off to the left to service the
Glen Finnan Lodge, don't take this but continue past Corryhully
Bothy, a rather luxurious doss complete with electric lighting, to
where the road ends at the stream which drains Coire Thollaidh and
Coire a' Bheithe. Just beyond this point an obvious spur leads to the
long ridge called Druim Coire a' Bheithe. This is where the climbing
begins. Easy grassy slopes lead to a small subsidiary top and then
north to the summit of Sgurr Thuilm. From here the Knoydart hills
fill the horizon to the north-west, fronted by the remote Loch
Morar. To the north Loch Arkaig gives way to the Loch Quoich
hills. In front of you, Sgurr nan Coireachan fills the view, at the end
of a broad and knobbly ridge, splattered with tiny lochans and lined
by old fence-posts.

From the summit descend south for a short distance before
continuing the traverse westwards. Some rocky outcrops offer
easy scrambles, and the views are continuously stunning.

Sgurr nan Coireachan is slightly lower than Sgurr Thuilm but is a much better summit – this Peak of the Corries is well named, being thrown up by a number of remote corries, craggy and wild.

The south-east ridge is steep and rocky and abuts on to some steep cliffs which drop into Coire Thollaidh, a craggy and tumbling place of immense character. The ridge continues, in form and interest, across the minor top of Sgurr a' Choire Riabhaich and down towards the River Finnan again. Drop off the ridge in an easterly direction to where a good stalker's path skirts the foot of the crags to link up with the main Land Rover track again. Return past Corryhully Bothy and back to Glenfinnan.

# KNOYDART AND LOCH QUOICH

## The Munros:

Sgurr nan Coireachan    Garbh Chioch Mhor    Sgurr na Ciche
Sgurr Mor    Gairich    Gleouraich    Spidean Mialach
Luinne Bheinn    Meall Buidhe    Ladhar Bheinn
Beinn Sgritheall    Sgurr a' Mhaoraich

The peninsula of Knoydart, jutting out into the Sound of Sleat with all the character of an island, is generally perceived to be a wilderness. When the MoD wanted to buy it at the end of the eighties there was public outcry. 'Scotland's last wilderness,' said the press proclamations. And yet, Knoydart is, and always was, less of a natural wilderness than the Cairngorms, Torridon, the Cuillin, Inverpollaidh, the Fannaichs, the Blackmount and many other mountain areas of Scotland. This is no savage or untamed land.

Just after the 1745 rebellion there were over 1000 young men, the area's fighting force, working the land, paying what was known as 'warrior rent.' Skiary and Barisdale, Doune, Airor and Glenguserain, Sandaig and Inverie were sizeable townships. Even inland, in Glen Dubhlochain and Glen Meadale there were farmlands growing grain and potatoes, and an etching from the last century clearly shows 40 to 50 trading ships at anchor in Barrisdale Bay.

But thanks to the Clearances, the townships have gone. Today, Inverie is the only remaining village with a pier, a cluster of whitewashed cottages, a pub and a guest house. Stretching out west from those rugged mountains which form the romantic sounding Rough Bounds of Knoydart, the peninsula is sequestered from the rest of the mainland by long, winding sea lochs. Common belief suggests that Loch Hourn and Loch Nevis are corruptions of the Gaelic words for Heaven and Hell, placing Knoydart in some sort of montane limbo.

Choice of access is limited – a long walk from Kinlochhourn in the north or from Glen Dessarry via the Mam na Cloich Airde in the south, or ferry from Mallaig or Arnisdale, the latter being the keeper's rowing boat. Perhaps it's no small wonder that people regard Knoydart as being as remote as anywhere on the mainland.

The three Munros of Knoydart itself, Ladhar Bheinn, Luinne Bheinn and Meall Buidhe are best climbed from Inverie in the south or from Barrisdale – reached by a lovely eight-kilometre coastal walk from Kinlochhourn, while the hills that fringe the Loch Quoich area can be climbed from Glen Dessarry in the south or from Loch Quoich-side in the north. Beinn Sgritheall is climbed from the Glenelg/Arnisdale road.

*Gleouraich and Spidean Mialach from high in Glen Quoich*

*The Knoydart hills and Beinn Sgritheall from Sgurr na Ciche*

**Route Summary:** Follow the track from Strathan to Glen Dessarry. Continue W past Upper Glendessarry (Route A) and about 200m beyond the Allt Coire nan Uth climb the S ridge of Sgurr nan Coireachan. From the summit descend W to the Bealach nan Gall. Climb W up increasingly rocky slopes to the ridge which leads to Garbh Chioch Bheag and then Garbh Chioch Mhor. Beyond the summit the ridge narrows considerably on the descent to Feadan na Ciche. From the pass take the obvious grassy ramp which leads to a succession of grassy ledges which lead through the rocky screes and blocks to the summit of Sgurr na Ciche. From the summit return to the Feadan Gap. From here descend SW down the course of the Allt Coire Ciche, steep in places, to

## Sgurr nan Coireachan (207), 953m/3127ft, Garbh Chioch Mhor (113), 1013m/3323ft, Sgurr na Ciche (89), 1040m/3412ft

Sgurr na Ciche is the highest point in the Rough Bounds of Knoydart, that area of hills and glens which forms a wild barrier between the rest of the Knoydart peninsula and the hinterland. It's a particularly dominant mountain, its prominent peak recognisable from many points distant. If you are staying at the bothy at Sourlies or approaching from the head of Loch Nevis the obvious route of ascent is up the Druim a' Ghoirtein, the long ridge which rises in one steepening swoop all the way from the head of the loch to the summit.

If your approach is from Glen Dessarry then follow the path up the glen for about 2.5km beyond the house at Upper Glendessarry and climb north up a steep and narrowing rocky corrie to the bealach, the Bealach nan Gall, on the west side of Sgurr nan Coireachan. A path weaves its way through a rocky landscape all the way to the summit.

Most walkers nowadays tend to climb Sgurr na Ciche along with its near neighbours, Sgurr nan Coireachan and Garbh Chioch Mhor, a sensible alternative since the three are linked by a long rocky ridge, making a very enjoyable expedition.

Take the path from Strathan into Glen Dessarry, past Glen Dessarry House and continue as far as Upper Glendessarry. It is possible to travel this distance (4km) by mountain bike. Beyond Upper Glendessarry a footpath continues above the forestry and crosses a footbridge over the Allt Coire nan Uth. Beyond the bridge continue on the footpath for a couple of hundred metres and then take to the steep south ridge of Sgurr nan Coireachan and follow its rough and rocky slopes to the summit.

Descend in a west-south-west direction down a steep path to the Bealach nan Gall and then continue westwards over the Garbh Chiochs. Cross Garbh Chioch Bheag, with the craggy slopes of Coire nan Gall dropping away to the north, and follow the narrowing ridge to Garbh Chioch Mhor. Beyond the summit the ridge continues westwards, then north-westwards down into the col of the Feadan na Ciche, the whistle of the peak! The path to Sgurr nan Ciche weaves an intricate path up through the crags but is fairly straightforward. Descend via the Feadan gap, down the narrow gully towards Coire na Ciche. Where the gully opens out below Garbh Chioch Mhor skirt its south-west slopes to descend steep grassy slopes down to the pass at the head of Glen Dessarry where the footpath takes you back to your starting point.

a grassy terrace from which easy slopes drop down to the Mam na Cloich' Airde pass. Follow the path back to Glen Dessarry and Strathan

**Map:** OS Sheets 33 and 40

**Access Point:** Strathan

**Distance:** 20.8km, 914m ascent

**Approx Time:** 6-8 hours

**Translation:** peak of the corries; big rough place of the breast; peak of the breast

**Pronunciation:** skoor nan korachan; garav kee-ach voar; skoor na keesh

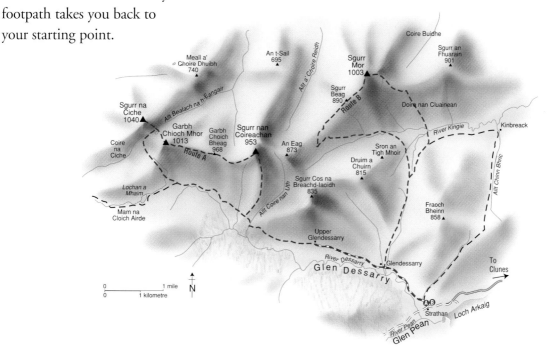

## Sgurr Mor (128), 1003m/3291ft

**Route Summary:** Follow the footpath which runs N from Glendessarry Lodge beside the Feith a' Chicheanais (Route B, p.149). Cross the obvious bealach and drop down into Glen Kingie. Cross the grassy slopes of Sron an Tigh Mhoir westwards. On the W side of the river a stalker's path runs from the upper reaches of Glen Kingie to a col between An Eag and Sgurr Beag. From here another path leads over Sgurr Beag to Sgurr Mor

**Map:** OS Sheets 33 and 40

**Access Point:** Strathan

**Distance:** 22.4km/1524m ascent

**Approx Time:** 9-10 hours

**Translation:** big peak

**Pronunciation:** skoor mor

This hill, and its near neighbour Gairich, are awkwardly placed in the upper reaches of Glen Kingie, a long and desolate glen which runs out eastwards into Glen Garry. There is a bothy at Kinbreak which provides a spartan base for climbing both peaks but it is possibly better to climb Sgurr Mor from Strathan at the end of Loch Arkaig, leaving Gairich to be climbed from the Loch Quoich dam.

A footpath runs north from Glendessarry Lodge beside the Feith a' Chicheanais and drops down into the head of Glen Kingie where it sweeps round eastwards towards Kinbreak bothy. Leave the path before it turns and traverse over the rough grassy slopes of Sron an Tigh Mhoir and into the wild upper reaches of Glen Kingie. On the north side of the river a stalker's path heads westwards before suddenly turning to zigzag its way up the col between An Eag and Sgurr Beag. From the col the path continues northwards towards Loch Quoich while another path follows the ridge over Sgurr Beag and up steepening slopes onto Sgurr Mor. The best way of descent is to continue over the summit and down to the ridge above Coire Buidhe. From here, long grassy slopes lead southwards to the River Kingie and the path back to Glendessarry Lodge.

*Gairich and Loch Quoich from the air*

## Gairich (265), 919m/3015ft

I've often driven along the road on the north side of Loch Quoich and thought that the finest way to climb Gairich would be to canoe across the loch and climb the hill by its broad north ridge. You could then canoe back over the loch and climb Sgurr a' Mhaoraich in the afternoon! As it is, most folk climb the two hills in a day, using a car between Loch Quoich dam and the foot of Sgurr a' Mhaoraich.

The normal approach to Gairich is from Loch Quoich dam. From the dam follow a path southwards across the boggy moor to the edge of the forestry plantation in Glen Kingie and then take the stalker's path westwards along the length of the Druim na Geid Salaich. As the ridge widens out on to the Bac nam Foid it becomes increasingly boggy and cut up by peat hags. Continue right up this ridge which is broad at first but which soon steepens as the path begins to climb through rocky outcrops and crags. Various tracks cross the south-east slopes of the hill and it's easy to follow these too far west, but by keeping on a rising traverse as close to the crest as you can it is possible to pick a line through the difficulties to the surprisingly broad summit ridge and massive cairn.

An alternative route to Gairich is from Glen Kingie in the south, using Kinbreack bothy as a base. A good stalker's path climbs Gairich Beag from the A' Mhaingir pass between Glen Kingie and Loch Quoich from where a rough path follows the ridge east-north-east to the summit.

**Route Summary:** From the S end of the Loch Quoich dam a path leads to an old stalker's path which runs S over boggy moorland to the edge of a forestry plantation (Route A). Here, another path runs due W, up the Druim na Geid Salaich. Once the broad ridge crest is reached the path peters out. The going is easy, however, and the broad ridge should be followed W to the final steep pull to Gairich. At the foot of this final rise a path reappears, but after a while it runs out on to the S face. Don't be tempted by it but continue climbing on the crest of the ridge to the spacious summit and large cairn

**Map:** OS Sheet 33

**Access Point:** Loch Quoich dam

**Distance:** 14.4km, 762m ascent

**Approx Time:** 4-6hours

**Translation:** roaring

**Pronunciation:** gaareech

*Looking west towards the Inner Hebrides from Meall Buidhe*

## Gleouraich (94), 1035m/3396ft, Spidean Mialach (143), 996m/3268ft

Another fine round which makes the most of excellent stalkers' paths, one of the great features of this entire area. Both Gleouraich and Spidean Mialach have several great corries biting into their steep flanks from the north and the walker, traversing both hills, can admire them from best advantage. Snow cornices lie deep into the early summer and the views north to the Glen Shiel hills are particularly fine.

While the south-facing slopes of both hills are fairly uniform and uninteresting, an amazing stalker's path leaves the road near the Allt Coire Peitireach. A roadside cairn marks its start. This fantastic example of footpath engineering makes a series of rising traverses onto Gleouraich's south ridge where it continues above the hill's precipitous western slopes. Further on the path follows the ridge to the right and stops at the foot of the final steep rise to Gleouraich's summit.

From the top, the route onwards to Spidean Mialach follows the rim of several huge corries which fall away to the north in spectacular fashion. There is a considerable drop between the two Munro summits, but there is plenty of interest. From the summit of Spidean Mialach continue in a south-east direction for a while before dropping down an obvious spur towards Loch Fearna. From the small saddle above the loch make your way across Coire Mheil to pick up the stalker's path on the west side of the burn, a path which can then be followed back to the road near the starting point.

## Luinne Bheinn (230), 939m/3081ft, Meall Buidhe (215), 946m/3104ft

These two hills, along with Ladhar Bheinn, are the real hills of Knoydart. The first two rise from extremely rough and rocky corries and are separated from their western neighbour by the high pass of the Mam Barrisdale. A path which runs from Inverie to Barrisdale, crosses the pass, the summit of which gives excellent access to the north-west ridge of Luinne Bheinn. Barrisdale is reached by a wonderfully scenic footpath which follows the south shore of Loch Hourn from Kinlochhourn, while Inverie is reached either by ferry from Mallaig, or by a long walk-in from Glen Dessarry to the head of Loch Nevis and then through the Mam Meadail.

From the summit of the Mam Barrisdale, easy slopes lead eastwards to the Bachd Mhic an Tosaich, from where the ridge to Luinne Bheinn both narrows and steepens in a rough and rocky climb to the summit ridge. It's interesting that the name has been translated as meaning the hill of anger, or the hill of melody, or even the hill of mirth – a fair range of emotions. One Gaelic-speaking friend suggested it perhaps should just be hill of moods!

The summit sits proudly at 939m, offering fine views down the length of Gleann an Dubh-Lochain and out to Loch Nevis. Beyond, shimmering on a flat sea, lie the contrasting outlines of Rum and Eigg.

At the east end of the summit ridge a steep southern flank drops down to a broad knolly ridge which eventually forms Druim Leac a' Shith. This ridge borders the remote and desolate north corrie of Meall Buidhe, and eventually leads you to the obviously defined NE summit ridge. The highest of the two tops is the westernmost one, at 946m.

A long ridge, high above Gleann Meadail, eventually brings you down from the high tops and into the lower reaches of Gleann an Dubh-Lochain, where a good Land Rover track swiftly carries you down into Inverie, or alternatively, back over the Mam Barrisdale to Barrisdale itself.

## Ladhar Bheinn (108), 1020m/3346ft

Ladhar Bheinn can be climbed from Folach in Gleann na Guiserein, south west of the mountain, by Coire a' Phuill from the Mam Barrisdale or by the magnificent Coire Dhorcaill from Barrisdale. The latter route is by far the finest.

While every possible advantage points to Barrisdale as being the best approach, walkers who are staying at Inverie may find the Gleann na

**Route Summary:** Take the Inverie path to the head of Mam Barrisdale (Route A, p.155). Above the pass, the NW ridge of Luinne Bheinn drops down in a sharp even line. Follow this ridge to the summit. At the E end of Luinne Bheinn a steep S flank drops to a broad knolly ridge which eventually forms Druim Leac a' Shith. This ridge borders a remote and desolate N corrie of Meall Buidhe. Follow this ridge, over its complex bumps and knolls, and climb gradually to the more obviously defined NE ridge of Meall Buidhe which takes you to the E summit. The true summit is a few hundred metres to the W

**Map:** OS Sheets 33 and 40

**Access Point:** Inverie

**Distance:** 19.2km, 1372m ascent

**Approx Time:** 6-9 hours

**Translation:** hill of anger, or hill of melody; yellow hill

**Pronunciation:** loonya vyn; myowl booee

**Route Summary:** A bridge crosses the river above Barrisdale to a path which in turn crosses the saltings to meet a stalker's path below Creag Bheithe (Route B, p.155). Follow this path up zig-zags, round the nose of Creag Bheithe and through some woodland into Coire Dhorrcail. Cross the Allt

*Ladhar Bheinn from the north-east*

Coire Dhorrcail and climb grassy slopes W to the ridge of Druim a' Choire Odhair. Follow this narrowing ridge to the crest of Stob a' Choire Odhair, then on to the summit ridge of Ladhar Bheinn. A cairn at this point is often mistaken for the summit, but the true summit lies a few hundred metres to the west. To complicate matters further an OS trig point lies at the W end of the ridge at a height of feet. The best descent lies SE, over the ridges above Coire Dhorrcail and Coire na Cabaig, over Aonach Sgoilte and down the E ridge to Mam Barrisdale

**Map:** OS Sheet 33

**Access Point:** Barrisdale

**Distance:** 14.4km, 1067m ascent

**Approx Time:** 4-6 hours

**Translation:** hoof or claw hill

**Pronunciation:** laarven

Guiserein approach quicker, if duller. From the village a road runs through the forest and over the Mam Uidhe pass. About a kilometre beyond the summit of the pass a footpath leaves the road in a north-east direction and into Gleann na Guiserein. From the ruins at Folach, long and interminable slopes lead to the summit ridge, but a better route follows a footpath northwards beside the Abhainn Bheag to reach the western ridge of the mountain above the forestry plantations. This ridge can easily be climbed, over An Diollaid to the narrow summit ridge and cairn.

The Coire a' Phuill route climbs grassy slopes and then increasingly rocky ground to reach the narrow ridge between Stob a' Chearchaill and the top of the Aonach Sgoilte from where the ridge can be followed north-westwards to the summit ridge, high above the craggy walls of Coire Dhorrcail.

Coire Dhorrcail itself is enclosed by the subsidiary peaks of Stob a' Chearcaill on the east and Stob a' Choire Odhair on the west and a circuit of the corrie makes a superb expedition. A zigzagged stalker's path climbs on to the lower reaches of Creag Bheithe from Barrisdale, before turning south-westwards and through the trees in the lower reaches of Coire Dhorrcaill. This side of Ladhar Bheinn is owned by the John Muir Trust, who purchased it a number of years ago after the threatened purchase of Knoydart by the MoD fell through. On Ladhar Bheinn the Trust is primarily trying to regenerate the native Caledonian pine woods.

A horseshoe of ridges and peaks encloses the corrie to form this high cirque of riven cliffs and buttresses still rimmed by sparkling snow cornices well into the spring. Our route is by the long, bumpy ridge of the Druim a' Choire Odhair which rises gently in stages, each protuberance offering grander and wider views out over Loch Hourn towards Beinn Sgriol and Skye.

The summit, 1020m, is close to where this long ridge abuts onto the main ridge. The cairn itself is on the west-north-west ridge just a short distance from the junction.

Ladhar Bheinn is not only a magnificent mountain, but a complex one, rising above a series of corries which bite into its steep north eastern slopes. A good descent to the Mam Barrisdale follows the line of these corries, down to the Bealach Coire Dhorrcail, round the head of another steep corrie before the junction with the long Aonach Sgoilte ridge, and then down to another bealach before Stob a' Chearcaill and the long, wet slippery slopes which lead down eastwards to the Mam Barrisdale.

# Beinn Sgritheall (180), 974m/3196ft

**Route Summary:** Follow the old hill track to Glenelg up through some scattered woods and make for an obvious break in the rocky escarpment above you. Above the crags turn right and cross some moorland with scattered lochans. The W ridge of Sgritheall is now quite obvious and leads to the summit. Continue E on the ridge which soon narrows again. Follow it to the Bealach Arnisdale; a stream offers the best guide back to Arnisdale itself and the Loch Hourn road

**Map:** OS Sheet 33

**Access Point:** Opposite Eilean Rarsaidh on the Arnisdale road, GR815120

**Distance:** 9.6km, 975m ascent

**Approx Time:** 4-6 hours

**Translation:** hill of screes

**Pronunciation:** byn skreehal

This shapely hill dominates the rough quarter between Loch Hourn and the glens which run inland from Glenelg. It is, by association, Gavin Maxwell's hill, for the author's Camusfearna was near Sandaig on the very western tip of the peninsula. It was here that he wrote that classic of nature writing, *Ring of Bright Water*.

The south face of the mountain is scree girt and very steep, rising almost 1000m above the shore of Loch Hourn in only 1.6km. Despite that, the easiest routes of ascent are on this side of the hill though they do avoid the worst of the screes.

The most straightforward route leaves the road below the wooded hillside called Coille Mhialairigh at a point roughly opposite Eilean Rarsaidh. Clamber uphill through the trees until a faint path is found, which leads to an old shieling on the hillside and continues in a north-westerly direction to cross a rough escarpment on to the west ridge of the mountain, near a tiny lochan. From there the increasingly steep ridge is climbed to the summit over rocky terrain.

Another route of ascent goes uphill behind Arnisdale village to the Bealach Arnasdail then north-west up steep screes to a subsidiary peak and finally along the connecting ridge to the summit. This also makes a good descent if you want to enjoy a complete traverse of the mountain, although you will have a 5km walk back along the road at the end.

*The summit of Beinn Sgritheall from its east top*

## Sgurr a' Mhaoraich (101), 1027m/3369ft

Often climbed together in one day with Gairich, Sgurr a'
Mhaoraich is a big, bluff hill which rises in a series of broad
muscley shoulders above Kinlochhourn. Perhaps not surprisingly,
very few climb it from the village, maybe preferring to gain some
height by starting from the road which runs along the length of
Loch Quoich.

Another route which is rarely climbed is from Glen Quoich,
beyond the loch's northern finger. A stalker's path runs up the
length of Coire a' Chaorainn, while another takes the east ridge
of An Bathaich in a series of tight zigzags and crosses a narrow ridge
to the rocky summit of An Bathaich. From there a high bealach
separates this summit from Sgurr a' Mhaoraich.

Another stalker's path can be used to advantage following the line
of the Bac nan Canaichean on to Sgurr Coire nan-Eiricheallach,
Sgurr a' Mhaoraich's eastern top. A narrow, rocky ridge connects
the two summits and a fine round can be completed by descending
from Am Bathaich.

Finally, probably the most straightforward, and certainly the
quickest, ascent is up the line of the Allt Coire nan Cnamh (leave
the road opposite Loch a' Choire Bheithe on the Kinlochhourn
road) and into the upper corrie. Climb the rough grassy slopes in a
north-north-east direction to the summit.

**Route Summary:** Follow a
stalker's path which starts just
SW of the bridge (Route C,
p.150). Follow the path N up
the ridge of Bac nan Canaichean
to Sgurr Coire nan Eireallach
and then across a slight dip to
its NW top. From here another
ridge leads W to the summit of
Sgurr a' Mhaoraich

**Map:** OS Sheet 33

**Access Point:** Quoich Bridge,
GR014040

**Distance:** 11.2km, 975m ascent

**Approx Time:** 4-6 hours

**Translation:** peak of the shellfish

**Pronunciation:** skoor a
vooreach

# GLEN SHIEL HILLS

## The Munros:

The Saddle   Sgurr na Sgine   Saileag   Sgurr a' Bhealaich Dheirg
Aonach Meadhoin   Ciste Dhubh   Sisters of Kintail (Sgurr na Ciste Duibhe;
Sgurr Fhuaran)   The South Glen Shiel Ridge (Creag a' Mhaim; Druim
Shionnach; Aonach air Chrith; Maol Chinn-dearg; Sgurr an Doire Leathain;
Sgurr an Lochain; Creag nan Damh)   A' Chralaig   Mullach Fraoch-choire
Carn Ghluasaid   Sgurr nan Conbhairean   Sail Chaorainn

With no fewer than 20 Munros accessible from the A87 road which runs down its length, it's no wonder than Glen Shiel is popular with hillwalkers. With nine Munros on the south side, seven of them capable of being climbed in one day-long expedition, and 11 on the north side, the area is not only convenient for the car-borne enthusiast but boasts some of the finest hills in the Western Highlands.

The Saddle is generally recognised as being the finest mountain in the area, and its long eastern ridge, known as the Forcan Ridge, is a classic scramble in its own right.

The mountains on the north side of the glen have a much more complex topography than those of the south and break down into several groups, the most famous of them, The Five Sisters of Kintail, also comprising one of the great picture postcard views of Scotland. Unfortunately, only two of the Five Sisters are Munros, but the traverse of the ridge over Munros and tops makes a very worthwhile expedition.

## The Saddle (118), 1010m/3314ft, Sgurr na Sgine (220), 945m/3100ft

The Saddle is a peak of narrow ridges, deep corries and superb views. The best feature of the mountain and one that shouldn't be missed, is the Forcan Ridge, a great scrambling route which follows The Saddle's east ridge. Approach by the stalker's path which leaves Glen Shiel just south-east of Achnangart, and from the end of this path climb south over Meallan Odhar and then continue south west across a grassy col to reach the foot of the rocky Forcan Ridge.

As you gain height the ridge becomes narrower and tighter, and

**Route Summary:** Start SE of the quarry at Achangart. A stalker's path leads W to a bealach between Biod an Fhithich and Meallan Odhar (Route A, p.161). From here go S then SW to the bottom of the Saddle's E ridge, known as the Forcan Ridge. Follow this ridge, knife edged and exposed in places, to Sgurr na Forcan. Continue W down a steep rock pitch with good holds and traverse a narrow ridge to the E top of the Saddle and then the

*Looking west towards Sgurr na Ciste Duibhe, Sgurr na Carnach and Sgurr Fhuaran*

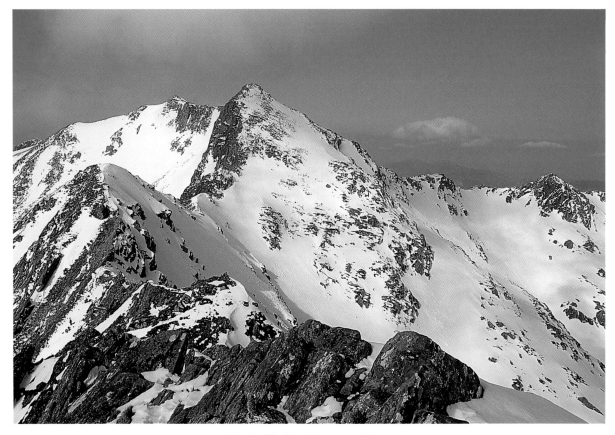

*The Saddle from Sgurr nan Forcan*

summit. The OS trig point is further on and lower than the cairn which marks the summit. Descend to the Bealach Coire Mhalagain down rough bouldery slopes and climb to the NW top of Sgurr na Sgine. Follow a rocky ridge SE to the summit cairn. Descend by way of Faochag and its fine NE ridge

**Map:** OS Sheet 33

**Access Point:** Achnangart, GR968142

**Distance:** 16km, 1430m ascent

**Approx Time:** 5-7 hours

**Translation:** the saddle; peak of the knife

**Pronunciation:** the saddle; skoor na skeena

for good stretches it's very rocky with some great scrambling if you stick with the crest. A rough path avoids the best of the scrambling up the right-hand side of the ridge but this really is an inferior way of climbing the hill. The continuation to The Saddle from the top of the Forcan Ridge, Sgurr nan Forcan, is narrow and steep in places and care should be taken.

Descents can be made down the north ridge over Sgurr na Creige, or west and then north round Coire Uaine but most visitors will want to add Sgurr na Sgine to their day's tally and this Munro, and its outlier, Faochag (The Whelk) are situated about 1.6km south-east of the summit.

Sgurr na Sgine can be easily climbed from the Bealach Coire Mhalagain – up on to the north ridge which is then followed round the head of Coire Toileil to the summit. Descend northwards again, and then round the corrie rim to Faochag whose steep uniform north-east ridge can be followed back to the A87.

# Saileag (195), 959m/3146ft, Sgurr a' Bhealaich Dheirg (92), 1038m/3405ft, Aonach Meadhoin (129), 1003m/3291ft, Ciste Dhubh (163), 982m/3222ft

These hills are generally referred to as the North Glen Shiel Ridge. They have very similar characteristics to their southerly sisters.

It's possible to climb the hills of this group with the Five Sisters, but that's a long, strenuous day. Taken on its own the North Glen Shiel Ridge route offers a straightforward traverse between An Caorann Mor, the pass between Cluanie Inn and Glen Affric, and the Bealach an Lapain.

If tackling the ridge from west to east ascend the grassy wall of Meall a' Charra from Glenlicht House in Glen Lichd (access by track from Morvich near Loch Duich) to Saileag, traverse the ridge, and return westwards by the Glen Affric track. Ciste Dubh is a steep and fairly isolated peak which lies about 5km north of Cluanie Inn and which is easily accessible when approached from An Caorann Mor. Climb to the Bealach a' Choinich and up the south ridge of the peak which becomes very narrow near the summit.

The ridge can then be tackled by returning to the Bealach a' Choinnich and following the ridge over the top of Sgurr Fhuarail, Aonach Meadhoin and westwards to Sgurr a' Bhealaich Dheirg and Saileag.

**Route Summary:** From Glenlicht House climb SE up Meall a' Charra, then up the long grassy spur which leads to Saileag (Route B). Follow the ridge E above the Fraoch-choire to Sgurr a' Bhealaich Dheirg. The summit cairn lies about 50m N of the main ridge. Return to the ridge and continue ESE to Aonach Meadhoin, then to another top on Sgurr an Fhuarail. A wide ridge now runs N and dips to a green bealach. Above this pass a steep and narrow ridge runs north to Ciste Dhubh from where the NW ridge can be descended to the Allt Cam-ban

**Map:** OS Sheet 33

**Access Point:** Glenlicht House

**Distance:** 17.6km, 1676m ascent

**Approx Time:** 6-8 hours.

**Translation:** little heel; peak of the red pass; middle hill; black chest

**Pronunciation:** saalak; skoor a vyaleech yerak; oenach vain; keesta doo

*The Five Sisters of Kintail and Loch Duich*

**Route Summary:** From Glenshiel Bridge climb the steep and unrelenting slopes of Sgurr na Ciste Duibhe (Route C). Make for the ridge W of Sgurr nan Spainteach. From here follow the narrow ridge W to Sgurr na Ciste Duibhe's summit. Avoiding a false ridge which runs N of the peak continue NW and descend to the Bealach na Craoibhe. Turn and climb over Sgurr na Carnach to a V-shaped gap of the Bealach na Carnach. From here a short and steep ascent leads to the summit of Sgurr Fhuaran

**Map:** OS Sheet 33

**Access Point:** Glenshiel Bridge

**Distance:** 16km, 1524m ascent

**Approx Time:** 6-8 hours

**Translation:** peak of the black chest; meaning obscure

**Pronunciation:** skoor na keesta ghoo; skoor ooaran

# Sisters of Kintail (Sgurr na Ciste Duibhe (102), 1027m/3369ft, Sgurr Fhuaran (66), 1068m/3504ft)

The mountains which stretch along the north side of Glen Shiel form a barrier some 16km long and the peaks at the north west end of this long ridge are known as the Five Sisters of Kintail, although only two are Munros. One of the notable features of these hills is the fact that their western flanks rise for over 1000m in one fell swoop from glen floor to the rocky crest. The average angle is about 30°!

The traverse of the Five Sisters of Kintail must be considered as one of the real classic hill walks in the UK. The best direction is from south-east to north-west and the best route is to leave the Glen Shiel road below the Bealach na Lapain. The ascent northwards to the bealach is a steep one but relatively short, and from the col the ridge, which is grassy and narrow at this point, rises gradually over two minor tops to Sgurr na Ciste Duibhe. Continue north west and then north where the ridge begins to broaden out considerably. A steep climb continues to the next Munro, Sgurr Fhuaran, the highest of the Five Sisters. The next top, Sgurr nan Saighead, is tight and exposed and is in many ways the finest of the group, although it's not even of Munro status! Descend to Loch Duich down Coire na Criche or down the west ridge of Sgurr nan Saighead, followed by a steep descent to Loch Shiel where a footbridge carries you over the river.

# The South Glen Shiel Ridge: Creag a' Mhaim (214), 947m/3107ft, Druim Shionnach (155), 987m/3238ft, Aonach air Chrith (107), 1021m/3350ft, Maol Chinn-dearg (166), 981m/3218ft, Sgurr an Doire Leathain (116), 1010m/3314ft, Sgurr an Lochain (126), 1004m/3294ft, Creag nan Damh (268), 918m/3012ft

Possibly the best way to begin this traverse is to walk up the old road which goes south-east from the Cluanie Inn towards the eastern end of the ridge. From the high-point of the road a stalker's path leads to the summit of Creag a' Mhaim. From here the whole of the ridge stretches out before you to end at Creag nan Damh, some 11km away. The main problem of the day is how to get back to your starting point from the far end of the ridge. Ideally you can get a lift, if you can't it's a long walk back to Cluanie – it's mostly uphill too!

While many will want to climb all seven Munros in one outing, others may be happier breaking the route down into two easier sections. The most obvious breakdown is probably to climb Creag a' Mhaim by the route mentioned above, then follow the ridge over Druim Shionnach, Aonach air Chrith, and Maol Chinn-dearg and descend back to the road in Glen Shiel by the north ridge, which is steep at first but eases off lower down where a stalker's path takes you to a point about 4km west of your starting point.

The other section takes in Sgurr an Doire Leathain, Sgurr an Lochain and finally, Creag nan Damh. The ridge is gained by the long spur of the Druim Thollaidh to Sgurr Coire na Feinne then north west along the main ridge to Sgurr an Doire Leathain.

**Route Summary:** Take the old road from Cluanie Inn to Glen Loyne and climb Creag a' Mhaim by the streams which flow down Coirean an Eich Bhric. Follow the broad ridge NW to Druim Shionnach, descend a short dip then a gradual rise brings you to Aonach air Chrith. Continue on the narrowest section of the ridge towards Maol Chinn-dearg. Continue NW to the minor top of Sgurr Coire na Feinne, then W to the flat topped Sgurr an Doire Leathain. From here the ridge dips again, before rising to Sgurr an Lochain. Another minor top follows, Sgurr Beag, before the last Munro of the ridge, Creag nan Damh. From here a fence leads W to the Bealach Duibh Leac and a stalker's path to Glen Shiel

**Map:** OS Sheet 33

**Access Point:** Cluanie Inn

**Distance:** 24km, 1829m ascent

**Approx Time:** 7-11 hours

**Translation:** rock of the large round hill; ridge of the fox; trembling hill; bald red hill; peak of the broad thicket; peak of the little loch; rock of the stags

**Pronunciation:** crayk a vaim; drim heeanach; oenach ayr chree; moel chan dyerack; skoor an dira lehan; skoor an lochan; creag nam dav

## A' Chralaig (32), 1120m/3674ft, Mullach Fraoch-choire (46), 1102m/3615ft

**Route Summary:** Leave the A87 near the W end of Loch Cluanie (Route A) where a stalker's track leaves the road to run through the An Caorrann Mor to Glen Affric. Don't follow the track but climb steeply NE up grassy slopes on A' Chralaig. Continue until the angle eases on the S ridge, and follow this ridge to the large summit cairn. Continue N along a grassy ridge and cross the top of Stob Coire na Cralaig. After this the ridge narrows considerably and several pinnacles have to be crossed before reaching the summit of Mullach. Either return to the start the way you came, or alternatively drop down into Coire Odhar (steep at first) and return by the track in An Caorrann Mor

**Map:** OS Sheet 33 and 34

**Access Point:** West end of Loch Cluanie

**Distance:** 12.8km, 1067m ascent

**Approx Time:** 5-8 hours

**Translation:** basket or creel, heather-corrie peak

**Pronunciation:** a chraalik, moolach froech-chora

These two hills are best climbed from the Cluanie Inn, taking a rising traverse over grassy slopes up a wide and open corrie to the stony summit ridge of A' Chralaig. The route continues north to Stob Coire na Cralaig, with deep corries, Coire Odhar and Coire na Cralaig, on either side of the rock-strewn ridge. From Stob Coire na Cralaig the ridge veers suddenly to the north-east and then north again towards Mullach Fraoch-choire. This next section is the finest feature of all these hills, a ridge which is narrow and contains a number of fine rocky pinnacles which give the ridge such character. In snowy conditions this ridge can be extremely tricky, but when clear a footpath is obvious, weaving its way around the major difficulties.

The best route of descent is to follow your footsteps back around the ridge to Stob Coire na Cralaig and then drop down its broad grassy western ridge which leads back down to the footpath in An Caorann Mor and the Cluanie Inn.

*The Glen Shiel Hills from Sgurr nan Conbhairean*

## Carn Ghluasaid (201), 957m/3140ft, Sgurr nan Conbhairean (42), 1110m/3642ft, Sail Chaorainn (131), 1002m/3287ft

These three mountains form a compact little group on the north side of Loch Cluanie. Viewed from the north and east, from the headwaters of the River Doe you'll see great corries biting into the hillsides, culminating in crag-girt eastern facing cliffs.

From Lundie on Cluanie-side, a footpath, an old military road, runs westwards, parallel to the road for some distance and should be followed for about 500m or so to where a stalker's path climbs northwards all the way on to the flat stony plateau of Carn Ghluasaid. Cross the flat summit to find the cairn which is fairly close to the edge of the north face.

Head westwards then north-west along the broad ridge crossing the rise of Creag a' Chaorainn, across a col and then the final stony slopes to Sgurr nan Conbhairean.

By descending northwards down a distinctly curving ridge you'll reach a shallow col and gently rising slopes which lead northwards to the summit of Sail Chaorainn.

To return, follow the route of ascent but rather than climb back on to the summit of Sgurr nan Conbhairean, follow the rough path across its western slopes to reach the ridge above Gorm Lochan and the summit which is to the north west of the lochan, Drochaid an Tuill Easaich (unnamed by the OS). Turn south from the summit and descend the easy grass slopes down the shoulder of Meall Breac, eventually veering south east to cross the Allt Coire Lair. Follow the old military road back to Lundie.

**Route Summary:** Leave the A87 at Lundie (Route B) and follow the old military road W for a few hundred metres then take the obvious stalker's path which climbs the S slopes of Carn Ghluasaid. Cross the plateau to the summit. Continue W then NW along the broad ridge, crossing Creag a' Chaorainn then W to cross a col and the final climb to Sgurr nan Conbhairean. From here descend N down an easy ridge to a col and climb Sail Chaorainn. To return follow the ridge back towards Conbhairean but bypass the summit on its W side. Continue SW to a col above Gorm Lochan and continue a short distance to Drochaid an Tuill Easaich. Descend the S ridge to the old military road which will take you back to Lundie

**Map:** OS Sheet 34

**Access Point:** Lundie; Loch Cluanie

**Distance:** 16km, 1067m ascent

**Approx Time:** 6-8 hours

**Translation:** hill of movement; peak of the keeper of the hounds; hill (heel) of the rowan

**Pronunciation:** kaarn ghlooasat; skoor nan konavaran; sale choeran

# GLEN AFFRIC AND STRATHFARRAR

## The Munros:

Beinn Fhada (Ben Attow)    A' Ghlas-bheinn    An Socach
Sgurr nan Ceathreamhnan    Mullach na Dheiragain    Toll Creagach
Tom a' Choinich    Carn Eige (Eighe)    Beinn Fhionnlaidh
Mam Sodhail (Mam Soul)    Carn nan Gobhar    Sgurr na Lapaich
An Riabhachan    An Socach    Sgurr Fhuar-thuill    Sgurr a' Choire Ghlais
Carn nan Ghobhar    Sgurr na Ruaidhe.

Glen Affric, Glen Cannich and Strathfarrar are the three great inland glens which feed the River Glass, which becomes the River Beauly in its lower reaches. All three glens can be best reached by road from the east, for all lead to the roadless west, although rights of way run through all of them. A remote youth hostel, Alltbeithe, offers access to the Sgurr nan Ceathreamhnan hills, while a side glen, the Gleann nam Fiadh, gives access to the Carn Eighe hills. The Sgurr na Lapaich group can be reached from Glen Cannich in the east or by a long overland route from Glen Elchaig in the west. Further north, Glen Strathfarrar is entered via a locked gate at Struy, giving access to the four Munros which lie just north of the glen. All three glens are well wooded in their lower reaches, with the Caledonian pines of Glen Affric particularly splendid, but forestry and hydro electricity activities have spoiled the intimacy of these places, once reckoned to be the three finest glens in Scotland. But having said that, the hills tend to remain comparatively inviolate, and offer long days on high winding ridges well away from the signs of man's activities, big remote hills in a particularly beautiful corner of the Scottish Highlands.

**Route Summary:** From the car park near Dorusduain take the stalker's path which runs up to the Bealach an Sgairne (Route A). After crossing the stream which flows down from Coire an Sgairne take another path which runs up into the corrie and climb the slopes of Meall a' Bhealaich. Follow this ridge S to where it abuts on to the great summit plateau of Beinn Fhada known as the Plaide Mor. Continue SE along the edge of the plateau to the summit cairn. Return to the Bealach an Sgairne and climb directly to the summit of A' Ghlas-bheinn (Route B)

## Beinn Fhada (Ben Attow) (97), 1032m/3386ft, A' Ghlas-bheinn (269), 918m/3012ft

Beinn Fhada has two distinct characters. Seen from Glen Affric it appears quite unremarkable – a long grassy ridge leading all the way from glen floor to summit. But, go west and see its finest features from that angle – steep cliffs, narrow ridges and wild corries and the best route of ascent. It's well named the 'long mountain' for it occupies much the same length as all of the Five Sisters of Kintail!

Take the track up Strath Croe from the Forestry Commission car park at Dorusduain. Cross the river by the footbridge and continue eastwards up Gleann Choinneachain below the steep north face of Sgurr a' Choire Ghairbh until you reach the zigzags near the foot of the little Coire an Sgairne. Follow a branch path up this corrie to the top. Finally, cross the summit plateau, the Plaide Mhor, and continue in a south-east direction to the highest point and the summit cairn. The descent can be varied by going out along the ridge northwards to Meall a' Bhealaich which overlooks the narrow pass from Glen Affric, the Bealach an Sgairne. The descent to the pass is steep and some careful route selection is called for. From the path you can easily climb A' Ghlas-bheinn by its rather rough and rocky south ridge, past Loch a' Chleirich. Descend its west ridge to join the track through the forest to Dorusduain or continue north past the summit, down easy grassy slopes to pick up the path through the Bealach na Sroine. Follow this path, and later forestry tracks, back to Dorusduain.

**Map:** OS Sheet 33
**Access Point:** Strath Croe
**Distance:** 17.6km, 1143m ascent
**Approx Time:** 6-8 hours
**Translation:** long hill; the greenish/grey hill
**Pronunciation:** byn ata; a glash vin

**Route Summary:** Reach Alltbeithe from either Loch Beinn a' Mheadhoin in Glen Affric (16km) or a shorter route through the An Caorrann Mor from Cluanie. From Alltbeithe a footpath beside the Allt na Faing leads directly to the ridge just W of An Socach (Route C). Go E to the summit. Return to the ridge and follow it W again. Climb grassy terraces to the top of Stob Coire nan Dearcag. Continue on the gently rising ridge to the E top of Ceathreamhnan. Continue over rocky ground to the summit. Rough ground to the NE of the summit leads to a descent to a sharp rib above An Gorm Lochan. The ridge now broadens and offers an easy walk along the length of Creag a' Choir Aird to Mullach na Dheiragain. Return to Ceathreamhnan and descend to Alltbeithe by the S ridge of the W top

**Map:** OS Sheets 25 and 33

**Access Point:** Alltbeithe, GR080202

**Distance:** 26km, 1680m ascent

**Approx Time:** 7-12 hours

**Translation:** the snout; peak of the quarters; possibly summit of the hawk

**Pronunciation:** an sochkach; skoor nan keroanan; moollach na yerakan

## An Socach (264), 920m/3018ft, Sgurr nan Ceathreamhnan (21), 1151m/3776ft, Mullach na Dheiragain (164), 982m/3222ft

Sgurr nan Ceathreamhnan is a magnificent mountain of many peaks and ridges at the head of Glen Affric. It is fairly remote and all approaches to it tend to be long unless you happen to be staying at Alltbeithe Youth Hostel which conveniently lies right at the foot of the mountain. Otherwise you'll have to tackle Ceathreamhnan from Cluanie Inn or the head of Loch Duich over the Bealach an Sgairne. Probably the shortest approach is from Glen Elchaig in the north and this route has the added advantage of climbing up past the spectacular Falls of Glomach. Once above the falls you continue up the Allt Coire-lochain and on to the ridge on the west side of Coire Lochan which leads to the summit. Most Munro collectors will also want to climb Mullach na Dheiragain which lies about 4.5km north-east of Ceathreamhnan near the end of a long curved ridge and while both hills are in a sense connected, there is good justification in climbing Mullach na Dheiragain on its own from the north, from Glen Elchaig and the Iron Lodge to the head of Loch Mullardoch. Long grassy slopes up Coire Aird give easy access to the rockier north west ridge and a short distance after that the summit cone.

Another, longer, alternative is to tackle an entire horseshoe circuit of Gleann a' Choilich, the long and curved glen which separates the Beinn Fhionnlaidh/ Carn Eighe/Mam Soul massif from the Ceathreamhnan/ Dheiragain ridge. This entails about 25km of walking with about 2000m of climbing – and you still have to get to the start at the head of Loch Mullardoch! Alltbeithe Youth Hostel can be reached fairly comfortably through the An Caorrann Mor from Cluanie Inn. The route tends to be fairly boggy both in its upper reaches and lower down in Glen Affric. A footpath follows the line of the Allt na Faing into the higher, rocky reaches of Coire na Cloiche and on to the bealach just west of An Socach (unnamed on the OS map). This hill is dramatically dwarfed by its bigger neighbours and it's hard to believe it's of Munro status. It is often climbed on its own from Affric Lodge via the Bealach Coire Ghadheil. The ridge, which runs west from An Socach, narrows appreciably and offers an interesting route over Stob Coire nan Dearcag, then takes you high above Coire nan Dearcag with its high-level lochan and over Ceathreamhnan's east top to finish eventually on the suitably rocky summit of Sgurr nan Ceathreamhnan – one of the great hills of the Western Highlands.

*Carn Eige, Mam Sodhail and Coire Lochan from Beinn Fhionnlaidh*

## Toll Creagach (73), 1054m/3458ft, Tom a'Choinich (40), 1111m/3645ft, Carn Eige (Eighe) (11), 1183m/3881ft, Beinn Fhionnlaidh (125), 1005m/3297ft, Mam Sodhail (Mam Soul) (13), 1180m/3871ft

Mam Soul and Carn Eige are the two highest hills in the area and both can be climbed in a fairly big hill day from the west end of Loch Beinn a' Mheadhoin, at the foot of Gleann nam Fiadh. A footpath runs up this glen and after 4-5km another footpath leaves the riverside and climbs steadily in a north-west direction to the Bealach Toll Easa between Tom a' Choinich and Toll Creagach. The latter summit can be easily reached from the bealach by a steep initial climb then a long pull on to Toll Creagach's summit dome. From the bealach Tom a' Choinnich is easily reached by a steep climb which threads its way through rocky outcrops. The summit gives access to a long and winding ridge with steep drops on either side. Cross the deep notch of the Garbh-bhealach and continue past the needles of Stob Coire Dhomhnuill (easily avoided on the left), round the head of Coire Dhomhain to Creag na h-Eige and then to

**Route Summary:** From the car park near the head of Loch Affric a path runs N into Gleann nam Fiadh. As it turns W into the glen another path leaves the riverside and climbs NW over the Bealach Toll Easa. Toll Creagach can easily be climbed from the summit of this pass, and so can Tom a' Choinich. From here continue W over the undulating, and in places rough, ridge. Cross the deep notch of the Garbh-bhealach and continue past the needles of Stob Coire Dhomhnuill (easily avoided on the left), round the head of Coire Dhomhain to Creag na h-Eige and then to the great dome of Carn Eige itself. From the summit head N to Beinn Fhionnlaidh, a long pull involves a 305m drop and a pull up the other side. Return towards Carn Eige but the climb back to the summit can be avoided by a traverse up the W slopes to the pass between Carn Eige and Mam Sodhail. Continue to the summit cairn, a massive structure built round the OS pillar. Return to Glen Affric via the ridge which runs SE over Mullach Cadha Rainich and Sgurr na Lapaich avoiding the latter's craggy E cliffs.

**Map:** OS Sheet 25

**Access Point:** Glen Affric, GR215242

**Distance:** 36.8km, 2316m ascent

**Approx Time:** 10-16 hours

**Translation:** rocky hollow; hill of the moss; file hill; Finlay's hill; hill of the barns

**Pronunciation:** tow kraykach; towm a choanyeech; kaarn aya; byn yoony; mam sool

the great dome of Carn Eige itself.

North of Carn Eige, way out on a sinuous limb, Beinn Fhionnlaidh sits proudly above Loch Mullardoch, mocking the Munro-bagger in its isolation and remoteness. It takes willpower, and lots of it, to turn your back on the easy ridge which runs south to Mam Soul and drop down the rocky slopes to the peaty bealach below Beinn Fhionnlaidh. The summit ridge is welcome after a steep climb from the bealach and you are suddenly aware of the comparative remoteness of this hill. Loch Mullardoch is at your feet and across the blue waters the slopes of An Socach, An Riabhachan and Sgurr na Lapaich rise steeply. Westwards, another long limb holds a Munro – Mullach na Dheiragain involves an even longer diversion to reach its summit cairn, all the way north from Sgurr nan Ceathreamhain. The summit of Carn Eige can be skirted on the return and a rising traverse soon reaches the ridge just north of Mam Soul. A rocky slope leads to the gigantic summit cairn. From here the best descent follows the excellent grassy ridge to Sgurr na Lapaich and down to Loch Affric or directly down Coire Leachavie to Glen Affric and a footpath back to your starting point.

*Sgurr na Lapaich from the slopes of Carn nan Gobhar*

## Carn nan Gobhar (149), 992m/3255ft, Sgurr na Lapaich (22), 1150m/3773ft, An Riabhachan (28), 1129m/3704ft, An Socach (64), 1069m/3507ft

North of Glen Affric, Glen Cannich also runs in an east/west direction and like Affric, also boasts a loch. The lower reaches of Glen Cannich are beautifully wooded and the view up the glen is only marginally spoiled by the Mullardoch dam. Beyond it on the north side of the loch, a great ridge rises from Carn nan Gobhar and Sgurr na Lapaich and runs westwards to An Riabhachan and An Socach.

**Route Summary:** Follow the path beside the Allt Mullardoch into Coire an t-Sith. Climb N up the steep slopes of Creag Dhubh to the ridge. Follow the ridge WSW to the summit of Carn nan Gobhar. Follow the ridge NW over a wide saddle beyond which a rib leads to the summit of Sgurr na Lapaich. Leave the summit by the SW shoulder and descend to the Bealach Toll an Lochain. Follow the rim of An

171

*The Strathfarrar hills, looking west from Carn nan Gobhar*

Riabhachan's NE corrie to the top and then across to the summit. Cross to the SW top, here the main ridge turns NW to where a twist in the ridge leads down to another bealach below An Socach. Climb to the summit

**Map:** OS Sheet 25

**Access Point:** Mullardoch Dam

**Distance:** 30.4km, 1890m ascent

**Approx Time:** 9-13 hours

**Translation:** hill of the goats; peak of the bog; the brindled, greyish one; the snout

**Pronunciation:** kaarn nan gower; skoor na lahpeech; an reeavachan; an sochkach

From the Mullardoch dam you can make a fairly straightforward circuit of Carn nan Gobhar and Sgurr na Lapaich returning by the south ridge of the latter. The other two hills of this group, An Riabhachan and An Socach, can be climbed from the west end of Loch Mullardoch after a long walk-in, or cycle in to Iron Lodge, but by far the best way to treat these hills is to walk along the north shore of Loch Mullardoch for 10km to the buildings at the foot of the Allt Socach and the Allt Coire a' Mhaim. Easy slopes climb out of Coire Mhaim and form the long curving south ridge of An Socach. From the summit fine grassy ridges lead east, over the broad summit of An Riabhachan, through the rocky pinnacles of Sgurr na Lapaich and down over the bumpy afterthought of Carn nan Gobhar. It's a long walk, but a highly satisfying one. It can, as described in the route summary, be climbed from east to west, returning to the dam by the lochside footpath which is sketchy in places.

## Sgurr Fhuar-thuill (79), 1049m/3442ft, Sgurr a'Choire Ghlais (56), 1083m/3553ft, Carn nan Gobhar (150), 992m/3255ft, Sgurr na Ruaidhe (148), 993m/3258ft

Glen Strathfarrar is the third of the three glens which join up in Strath Glas. It's almost as long as Glen Affric though much less popular, probably because the gate across the road at Struy is usually locked and you have to ask permission to have it unlocked to allow you to continue up the glen. Once past this obstacle though, you can drive as far as the Loch Monar dam a distance of some 19km through the glen, one of the most beautiful in these Northern Highlands. The main interest for the Munro collector is the four hills which rise to the north side of the glen. The path up the Allt Toll a' Mhuic offers an easy ascent as far as the loch, beyond which it disappears. It can be picked up again higher in the corrie just below the first peak, Sgurr na Fearstaig. The traverse eastwards follows a well defined ridge as far as Sgurr a' Choire Ghlais but beyond this summit the last two peaks, Carn nan Gobhar and Sgurr na Ruaidhe, are rounded and rather featureless. The descent from the latter takes you down to the path by the Allt Coire Mhuillidh. The Glen Cannich mountains can also be climbed by Strathfarrar by the hydro road up the Uisge Misgeach, but this approach is probably longer than that by Loch Mullardoch in the south.

**Route Summary:** Access to Glen Strathfarrar is via a locked gate at Struy. Permission to enter and a key can be obtained from the cottage beside the gate. A stalker's path climbs N into the corrie of Loch Toll a' Mhuic and on up the steep back wall of the corrie to finish just below the crest of Sgurr na Fearstaig. From here continue E to Sgurr Fhuar-thuill. The crest of the ridge is broad so follow the rim E, over the undulation of Creag Ghorm a'Bhealaich and down to the narrow saddle before Sgurr a' Choire Ghlais. Return to the main crest and descend to a saddle at the foot of Carn nan Gobhar, from where an easy 122m climb leads to the stony summit. Continue E, then SE, and down into the Bealach nam Bogan then slopes to Sgurr na Ruaidhe

**Map:** OS Sheet 25

**Access Point:** Braulen Lodge, GR237387

**Distance:** 22.4km, 1524m ascent

**Approx Time:** 6-10 hours

**Translation:** peak of the cold hollow; peak of the greenish-grey corrie; hill of the goats; peak of redness

**Pronunciation:** skoor ooar hil; skoor a chor a ghlash; kaarn nan gower, skoor na rooy

**Stalking Information:** Broulin Estate Tel: Struy 260.

# THE ACHNASHELLACH AND TORRIDON HILLS

## The Munros:

Moruisg   Sgurr nan Ceannaichean   Sgurr Choinnich
Sgurr a' Chaorachain   Maoile Lunndaidh   Bidein a' Choire Sheasgaich
Lurg Mhor   Beinn Liath Mhor   Sgorr Ruadh   Maol Chean-dearg
Fionn Bheinn   Beinn Alligin   Liathach (Spidean a' Choire Leith,
Mullach an Rathain)   Beinn Eighe (Ruadh-stac Mor)

For many, this is the finest hillwalking area in the country – indeed there's a heart-strumming sound to the very name of Torridon. It's an evocative name, conjuring up an image of something unique, a symbolism of what fine mountains are all about. These are leviathan hills, ancient beasts which rise sheer from sea level with long lines of mural precipice, rounded and terraced bastions topped by sharp-pinnacled ridges, summits capped by grey Cambrian quartzite.

These great hills are possibly among the oldest in the world. Raised as a vast plateau, believed to be some 30 million years ago, it's now thought that the quartzite peaks, the rock of the original chain of mountains, could well be 60 million years old and if that's not old enough for you the sandstone below them is even older and the platforms of gneiss on which they stand could well be in the region of 2600 million years old.

If the enduring quality of these hills doesn't take your breath away, their appearance certainly will. All are individual, idiosyncratic, primeval – all are rugged, all are different. Beinn Alligin is elegant, shapely, bejewelled. Liathach is a monster and breathtakingly huge, while Beinn Eighe isn't so much a single hill as a chain of hills, a complex mini-range.

While Torridon is the jewel in the crown of Scotland's hills, the hills of the Ben Damph and Coulin Forests, to which ancient stalker's paths provide quick access, are also impressive. South of Glen Carron, Lurg Mhor is splendidly remote. Land-locked away beyond the head of lonely Loch Monar and girdled by track-less kilometres, it shares with its Munro neighbour, Bidein a' Choire Sheasgaich, the reputation of being one of Scotland's most isolated and inaccessible hills.

*Liathach from the north-east*

# Moruisg (252), 928m/3045ft, Sgurr nan Ceannaichean (275), 915m/3002ft

These two hills rise above Glen Carron and from their summits you can gaze north into the jumble of shapely hill features that make up the Torridon mountains. You have a choice here which mountain you climb first – Sgurr nan Ceannaichean can be climbed from the Allt a' Chonais track from Craig, directly and steeply up the north-west shoulder. Alternatively, you can leave the best till last and climb the long and relentless uniform slopes of Moruisg from a car park on the A890, just west of Loch Sgamhain.

The summit of Moruisg is flat and mossy and the ridge westwards offers easy walking with marvellous views both north, to the Torridons, and south to the Loch Monar hills.

Cross a subsidiary top and drop down steeper grassy slopes to the col. To the right, Coire Toll nam Bian is a great rounded corrie, deep and steep with a headwall of broken crags. From the top of the corrie, a broad grassy ridge climbs westwards for about 500m before swinging south-west to climb the last few metres to the flat summit of Sgurr nan Ceannaichean. The summit cairn is the most southerly one.

Take care on this climb from the col in winter conditions, for several times I've encountered great slabs of ice on these final slopes. On one memorable occasion, without crampons, I was reduced to cutting steps to reach the top of the north ridge, which is the usual descent route back to the Alltan na Feola. Cross the burn at the first convenient spot to reach the stalker's path on the east bank. This can then be followed back to the starting point.

# Sgurr Choinnich (136), 999m/3278ft, Sgurr a' Chaorachain (74) 1053m/3455ft, Maoile Lunndaidh (122), 1007m/3304ft

An excellent forestry road leads from Craig on the A890, 4km east of Achnashellach, up the Allt a' Chonais and makes a good approach to these hills, as well as for Lurg Mhor and Bidein a' Choire Sheasgaich. In fact the forest track is so good that I would strongly advise the use of a mountain bike for access to these hills. It can be ridden up as far as the bridge over the Allt a' Chonais, hidden in the heather, and picked up on your way back down. A long downhill freewheel through the forest is a fine alternative to a long footsore descent on forest tracks.

As you walk, or cycle, up the glen below the rocky west face of

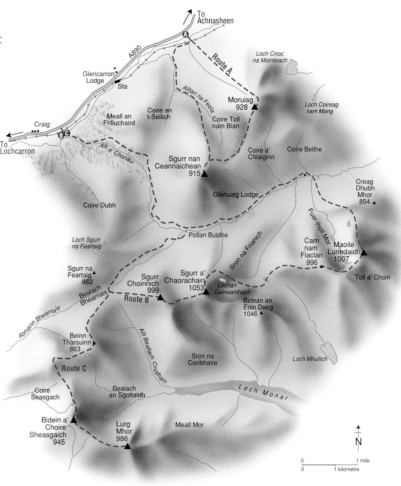

Sgurr nan Ceannaichean the mountains that appear in front of you are Sgurr Choinnich and Sgurr a' Chaorachain, divided by a steep col. It is possible to cross the river at Pollan Buidhe and climb up through the rough corrie to the col, but a more satisfying route follows a footpath south-westwards up to the Bealach Bhearnais to where Sgurr Choinnich's west ridge can be picked up. Climb this ridge which becomes increasingly rocky as you climb higher to the narrow level summit ridge.

Walk south-east along the summit ridge and descend for a short distance in the same direction before turning west-north-west where the corrie edge is followed down to the col below Sgurr a' Chaorachain. Follow the ridge directly to the summit where you can continue eastwards to Bidean an Eoin Deirg which can be descended steeply north-north-east to a col at about 600m. It is far better, though, to descend from Sgurr a' Chaorachain's north ridge for 500m before turning north east on to the Sron na Frianich above the waters of the dark Lochan Gaineamhach. Drop down the eastern slopes of the Sron to the peat-hag ridden bealach.

To continue to Maoile Lunndaidh, climb the long western ridge of Carn nam Fiaclan and follow the narrowing neck of ridge between the head of the impressive Fuar-tholl Mor in the north and Toll a' Choin in the south, to the huge, gravelly plateau of Maoile Lunndaidh.

Descend the broad heather covered slopes of the north ridge into Gleann Fhiodhaig just east of the ruined Glenuaig Lodge. Follow the track back to the Allt a' Chonais and your awaiting bike.

ridge and then by the Sron na Frianich before dropping down its E slopes to the bealach at the foot of the W ridge of Carn nam Fiaclan. Ascend this ridge to a plateau at the head of Fuar-tholl Mor and cross it in a NE direction to the summit of Maoile Lunndaidh. Descend N along the E rim of the Fuar-tholl Mor and down into Glen Fhiodhaig

**Map:** OS Sheet 25

**Access Point:** Craig

**Distance:** 32km, 1676m ascent

**Approx Time:** 8-12 hours

**Translation:** moss peak; peak of the little field of the berries; hill of the wet place

**Pronunciation:** skoor choany-eech; skoor a choerachan; moela loondy

**Route Summary:** From the footbridge over the Allt a' Chonais follow the footpath to the summit of the Bealach Bhearnais. From the boggy summit leave the path and climb the NE ridge of Beinn Tharsuinn (Route C) crossing several undulations before reaching the summit. Descend SW to a small lochan and then WSW to an obvious col between the summit and the W top. From here drop down steep slopes for a considerable distance to reach the floor of the Bealach an Sgoltaidh. Steep and craggy flanks guard Bidein a' Choire Sheasgaich but an easier route can be found by traversing slightly to the right and so avoiding the steepest of the crags. A steep path zigzags its way up and you will top out beside a small lochan. Continue S to the pointed summit of Sheasgaich. From the summit descend S, then SE and follow the broad ridge to Lurg Mhor. To return you have to retrace your steps all the way to the Bealach Bhearnais and the Allt a' Chonais

**Map:** OS Sheet 25

**Access Point:** Craig

**Distance:** 28.8km, 1585m ascent

**Approx Time:** 8-12 hours

**Translation:** peak of the corrie of the milkless cattle, big ridge stretching into the plain

**Pronunciation:** beetyan a chora haysgeech; loorak voar

# Bidein a' Choire Sheasgaich (218), 945m/3100ft, Lurg Mhor (158), 986m/3235ft

The remotest hills in the area, these are among the most isolated Munros in the country, and rise to the south-west of the head of Loch Monar in a wild and uncompromising setting. In effect, Bidein a' Choire Sheasgaich and Lurg Mhor form the southern arms of a horsehoe of big hills which enclose the western end of Loch Monar. Immediately to their north the long ridge of Beinn Tharsuinn, the Transverse Mountain, forms a continuation of this horseshoe with Sgurr Choinnich at the Bealach Bhearnais. Because of their remote position, you have to cross Beinn Tharsuinn, a Corbett, to reach Bidein a' Choire Sheasgaich and Lurg Mhor.

Follow the preceding route as far as the Bealach Bhearnais, and then climb the grassy ridge to the bumps and knolls of Tharsuinn's twisting summit ridge. Continue the traverse of this hill before dropping down its steep southern slopes to reach the narrow Bealach an Sgoltaidh at the foot of the rocky north ridge of Bidein. The way ahead looks forbidding, broken cliffs and rocky crags seem to bar the way, but there is a route through the hill's defences. Bear right, scrambling up through some crags and gullies – there is a path of sorts!

At the top of the steep section a fine ridge leads past a little lochan and tapers beautifully to the summit. The continuation to Lurg Mhor lacks the interest of what has gone before, descending around the head of a large corrie to a lochan before climbing a broad ridge to the rather featureless summit of Lurg Mhor.

It is possible to continue eastwards to Meall Mor over a narrow neck of ridge before descending to the head of Loch Monar and climbing back to the Bealach Bhearnais, but it is a lot of height to lose and a long pull up a wide corrie back to the Bealach. Alternatively, you can always try and head due north from Lurg Mhor to Bealach Bhearnais by a long traverse across the flank of Beinn Tharsuinn. Personally, I've always returned the way I came, and I suspect it's also quicker.

**Route Summary:** Take the path from Achnashellach station (Route A, p.180) through the pines above the River Lair. Climb above the forest on the path to a heathery hillside beneath the craggy terminal of Beinn Liath Mhor. Here the path separates, with one path running NW into Coire Lair and

# Beinn Liath Mhor (258), 925m/3035ft, Sgorr Ruadh (191), 960m/3150ft

Coire Lair, north-west of Achnashellach, is dominated by three splendid mountains, Fuar Tholl, the Cold Hollow at 906m, Sgorr Ruadh and Beinn Liath Mhor. The traverse of these hills offers a rewarding outing in a wonderful situation with the hills of Torridon and the Damph and Coulin Forest dominant in the north.

*Bidein a' Choire Sheasgaich from Beinn Tharsuinn*

From Achnashellach Station a path weaves its way up through the forest and then the pine woods, latterly climbing up some steep slabs before straightening out as it enters Coire Lair. Some way ahead there is a junction of paths – one carries on to the head of Coire Lair and down into Torridon, another comes down from the bealach between Fuar Tholl and Sgorr Ruadh while the third bears off north westwards over the south east slopes of Beinn Liath Mhor and eventually joins up with the Coulin Pass to Glen Torridon. This is the one we want.

Enjoy the short walk up to the high point of the path, because you have a steep climb ahead of you. Take a breather before you leave the path and enjoy the view back to Fuar Tholl, a hill well known to climbers for the routes on its immense Mainreachan Buttress.

A long and steep slope of heather and boulders leads to the long curving ridge of Beinn Liath Mhor – the summit is at its northern end and comes after a lovely undulating, quartzite ridge walk. The descent from the summit to the Bealach Coire Lair is awkward. The slopes are made up of sandstone blocks considerable care is required. Further down pass a small lochan and climb over a large knoll which is well protected by sandstone blocks. On the south-west side of the knoll is another lochan which marks the Bealach Coire Lair.

Climb out of the bealach towards the north-west ridge of Sgorr Ruadh, passing another small lochan before tackling the steep and rocky ridge to the summit. A path weaves its way through the crags and here and there the other running NE into the Easan Dorcha. Take the latter for a short distance to its highest point, and then take the steep and unrelenting heather slopes of Beinn Liath Mhor. Climb to its E top and follow the stony quartzite ridge WNW to the summit. Continue on the ridge, narrow in places and descend to the Bealach Coire Lair, taking care as there are some crags to bypass and a prominent knoll either to cross, or circumnavigate. From the bealach climb S on to the NW ridge of Sgurr Ruadh and follow this ridge SE to the steep and prominent summit. The descent SE is via the Bealach Mhoir and wide open slopes back to the River Lair

**Map:** OS Sheet 25

**Access Point:** Achnashellach

**Distance:** 14.4km, 1143m ascent

**Approx Time:** 5-8 hours

**Translation:** big grey hill; red peak

**Pronunciation:** byn leea voar; skoor rooa

*Maol Chean-dearg and An Ruadh-stac from the summit of Beinn Damh*

a bit of scrambling adds to the fun. The summit cairn is a wonderful view-point with the long jagged ridge of Liathach dominating the view to the north. The next hill, Fuar Tholl, although not a Munro, is probably the finest of the three. The mountain radiates three spurs, one north, one south and the other south-east, and it's on these spurs that the great rock features of the mountain are prominent.

Between the north and south-east spurs lies the Mainreachan Buttress, a magnificent mass of ter-raced sandstone which seems to be suspend-ed above a tiny lochan below the north face of the mountain. Here lies some of the finest sandstone rockclimbing in the country.

From the wide pass between Sgor Ruadh and Fuar Tholl a path drops down through the glaciated landscape back to the junction of paths at the foot of Coire Lair, but one word of warning – the River Lair can quickly rise in spate, making a crossing difficult. In such cases you'll have to follow the west bank of the river all the way back to Achnashellach.

180

## Maol Chean-dearg (241), 933m/3061ft

Along with Beinn Liath Mhor and Sgor Ruadh, Maol Chean-dearg makes up the rocky trio of Munros that lies between Strath Carron and Glen Torridon. Because of the Coulags Pass running between Maol Chean-dearg and Sgor Ruadh, the three Munros are rarely climbed in one outing and most folk treat Maol Chean-dearg as a single expedition, although it is best climbed along with its neighbouring rocky Corbett An Ruadh-stac.

It is the Coulags right-of-way that gives access to Maol Chean-dearg. From the little scattering of houses of the same name on the A890, make your way up the glen, which is fairly dull in its lower reaches but shows more promise as you climb higher. Cross the footbridge over the river, pass the bothy and the old stone of Clach nan Con-fionn to which the Celtic folk hero Fionn McCuill apparently used to tie his hounds. About 500m beyond the stone another path bears off to the left and begins to climb up to the high bealach between Maol Chean-dearg and Meall nan Ceapairean, with the rocky route to the Corbett An Ruadh-stac before you.

If you are intent only on Maol Chean-dearg turn north-west from the bealach and climb the broad scree-covered ridge over two large steps to the final summit slopes and the large cairn. The views from the summit are extensive with particularly good views of the very fine Corbett Ben Damh in the north west.

**Route Summary:** From Coulags follow the path on the E side of Fionn-abhainn (Route B). Cross the bridge to the W side after 2.4km or so and continue past the ruined cottage to the Clach nan Con-fionn. Shortly after this take the path which bears off W and climb to the col between Maol Chean-dearg and Meall nan Ceapairean. Turn NW here and climb the broad ridge to the summit

**Map:** OS Sheet 25

**Access Point:** Coulags

**Distance:** 12.8km, 914m ascent

**Approx Time:** 3-5 hours

**Translation:** bald red head

**Pronunciation:** moel chan dyerak

## Fionn Bheinn (240), 933m/3061ft

Kenneth MacKenzie, the Brahan Seer once predicted that 'the day will come when a raven, attired in plaid and bonnet, will drink his fill of human blood on Fionn Bheinn, three times a day, for three successive days.'

I've no idea what this prophesy means, and neither am I certain that the Seer was referring to the same hill, but never mind – the hill doesn't have a lot else going for it!

Fionn Bheinn is an uninspiring hill, rising behind Achnasheen, which, since its hotel burnt to the ground, doesn't have a lot going for it either. Negatives aside, Achnasheen is on the road and the railway line to many more interesting places, so Fionn Bheinn can easily be visited en route to Torridon or the Achnashellach hills and shouldn't take more than three or four hours of your time.

The Allt Achadh na Sine is the usual line of ascent. Stay on its

**Route Summary:** Follow the Allt Achadh na Sine from Achnasheen and keep to its NE bank. Follow the burn high up into a corrie W of Creagan nan Laogh and climb grassy slopes N to the ridge. Follow the ridge W to the summit

**Map:** OS Sheets 20 and 25

**Access Point:** Achnasheen

**Distance:** 6.4km, 914m ascent

**Approx Time:** 3-5 hours

**Translation:** pale coloured hill

**Pronunciation:** fyoon vyn

north-east bank and follow it high into a wide corrie west of Creagan nan Laogh. Climb the grassy slopes directly north to reach the broad summit ridge which is then followed westwards to the summit.

While it's easy to be disparaging about this hill there is no doubt that it stands on the edge of some superb country, with the Torridon giants to the west and the shapely Fannaichs, Sgurr nan Clach Geala and Sgurr Mor Fannaich to the north. Once you've drunk your fill of the views you can descend the way you came or vary it slightly by following the ridge above the Toll Mor for a short distance before descending the east side of the Creagan nan Laogh back to Achnasheen.

## Beinn Alligin (160), 985m/3232ft

The Torridon trio of Liathach, Beinn Eighe and Beinn Alligin must be one of the most magnificent groupings of small mountains anywhere, as well as being one of the oldest! Quartz-capped Torridonian sandstone offers an unusual mountain form, a landscape of ribs, buttresses and spires, intermingling with rounded battlements of immense bulk and while Liathach and Beinn Eighe are huge muscle-bound mountains in terms of visual mass, Beinn Alligin wears a more feminine robe – it's for good reason it's known as the Jewelled Mountain, or Mountain of Beauty.

Stretching in a gentle curve for almost five kilometres, the sandstone ridge of Beinn Alligin crosses four distinct tops and is split by a great natural cleft, the Eag Dubh. That great slash, along with Na Rathanan, the Horns of Alligin, are two of the most distinctive features of what is a very distinctive mountain.

A car park on the Torridon-Diabaig road makes a good starting point, and just across the road from it, at the right-hand side of the road bridge a fine footpath leads up through pine woods alongside the Abhainn Coire Mhic Nobuil and into Coire Mhic Nobuil itself. To

**Route Summary:** Cross the Torridon-Diabaig road from the car park and take the path which crosses the moorland towards Coir' nan Laoigh of Tom na Gruagaich (Route A, p.187). Climb to the head of the corrie and ascend Tom na Gruagaich itself. Descend N down a rocky ridge to a col beyond where the ridge becomes broader. Climb NNE over a knoll, drop a little height to a bealach and then climb NE to Sgurr Mhor, the summit of Beinn Alligin. From here descend steeply ENE then E down a narrow ridge to a col. Follow the well-marked path over the Horns of Alligin, using hands as well as feet in places. From the third 'Horn' continue the descent SE to the moorland and join the track in Coire Mhic Nobuil

**Map:** OS Sheets 19 and 24

**Access Point:** Coire Mhic

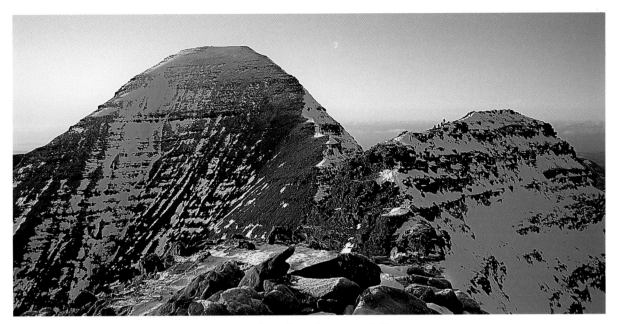

*Beinn Alligin from the Horns of Alligin*

the left of the bridge another path begins, a climber's path which is marked by cairns in a rough north-north-west direction across sandstone slabs to meet the Alltan Glas, which issues from the mouth of Coir' nan Laogh. The effort of climbing the steep slopes of Coir' nan Laogh is well rewarded by the views from the first summit, Tom na Gruagaich, the hill of the damsel, a name which confirms the feminine quality of this mountain. As you pull up out of the dark confines of the corrie the abruptness of the view hits you unexpectedly. To the west, close at hand, lies the Trotternish Ridge of Skye and beyond it, the hills of Harris and the low-lying profile of Lewis. The Alligin ridge now lies before you. A careful descent from Tom na Gruagaich round the rim of Toll a' Mhadaidh Mor, over a slight bump, and then a steepish climb leads you to the main summit, Sgurr Mhor, just beyond the great gash of Eag Dubh na h-Eigheachd, the rubble of which litters the corrie floor below you. From the summit you have the option of re-tracing your route to the start, but a complete traverse of a hill is always much more satisfactory, especially over Torridonian sandstone pinnacles like the Horns of Alligin. A footpath avoids the difficulties on the right above steep grassy slopes but the Horns themselves pose little technical difficulty, just good exposed scrambling. From the third, and last, Horn continue the descent in a south-east direction to the moorland below where a stalker's path can be picked up and followed back to the Coire Mhic Nobuil footpath.

Nobuil bridge car park
**Distance:** 9.6km, 1158m ascent
**Approx Time:** 4-6 hours
**Translation:** jewelled hill
**Pronunciation:** byn alligin

*Liathach and Glen Torridon from Beinn Damh*

**Route Summary:** Leave the road just E of Glen Cottage (Route B, p.187) and climb steeply up the craggy hillside into the Toll a' Meitheach. Higher up the corrie climb up to the right, NE, over steep ground to the col on the main ridge. Follow the ridge NW then W over two small tops to the cone of Spidean a' Choire Leith. Descend SW to a short and level grassy section. Continue over, or around the pinnacles of Am Fasarinen. An exposed path avoids the difficulties on the S side. Beyond the pinnacles it is an easy stroll on to Mullach an Rathain. From the summit the most interesting descent back to Glen Torridon is via the SW ridge, although there is a slightly quicker descent via the corrie of the Allt an Tuill Bhain

## Liathach (Spidean a' Choire Leith (72), 1054m/3458ft, Mullach an Rathain (105), 1023m/3356ft)

A number of years ago I sat on a high sandstone block on the south side of Glen Torridon and gazed across the glen towards the grey bulk of Liathach. I was overwhelmed by the sheer size and bulk of this, the Grey One, and it frightened the life out of me. As I looked at it, tier upon tier of sandstone cliff, I was convinced there was no route up the mountain from Glen Torridon, or down it. It looked impossible. In time, I realised that it wasn't.

Liathach is essentially an 8km ridge which crosses eight separate tops. Two of those tops are credited with Munro status. The southern flank of the mountain appears to be impregnable, but on closer inspection several breaches in its defences are discovered, not least the usual route of ascent, just east of Glen Cottage and climbing up to the steep upper slopes of Toll a' Meitheach. Another possibility is up beside the Allt an Tuill Bhain at the western end of the mountain. This leads up steep sandstone slopes to another upper corrie where a steep headwall leads to the summit of Mullach an Rathain. A traverse of the mountain using these two routes of ascent/descent, makes a fine outing with all the difficulties in the latter half of the traverse, between the two Munro summits.

The footpath which leads up into Toll a' Meitheach follows the Allt an Doire Ghairbh over rocky steps, heather and steep grass and leads over a break in a rock band which seems to cross the face of the mountain. It's a steep scramble into the upper reaches of the corrie where a scree gully gives access to the ridge just west of Bidein Toll a' Mhuic.

Enjoy the views eastwards towards Beinn Eighe, then follow the ridge towards the first of the two Munros, Spidean a' Choire Leith. It's not particularly easy going, over loose scree and rock, first of all in a north-westerly direction, then west over a couple of subsidiary tops before the final bouldery slope of Spidean's cone.

Spidean a' Choire Leith is Liathach's highest point and the views on a good day are extensive, all the way from Ben Hope in the north to Ben Nevis in the south. Even more spectacular is the ridge that lies ahead. All two kilometres of it are extremely narrow and for much of its length it is broken and shattered into a series of spectacular spires, the Fasarinen Pinnacles.

These shattered quartzite teeth fall away dramatically into Coire na Caime on the north side, one of Liathach's magnificent northern corries which are hidden from the tourist in Glen Torridon. A scramble across the summits of the Pinnacles is far from impossible, and the walker who has a head for heights and some experience of rock climbing will love the airy traverse. Others are advised to follow an exposed, but well-trodden footpath, now very much suffering from erosion caused by over-use, which hugs the southern side of the pinnacles. This path leads to the second Munro of the hill, Mullach an Rathain, the aptly named hill of the row of pinnacles.

A wide, grassy ridge carries you on to the summit and the OS pillar. To the north a short, stony arête runs out to the highest of the Pinnacles and the lower peak of Meall Dearg, again overlooking the wonderful Coire na Caime. A long ridge runs westwards down to the subsidiary top of Sgorr a' Chadail, with fabulous views across Loch Torridon, but the descent route goes westwards and south of the summit cairn, a narrow ridge dropping towards a broadening slope of broken, scree-filled gullies and worn terraces and down towards the road alongside the Allt an Tuill Bhain. It's then only a short walk back to the car beyond Glen Cottage in Glen Torridon.

**Map:** OS Sheet 25

**Access Point:** A896, 800m E of Glen Cottage

**Distance:** 11.2km, 1311m ascent

**Approx Time:** 5-8 hours

**Translation:** grey one; peak of the grey corrie; summit of the row of pinnacles

**Pronunciation:** leeahach; speetyan a chora lay; moolach an raahan

*Looking west along the main ridge of Beinn Eighe towards Sgurr Ban*

**Route Summary:** Leave the car park and follow the broad track which leads up Coire Dubh Mhor (Route C). At GR 934594 take another path which runs N round the prow of Sail Mor and traverses the hillside before climbing up into Coire Mhic Fhearchair. Cross the outflow of the loch and follow the E side of the loch before climbing screes and rough slopes SE to reach the ridge which leads to the summit, Ruadh-stac Mor. The traverse of Beinn Eighe can be continued to take in Coinneach Mhor, Spidean Coire nan Clach and along the main ridge to Sgurr Ban and Sgurr nan Fhir Duibhe

**Map:** OS Sheets 19 and 25

**Access Point:** Car park on A896

## Beinn Eighe (Ruadh-stac Mor) (117), 1010m/3314ft

Lying just south-west of Kinlochewe and Loch Maree, Beinn Eighe is separated from Liathach by Coire Dubh. It has seven peaks higher than 914m (3000ft) and a clutch of remarkable north-facing corries, of which the finest, Coire Mhic Fhearchair, is arguably the most impressive corrie in Scotland. With its lochan reflecting the sandstone tiers of the Triple Buttress, it has the awesome atmosphere of a great cathedral, especially on a quiet, windless day when the waters are mirror still.

The traverse of all seven peaks involves a long expedition but the most straightforward route to Beinn Eighe's highest summit, Ruadh-stac Mor, has the advantage of being able to visit Coire Mhic Fhearchair en route. The starting point is the car park by the A896 in Glen Torridon just west of the Allt a' Choire Dhuibh Mhoir. A signpost points out the route, and the path is worn and obvious as it takes its course up into Coire Dubh Mhor, round past the ramparts of Liathach. As you progress through Coire

Dubh Mhor, which is really more of a pass than a corrie, you become aware of the majestic and spectacular northern corries of Liathach. What a contrast to the huge forbidding flanks in the south.

Once past the obvious watershed, beyond a small lochan, a path peels off to the north around the great prow of Sail Mor. Follow it round, enjoying this great tract of wilderness landscape, as the path begins to climb again past some fine sparkling waterfalls, up a final rise and into the grand hall of Coire Mhic Fhearchair – one of the great mountain scenes of Scotland.

The route to the summit of Beinn Eighe's highest top is now straightforward, although it is made physically awkward by loose quartzite scree and boulder slopes. Ruadh-stac Mor is the end point of the ridge to your left, the eastern arm of Coire Mhic Fhearchair. Cross the outflow of the lochan and make your way round its eastern shores. A faint footpath weaves a route through the heather and jumbled boulders and eventually makes its way up the rough slopes towards the obvious col which separates the top from the main ridge of Beinn Eighe, and from there you'll find it an easy walk over quartzy screes to the summit.

**Distance:** 16km, 975m ascent

**Approx Time:** 4-6 hours

**Translation:** file hill, (big red peak)

**Pronunciation:** byn ay; roo-a stak more

# THE DUNDONNELL AND FISHERFIELD HILLS

## The Munros:

### Slioch    An Teallach (Sgurr Fiona, Bidein a' Ghlas Thuill)
### Ruadh Stac Mor    A' Mhaighdean    Beinn a' Chlaidheimh    Sgurr Ban
### Mullach Coire Mhic Fhearchair    Beinn Tarsuinn

Between the long arms of Loch Maree and Little Loch Broom in Wester Ross lies a great tangle of mountain country. Wild and remote, it boasts some of the most isolated Munros in Scotland, including An Teallach, arguably Scotland's finest mountain. In recent years there have been several attemps to discover which is Scotland's most popular mountain and in every published list this one hill, more than any other, stands aloof.

These days the word 'wilderness' tends to be over-used and often mis-applied, but the vast deer forests of Strathnashealag, Fisherfield and Letterewe have long been known to Scottish hill-goers as The Great Wilderness. The hills themselves are rocky, exposing the bare bones of the earth, folded into complex patterns and intermingled with a plethora of high-level lochans. A series of long sinuous lochs between Loch Maree in the south and Loch Broom in the north betrays the evidence of geological faults, subsequently carved out by massive glaciation. These basins, running from north-west to south-east, form the grain of the land, creating difficulties for those old travellers and drovers who wanted to move from north to south or vice versa. Ancient tracks avoid the lochs and the summits, weaving their way through glens and up over the bealachs at their heads. Even at that they have to cross rivers, which can be impossible when they are in spate, and make use of the man-made causeway between the Fionn Loch and the Dubh Loch.

## Slioch (169), 980m/3215ft

Slioch, the Spear, is a real fortress of a mountain – steep rocky crags present an almost impregnable air as you view it from the road which winds its way along the south shore of Loch Maree.

But while it is violently steep on three sides, its great corrie, the Coire Tuill Bhain, or White Hollow, carves into its eastern extremity and offers a break in its defences. Every year, hundreds, if not thousands, of hill-walkers make use of that breach to gain one of the two summit ridges and enjoy far flung views across the incredible landscape of Torridon, up

**Route Summary:** From the car park at Incheril follow the path which runs along the N bank of the Kinlochewe River. After 5km cross the Abhainn an Fhasaigh by a footbridge and turn right on the path which runs up Gleann Bianasdail. After 0.8km branch left on the well-worn path which climbs N towards Slioch's SE corrie. Continue to gain the SE ridge and climb to the trig point summit. From here follow the ridge which

*Looking south from the air along the ridge of An Teallach*

leads to the N top which is the same height. Descend by the Sgurr an Tuill Bhain.

**Map:** OS Sheet 19

**Access Point:** Incheril, Kinlochewe

**Distance:** 19.2km, 1067m ascent

**Approx Time:** 6-9 hours

**Translation:** from Gaelic sleagh, a spear

**Pronunciation:** slee-och

the length of an island-studded Loch Maree towards the sea and the Trotternish Peninsula of Skye, or across the slit trench of Lochan Fhada towards the jumble of remote mountains that make up the area known as the Great Wilderness.

But despite the panorama of mountains ranging out in all directions, it's Loch Maree which calls for attention. World famous for its beauty, this loch typifies all that is held in the phrase 'highland grandeur'. The largest loch north of the Great Glen, it covers 28 square kilometres with a backdrop that is as incredible as the Torridon hills on its south bank. Not only the mountains but the Caledonian pine forest which covers the slopes on those same southern shores is pretty ancient too, its generations of trees dating back some 8000 years. It's a miracle that these trees avoided the fate which befell other pine woods in the area, especially since 350 years ago local ironworks consumed 8 hectares of oakwoods daily for charcoal.

As you follow the path from Incheril along the riverbank to what is now the head of Loch Maree, you may well wonder at the size of the great flood plain, now scattered with broom and birch, which seems so out of proportion for an inland loch. This question runs alongside another – why is Kinlochewe (the Head of Loch Ewe) so named, since that particular sea-loch is some 24km to the west? Was it once connected to Loch Maree?

Loch Ewe is indeed the former name of Loch Maree, which suggests that the loch was once a great sea-loch, and that would explain the size of the flood plain at its head. Saint Maelrubha came to Eilean Maruighe, one of the loch's islands, in the seventh century and made it famous as a place of pilgrimage. In time the loch became associated with the island and the name of both were corrupted to Maree.

Once you've crossed the footbridge over the Abhainn an Fhasaigh, the path runs north-north-east up Gleann Bianasdail towards the mouth of Coire Tuill Bhain below Meall Each. The path is well worn but becomes fainter once the corrie is reached. The curving summit ridge which forms the corrie wall ahead of you may appear steep and intimidating, but the path breaches it just south of the main rise to the summit where twin lochans fill the ridge. Above the lochans the ascent steepens on rough and rocky ground before it

*Slioch and Lochan Fada*

*An Teallach from Sgurr Creag an Eich*

eases off. Pass a subsidiary knoll and climb to the trig point summit which is given the same height as the cairn immediately to the north.

While you could descend the same way, it's worth noting that the ridge between the summit and Sgurr an Tuill Bhain is a narrow and exhilarating traverse with superb views down to Lochan Fada below you. Continue over the summit and down steep slopes back into the corrie.

**Route Summary:** Leave the A832 road and take the track which runs up through the trees in Gleann Chaorachain and eventually crosses the Allt Chaorachain. Continue on the path across rocky slabs and heather towards Shenavall but before you begin the descent bear right and climb Sail Liath. From the summit follow the ridge of An Teallach to the Corrag Bhuidhe Buttresses (which can be avoided on the

## An Teallach (Sgurr Fiona (70), 1059m/3474ft, Bidein a' Ghlas Thuill (69), 1062m/3484ft)

This mighty mountain virtually fills the Strathnasheallag Forest, with 10 tops above the magic 914m contour. Its rocky crest reaches a high point on Bidein a' Ghlas Thuill of 1062m and another of its peaks, Sgurr Fiona, at 1059m also boasts Munro status. But more important than mere Munros is the four-kilometre ridge around the mountain's eastern corrie, a sinuous, sharp edge which offers the hillwalker an exhilarating day's outing, without doubt one of the best expeditions in the country.

The best view of An Teallach is probably that from the old

'Destitution Road' between Braemore Junction and Dundonnell. Three imposing ridges, Glas Mheall Mor, Glas Mheall Liath and Sail Liath form two corries, Glas Tholl and Toll an Lochain. The main summit, Bidein a' Ghlas Thuill, lies at the apex of the middle ridge and the main ridge, while Sgurr Fiona forms a bend on the main ridge as it curves round southwards and becomes a tight, pinnacled arête which ends on Sail Liath. This arête crosses a tall, leaning spire by the name of Lord Berkeley's Seat, a crumbling pile of sandstone which looks as though it could well topple over into Toll an Lochain below, and four high rock towers called the Corrag Bhuidhe Buttresses. The traverse of this arete is a fine one, but does call for some climbing experience.

The mountain can be traversed in both directions, from Dundonnell in the north, via the ridge of Meall Garbh and on to the high plateau north west of Glas Mheall Mor, or better still, from the A832 at the foot of Corrie Hallie. A track runs south-west through the trees of Gleann Chaorachain, crosses the Allt Gleann Chaorachain and climbs westwards over rocky slabs to the foot of the Sail Liath ridge.

Sail Liath eases you in gently. A rounded afterthought to the main ridge, her summit is dome shaped, and an eroded footpath leads down sharply to a high bealach from which the first of the ridge's summits is climbed. From here drop down to the Cadha Gobhlach where, unfortunately, evidence of An Teallach's popularity is all too clear. The soft sandstone of the hill has been ravaged by the passing of countless boots, not only an aesthetic problem but a practical one too. Secondary footpaths lead off in all directions and it's all too easy to follow the wrong track, especially in misty weather.

Most walkers avoid the Corrag Bhuidhe Buttresses, and that's a shame, for the traverse over these rocky pinnacles is one of the great outings of the

left). Scramble over the pinnacles to Lord Berkeley's Seat, descend and climb to the summit of Sgurr Fiona. Continue NNE to Bidein a' Ghlas Thuill.

**Map:** OS Sheet 19: GR064837, GR069844

**Access Point:** A832 Corrie Hallie

**Distance:** 22km, 1585m ascent

**Approx Time:** 6-10 hours

**Translation:** the forge; peak of wine; peak of the greenish-grey hollow

**Pronunciation:** an tyalach; skoor fee-ana; beetyan a ghas-hool

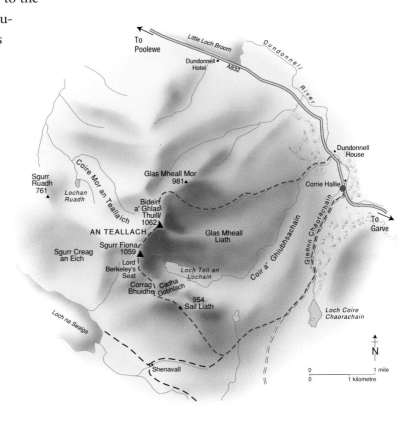

Scottish hills and is certainly the pièce de resistance of An Teallach. Ravaged footpaths skirt the Buttresses and Lord Berkeley's Seat before climbing Sgurr Fiona and the eroded state of these paths is a good enough excuse to take the higher, scrambling route.

From the Cadha Gobhlach a huge, terraced buttress seems to bar the way, but the route is clear enough, just follow the crampon scratches on the sandstone. A very steep slab, covered in good holds, marks the beginning of the scrambling. Higher still an awkward chimney marks the crux – an abseil sling decorates the top of it, and from there it's exposed ridge scrambling all the way to the top of the leaning, overhanging Lord Berkeley's Seat.

Descend the sandstone steps to the main footpath and climb the first of the hill's two Munros, Sgurr Fiona, the Peak of Wind. The route steepens again after Fiona as you descend north-north-east over some pretty rocky ground to the obvious col. There are no real obstacles left now, other than a long pull on to the highest summit, Bidean a' Ghlas Thuill. The normal descent route continues north from the summit to the obvious col and then drops down steep slopes eastwards into Coire a' Ghlas Thuill. Follow the north side of the stream to the Garbh Allt waterfalls from where a good path takes you back to the A832.

It's always a pity to traverse An Teallach and miss out on the cathedral-like grandeur of Toll an Lochain. On a recent visit the growing view down into the corrie encouraged us to find a descent route towards the lochan and after some slipping and sliding on loose sandstone and quartzy scree we hit the top of a great snow chute which gave some of the best glissading I've had for a long time. Within ten minutes we were standing by the lapping waters of the loch itself, exhilarated by our long glissade, having descended about 400m.

The prospect of the long walk back out to Corrie Hallie was overshadowed by the splendour of the surroundings, with the great riven cliffs above us rising to a stormy sea of rocky, sharp crests and bare, blank buttresses, possibly the finest corrie in Scotland.

Route Summary: A private road leaves Poolewe (Route A, p.197) and runs along the E side of the River Ewe to Inveran and Kernsary. From Kernsary go E then SE through woods to reach the path on the N bank of the Allt na Creige. This path is indistinct in places but soon

## Ruadh Stac Mor (267), 918m/3012ft, A' Mhaighdean (184), 967m/3173ft

Stand on the summit of Slioch and look north across Lochan Fada towards the great complexity of hills and deep glens that make up the heart of this, the most wonderful wilderness area in Scotland. There, in the centre of this heartland, lie the rock-bound twin peaks of

*Looking west across Fionn Loch and Dubh Loch towards Ruadh Stac Mor and A' Mhaighdean*

Ruadh Stac Mor and A' Mhaighdean, arguably the remotest of all Scotland's 277 Munros.

In many ways it's a shame to try and climb these hills in a single day – far better to carry a rucksack with tent and food and wander all these hills at leisure over a number of days – this is backpacking country par excellence. My own first introduction to this area was a long walk from Dundonnell in the north to Poolewe, over all the Munros. We enjoyed a superb high camp on A' Mhaighdean and I will never forget the view down the length of the Dubh Loch, the Fionn Loch and Loch Ewe out to sea and the long limb of Trotternish Ridge of Skye.

More recently, during another long walk for television, from Kinlochewe to Dundonnell, we failed to see any view from A' Mhaighdean because of mist, but the experience of remoteness and rocky splendour was almost just as great. These are special hills indeed.

From Poolewe, a private road runs alongside the River Ewe to Inveran and Kernsary. From here a track runs through woods and eventually runs alongside the Allt na Creige. It continues across flat and boggy terrain in a south-east direction, makes a slight divergence to cross the Strathan Buidhe, and continues across more flat ground to the causeway at the south-eastern end of the Fionn Loch.

Now this may sound, on the face of it, a fairly dull walk on featureless terrain, but all the time the great rocky bastion of the western faces of A' Mhaighdean grow in height and presence, and with the rocky buttresses of Beinn Lair filling the view to the south there is a feeling that you are approaching a very special place. And you are.

From the north side of the causeway a very good path continues past descends to pass Loch an Doire Chrionaich. Continue S to cross Strathan Buidhe then continue to SE end of Fionn Loch. Cross the causeway between Fionn Loch and Dubh Loch and follow stalker's path to Carnmore. Continue E, cross the Allt Bruthach an Easain and traverse SE across the hillside to reach the NW ridge of A' Mhaighdean. Follow the craggy ridge to the summit. From here descend NE to the grassy col below Ruadh Stac Mor. Climb the sandstone crags N to the summit trig point. Return to the col and take the stalker's path to Carnmore and the return journey to Poolewe

**Map:** OS Sheet 19

**Access Point:** Poolewe

**Distance:** 40km, 1189m ascent

**Approx Time:** 10-14 hours

**Translation:** big red peak; the maiden

**Pronunciation:** roo-a stak more; ah-vatyin

Carnmore and makes a rising traverse across the slopes of Sgurr na Laocainn. At its high point it turns north to follow the Allt Bruthach an Easain for almost 1km before turning south-east again to make the rocky climb up over great slabs and pavements to Fuar Loch More, a dramatic stretch of water enclosed in a tight grip of craggy cliffs.

From the lochside, continue on this path up into the rocky corrie to the bealach below the sandstone screes and crags of Ruadh Stac Mor and it takes little time, or effort, to thread your way up through the cliffs to the summit. Return to the bealach where there is a fine rocky howff and climb the north-east ridge of A' Mhaighdean to its summit plateau. Continue in a south-south-west direction for a final climb through gneiss boulders to the summit and some of the best mountain views in the country.

An alternative route of ascent follows the stepped north-west ridge of A' Mhaighdean from the west end of Fuar Loch Mor. There are plenty of crags on the ridge, but all the real difficulties can be avoided. For those who don't mind a bit of exposure, this is the recommended route to the summit.

**Route Summary:** From the bothy at Shenavall (GR 066810) cross the Abhainn Strath na Sealga (Route B). (Take care; the crossing of this river when in spate is not advisable and there is no bridge.) Climb the steep heather-covered slopes of Beinn a' Chlaidheimh to the SW. The slope becomes steeper as you reach the summit ridge and the final pull is up the ridge just E of the summit. Descend to the S on long scree slopes towards Loch a' Bhrisidh and follow the corrie rim to the summit of Sgurr Ban over white quartzite scree. Continue to another scree-filled col just S of Sgurr Ban where another steep climb takes you to the summit of Mullach Coire Mhic Fhearchair. Continue S to a prominent knob where the mountain's S ridge suddenly turns W to Beinn Tarsuinn. This can be turned by easy slopes to the E and S. Continue over rocky plat-

## Beinn a' Chlaidheimh (277), 914m/3000ft, Sgurr Ban (153), 989m/3245ft, Mullach Coire Mhic Fhearchair (109), 1019m/3343ft, Beinn Tarsuinn (234), 936m/3071ft

The traverse of these hills is a serious undertaking, and the best base for climbing them is Shenavall, although Sgurr Ban, Mullach Coire Mhic Fhearchair and Beinn Tarsuinn can be climbed in a fine, if long, circuit from Incheril near Kinlochewe, leaving Beinn a' Chlaidheimh to be climbed another day from the north.

Beinn a' Chlaidheimh lies south of the Abhainn Strath na Sealga. Once safely across it's best to tackle the steep heathery slopes in a south-west direction and so avoid the craggy north slopes of the hill. Gain the Creag Ghlas ridge and follow it to the fields of white quartzite which cap the summits of so many of these hills.

Beinn a' Chlaidheimh sits spot on the 914m Plimsoll line. Below, to the south, Loch a' Bhrisidh is set in a craggy cirque before a dazzling white slope of quartzite stretches up to the summit of Sgurr Ban. Although splendidly quartz capped, Sgurr Ban can be ascended on grass for much of the 300m climb from the bealach to its broad plateau summit, but immediately to the south Mullach Coire Mhic Fhearchair presents a contrasting image – steep and bouldery, its slopes riven and seamed with long scree gullies and protuding crags running upwards to its narrow top and large cairn. The western face of the hill is of pink sandstone, split by great searing gullies. The summit cone, like Sgurr Ban, is of Cambrian quartzite. The main feature of Mullach is a 1.6km long ridge of gneiss which extends south-eastwards into the head of Gleann an Nid, terminating in a series of spiring pinnacles. Between Mullach and Beinn Tarsuinn is an intermediary top, Meall Garbh, but this can be avoided by following a very good path which runs along the foot of its north west-facing slopes. A boggy bealach leads on to the grassy slopes of Tarsuinn.

This mountain forms the red sandstone tiered headwall of Gleann na Muice and forms a marvellous curving ridge cradling a high lochan in its clench. From the summit the views northwards are superb, towards the castellated ridge of An Teallach. The narrow, sandstone crest of Beinn Tarsuinn is an interesting one, dropping from the summit on to a flat topped table, then a series of pinnacles, weathered and seamed. Follow the ridge almost to its end then drop down grassy slopes to a peat hag riven bealach. From here head north below the crags of Stac a' Chaorruinn and follow the infant waters of the Abhainn Gleann na Muice down grassy slopes into the glen where a stalker's path eventually meets up with the Gleann na Muice Beag path to Shenavall.

forms to the summit of Beinn Tarsuinn. To return to Shenavall take a line across the N slopes to reach the stalker's path in Gleann na Muice

**Map:** OS Sheet 19:

**Access Point:** Shenavall

**Distance:** 20.8km, 1768m ascent

**Approx Time:** 8-12 hours

**Translation:** hill of the sword; light-coloured peak; summit of the corrie of Farquhar's son; transverse hill

**Pronunciation:** byn a' shleev; skoor bawn; moolach mora veechk erachar; byn tarshin

# THE FANNAICHS
# AND ULLAPOOL HILLS

## The Munros:

An Coileachan    Meall Gorm    Sgurr Mor    Beinn Liath Mhor Fannaich
Meall a' Chrasgaidh    Sgurr nan Clach Geala    Sgurr nan Each
Sgurr Breac    A' Chailleach    Ben Wyvis (Glas Leathad Mor)
Am Faochagach    Beinn Dearg    Cona' Mheall
Meall nan Ceapraichean    Seana Bhraigh    Eididh nan Clach Geala

These hills make up two hill groups of very different character, with Ben Wyvis lying out on a limb to the east. Both groups have a splendid wilderness quality to them and although fairly close to the Garve/Ullapool road they offer a fine feeling of remoteness, created probably by the knowledge that to the north and north-east lie great chunks of wild country, roadless and without habitation.

The best of the Fannaichs undoubtedly lie to the west, with Sgurr nan Clach Geala in particular appearing almost Alpine in feature when viewed from Sgurr Mor. Sadly, the approach to these western Fannaichs is under threat. A small hydro-electric scheme has been proposed for lovely Loch a' Bhroain which would virtually drain the Abhainn Cuileig, see the construction of power lines and inflict a 'tideline' around the shores of the loch. Let's hope it never happens.

To the north of the Dirrie More, the Beinn Dearg group introduces the walker to the vast watery landscape of the north-west, especially Seana Braigh, which lies in isolated splendour in the midst of this wilderness. One of the remotest Munros, its ascent demands a considerable expedition, although it is probably more easily climbed, if by a less attractive route, from Oykel Bridge in the north-east.

Route Summary: Permission can be gained to drive from Grudie bridge to Fannich Lodge, a distance of 11.2 km. Telephone the Hydro Board, Grudie Power Station, Garve 209. From Fannich Lodge (Route A) climb the slopes of An Coileachan from where a broad ridge stretches in a NW direction to Meall Gorm where two tops appear as little more than the high spots on a broad and featureless ridge. The true summit is the one with a wind-break shelter built near it. Continue over the long pull to Meall nam Peithirean and

## An Coileachan (261), 923m/3028ft, Meall Gorm (210), 949m/3113ft, Sgurr Mor (41), 1110m/3642ft, Beinn Liath Mhor Fannaich (204), 954m/3130ft

A complete traverse of all the Fannaichs will give a trip in excess of 45km, a group which challenges the likes of the Mamores or the Grey Corries as being one of the great high-level traverses of Scotland. A long switch-backed route offering a great variety of hill and mountain features, most walkers will be happy to break the entire ridge down into day-sized chunks, taking these four hills in one go.

The hills can be climbed either from the north or the south and both approaches have advantages and disadvantages. From the north the best approach is from the west end of Loch Droma from where a footpath follows a pipeline to a small power station on the Allt a' Mhadaidh. From the power station take to the heather covered slopes on the south side of the river and climb on to the north ridge of Beinn Liath Mhor Fannaich. Descend steeply to the upper rim of Coire a' Mhadaidh and follow the ridge as it curves gently round to Sgurr Mor with steep craggy ground falling away to your right and more open slopes to the left. The final slopes are steep and lead to a huge summit cairn. Retrace your steps back down and continue in a south-south-east direction over the slabs of Meall nam Peithirean and around the crest of Coire Fhuar Thuill Mhoir to pick up a stalker's path on Creachan Rairigidh. Follow it south-east to the flat stony summit of Meall Gorm.

The wide ridge continues east, then south east as it drops down to the Bealach Ban, before rising to An Coileachan.

Now comes the chief disadvantage of this northerly approach. It's a long, long way back to the A835, over very rough and boggy ground. The best line is from the Bealach Ban, taking a diagonal line to reach the col between An Coileachan and its northern outlier, Meallan Buidhe. Head north down easy slopes to the Abhainn a' Ghiubhais Li and follow rough, tussocky and boggy ground back to

onwards towards Sgurr Mor. Just before the final rise to the summit of Sgurr Mor, however, a ridge breaks off E to the summit of Beinn Liath Mhor Fannaich

**Map:** OS Sheet 20

**Access Point:** Fannich Lodge, GR218660

**Distance:** 24km, 1981m ascent

**Approx Time:** 8-12 hours

**Translation:** the little cock; blue hill; big peak; big grey hill of Fannaich

**Pronunciation:** an kilyachan; myowl gorram; skoor more; byn leea voar fannich

**Stalking Information:** Eastern Munros – Kinlochluichart Estate. Tel: Garve 228. Western Munros–Fannich Estate. Tel: Almondbank 236

*Looking north-west from the summit of Beinn Liath Mhor Fannaich towards An Teallach and Loch Broom*

the A835. Follow the road back to the west end of Loch Droma.

The approach from the south is shorter and significantly easier, but you'll need to get permission to drive the 11km from the Strathbran/ Achnasheen road, the A832, to Fannich Lodge as the gate at Grudie Power Station is normally locked. It's worth remembering that this road is often blocked by snow in the winter.

An alternative route from Fannich Lodge follows an excellent stalker's path up the south ridge of Meall Gorm and gives easy access to An Coileachan. Sgurr Mor is also within easy reach and it's not a lot further to climb Beinn Liath Mhor Fannaich as well, though this hill is easily climbed on its own from the west end of Loch Droma.

**Route Summary:** From Loch a' Bhraoin cross the outflow and follow the footpath S. Cross the Abhainn Cuileig, leave the footpath and strike diagonally across the SW slopes of Meall a' Chrasgaidh (Route B) to the bealach between that hill and Sgurr nan Clach Geala. Climb Meall a' Chrasgaidh, return to the bealach, and climb to the high saddle SW of Carn na Criche. Climb the NE ridge of Sgurr nan Clach Geala, descend S and continue to the rocky

## Meall a' Chrasgaidh (239), 934m/3064ft, Sgurr nan Clach Geala (51), 1093m/3586ft, Sgurr nan Each (262), 923m/3028ft

Over the years I've become very fond of Loch a' Bhraoin. It's firmly wedged in a triangle of high moorland which skirts the western boundary of the Fannichs, and the huge upthrusts of the Letterewe hills. It's also the prelude to these western Fannaichs and their neighbours, A' Chailleach and Sgurr Breac.

There are nine Munros in the Fannichs all to the north side of the remote Loch Fannich and south of the Dirrie Mor, one of which, Sgurr Mor, at 1111m is the highest hill in the Northern Highlands. But the most attractive, without any doubt, is Sgurr nan Clach Geala, the Peak of the White Stones. With its near neighbours, Sgurr nan Each and Meall a' Chrasgaidh, Sgurr nan Clach Geala lies on the east side of the footpath which runs from Loch Fannich to Loch a' Bhraoin, a stalker's path which offers a fine exit from Sgurr nan Each after a traverse of all three Munros.

Take the private road to Loch a' Braoin, cross its outlet and continue on the stalker's path beside the Allt Breabaig. After a kilometre cross the burn and take the steep heathery west slopes of Meall a' Chrasgaidh. This hill is, in many respects, a rather dull foretaste of the grandeur to come. As its name, the Rounded Hill of the Crossing would perhaps suggest, it lacks the ruggedness of some of its neighbours but its summit is most certainly a viewpoint par excellence. Out west, the pinnacles of An Teallach rise to its broken crest, one of Scotland's finest hills. Northwards, Beinn Dearg fronts that high upland which leads to Seana Braigh and to the south the skyline is dominated by the outline of the Torridon hills, Slioch and the Letterewe giants.

From Chrasgaidh a long slope leads to a wide bealach. One ridge heads off to the NE to climb Sgurr Mor while another becomes the rough NE ridge of Sgurr nan Clach Geala. This is the finest of the Fannichs with its high, hanging corrie and steep buttresses. Follow the graceful curved ridge to the narrow summit ridge and then descend to another bealach, the Cadha na Guite before climbing the slopes to the shapely summit of Sgurr nan Each. Return to the Cadha na Guite, drop down the slopes to the WNW and follow the stalker's path back to Loch a' Bhraoin.

**Route Summary:** ridge of Sgurr nan Each. Return to the bealach S of Sgurr nan Clach Geala and drop down W to the path which runs back to Loch a' Bhraoin

**Map:** OS Sheet 20

**Access Point:** A832, near Loch a'Bhraoin

**Distance:** 20km, 220m ascent

**Translation:** hill of the crossing; peak of the white stones; peak of the horses

**Pronunciation:** myowl a chras-kee; skoor nan klach gee-ala; skoor nan yaach

## Sgurr Breac (135), 1000m/3281ft, A' Chailleach (137), 999m/3278ft

The most westerly of the Fannaichs, these two hills are joined to the rest of the ridge by a high col at the head of the Allt Breabaig. A footpath runs south from Loch a' Bhraoin to this col where Sgurr Breac can be climbed by its eastern ridge. A good high-level ridge runs west from Sgurr Breac over the subsidiary top of Toman Coinich and onto A' Chailleach. This ridge is like the upright of a letter F with two projecting spurs, Sron na Goibhre and Druim Reidh running out in a northerly direction forming the arms of the corrie of Toll an Lochain.

One of these spurs, the Druim Reidh, rises steeply from the eastern end of Loch a' Bhraoin and once the initial height is gained, runs gently southwards towards Toman Coinich and its central position between the two Munros. Climb both Munros from this top and return by way of the Druim Reidh.

**Route Summary:** Follow the path to the bealach which leads to Loch Fannaich (Route C). Climb the E ridge of Sgurr Breac. Traverse Toman Coinich and descend to the col below its W slopes. Follow the rim of Toll an Lochain to its junction with Sron na Goibhre spur, then continue SW to the summit of A' Chailleach

**Map:** OS Sheets 19 and 20

**Access Point:** A832 near Loch a' Bhraoin

**Distance:** 16km, 1143m ascent

**Approx Time:** 5-8 hours

**Translation:** speckled peak; the old woman

**Pronunciation:** skoor brechk; a chalyach

## Ben Wyvis (Glas Leathad Mor) (83), 1046m/3432ft

**Route Summary:** Take the muddy track which runs alongside the Allt a' Bhealaich Mhoir. Continue past the forest plantation and turn uphill to climb the steep slopes of An Cabar. From the top the summit lies 1.6km in a NE direction over a rolling mossy ridge

**Map:** OS Sheet 20

**Access Point:** Garbat

**Distance:** 22.4km, 1311m ascent

**Approx Time:** 6-10 hours

**Translation:** from Gaelic fuathas, possibly hill of terror; big greenish grey slope

**Pronunciation:** byn wivis; glas lehat moar

It's not the most dramatic mountain in Scotland and neither is it the prettiest, but it can nevertheless throw down a challenge which can cause problems for the unwary. Ben Wyvis is Inverness's mountain, just as Ben Lomond is Glasgow's and just as generations of hillwalkers from the Central Belt have first scuffed their boots above the bonnie, bonnie banks, so many local folk have battled up the heather clad slopes of Tom a' Choinnich, Glas Leathad Mor and An Cabar, the tops which collectively make up Ben Wyvis.

The flat summit skyline and rather featureless western slopes, those seen from the Garve-Ullapool road, don't immediately suggest any sense of threat, but when Martin Moran from Lochcarron was climbing all the Munros during the winter equinox a few years ago it was here that he came closest to getting the chop – he was avalanched off Glas Leathad Mor.

My own first attempt on Ben Wyvis wasn't quite as dramatic, but didn't lack excitement. We had struggled up the track on to An Cabar, to a height of 950m only a couple of kilometres away from the summit and 96m lower, but gale force winds had us, literally, on our knees, and from time to time sudden gusts threatened to lift us off the ground. Swallowing our pride, we made a hasty retreat and left the summit for another, more benevolent, day.

The main physical features of the hill are the two great corries which are gouged out of the eastern flanks of the hill, the dark side of the mountain which is relatively unseen, and unfrequented. Here the snow lies late into the summer and mountaineer John Mackenzie, Earl of Cromartie, told me that his ancestors used to rent their land from the Crown on condition that they could gather a snowball at any time of the year.

The popular route up the hill begins at the bridge over the Allt a' Bhealaich Mhoir near Garbat on the Garve-Ullapool road. This is a path which has suffered extensively from erosion and the Forestry Commision have tried various methods of path

*Looking south from the summit of Ben Wyvis*

maintenance to keep a solid route over the bogs. The path follows the line of the forest before climbing a better path up the steepening ridge of An Cabar, Ben Wyvis's southern top. From here, wind permitting, it's an easy walk over a moss-covered ridge to the summit cairn, where the views to the west make every bit of effort so worthwhile.

## Am Faochagach (206), 954m/3130ft

This is the high point of a great tangle of hills which lie between Loch Glascarnoch and Strath Vaich. Like its outliers, Am Faochagach is a big, bluff, rounded hill and is well protected by big walk-ins from the Glascarnoch Dam or from Strath Vaich in the east. The obvious approach, from the A835 at Loch Droma, is both pathless and exceedingly wet and the crossing of the Abhainn a' Gharbhrain can be very difficult in wet weather

In such conditions it's worth trying to cross above Loch a' Gharbhrain, but bear in mind that you'll have two burns to cross – the Allt a' Gharbhrain and the outflow from Loch Coire Lair. This hill is best kept

**Route Summary:** Start at the bridge over the Abhainnan an Torrain Dubh. Cross the moorland E passing between Loch Glascarnoch and Loch a' Gharbhrain. The crossing of the Abhainn a' Gharbhrain will entail wading to a greater or lesser degree depending on the weather conditions. Once across the river turn NE and climb the steep heather slopes to reach the main ridge just S of the summit. From there the going is easy along a broad and obvious ridge.

**Map:** OS Sheet 20

**Access Point:** A835 NW end of Loch Glascarnoch

**Distance:** 14.4km, 701m ascent

**Approx Time:** 4-6 hours

**Translation:** place of the shells

**Pronunciation:** am foechakach

for a period of dry weather.

Once over the waterways the ascent is easy. A north-easterly line climbs steep heather covered slopes on the south bank of the Allt na h-Uidhe and then a more easterly direction climbs steeper slopes to the summit spine. Follow the broad ridge north-wards, over a rounded subsidiary top to the final summit slopes. Two cairns, a few metres apart, adorn the flat summit dome.

**Route Summary:** Take the private road through the forest into Gleann na Sguaib (Route A, p.206). Follow the stalker's path up the glen to the broad saddle at its head. From the saddle go S by a massive drystone dyke and follow it up Beinn Dearg's N ridge. Where the dyke turns W go through a gap and cross the bald summit dome in a SSW direction to the cairn. Return to the saddle and climb the easy angled ridge to the E to Cona' Mheall. Return to the saddle and climb the broad SE ridge of Meall nan Ceapraichean

**Map:** OS Sheet 20

**Access Point:** Inverlael

**Distance:** 24km, 1524m ascent

**Approx Time:** 7-11 hours

**Translation:** red hill; hill of the joining; possibly from ceap; meaning a rounded hilltop

**Pronunciation:** byn dyerak; konival; myowl nan kyapreechan

## Beinn Dearg (55), 1084m/3556ft, Cona' Mheall (170), 980m/3215ft, Meall nan Ceapraichean (172), 977m/3205ft

You notice the great bulk of Beinn Dearg as you drive over the A835 Ullapool road from Garve. It rears a lofty head beyond the foot of Loch Glascarnoch beside its near-neighbour, Cona' Mheall, the enchanted hill! It's a straightforward walk to climb the two hills from this approach and perhaps also take in the ascent of Am Faochagach which lies slightly to the east, but beware. The flat area between the foot of Loch Glascarnoch and these hills is very wet and boggy indeed and the river which flows into the loch can often be difficult to cross. Further down the A835, a few hundred metres north of Inverlael House, a private forestry track runs up through the Lael Forest into the lower part of Gleann na Sguaib.

This glen, particularly in its upper reaches, offers a much more interesting approach to Beinn Dearg, up a long stalker's path which twists and turns past some lovely waterfalls and pools in its upper reaches. The path soon takes you on to a high, broad pass, a stony place with scattered lochans. To climb Beinn Dearg, which is on your right, follow the line of a massive dry stone dyke which runs up the shoulder of the hill virtually all the way to the summit. Near the top, where the dyke bears west, is a gap in the wall. Go through

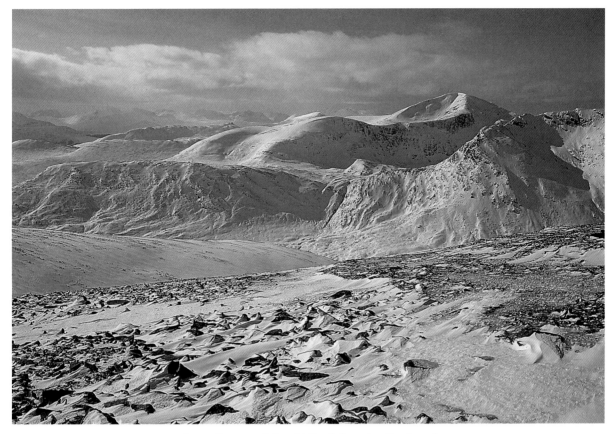

*Beinn Dearg and Cona' Mheall from Am Faochagach*

it and follow a south-south-west bearing for about 300m and you'll cross the bald dome of the summit slopes and find the 1084m summit itself.

Directly east of Beinn Dearg's summit, the slopes steadily steepen, eventually to form the sheer western wall of Coire Ghranda, a spectacular, crag-girt corrie with its high-level lochan, sheer walls and Cuillin-like atmosphere. The north-east wall of this corrie supports the flat-topped ridge of Cona' Mheall and it can be reached either by a long and wet walk-in from Loch Droma on the A835, or from the Bealach Coire Ghranda at the head of Gleann na Sguaib. The first route involves a spectacular scramble up the south-east ridge, probably the mountain's finest feature.

The route from the Bealach Coire Ghranda is a straightforward walk over rocky terrain and the summit cairn is found on the north-east corner of the flat topped summit ridge.

Back at the Bealach Coire Ghranda it's an easy climb up the south-east ridge of Meall nan Ceapraichean.

**Route Summary:** Follow the forest track as far as Glensguaib. Continue by the track which leads on to the Druim na Saobhaidhe ridge (Route B). From this ridge cross Gleann a' Mhadaidh and round a spur above to continue up Coire an Lochain Sgeirich. Continue across boggy terrain towards Loch a' Chadha Dheirg from where a N direction will take you to the easy slopes of the SW top. Follow the cliff edge to the summit of Seana Bhraigh. On the return route, pass the inward track in Coire an Lochain Sgeirich and continue in a SW direction to climb Eididh nan Clach Geala. Return by Gleann na Sguaib

**Map:** OS Sheet 20

**Access Point:** Inverlael

**Distance:** 25.6km, 1128m ascent

**Approx Time:** 7-10 hours

**Translation:** old upper part; web of the white stones

**Pronunciation:** shena vry; aydyee nan klach gyala

## Seana Bhraigh (254), 927m/3041ft, Eididh nan Clach Geala (249), 928m/3045ft

Since Seana Bhraigh lies very much in isolation to the north of the Beinn Dearg group it makes a lot of sense to climb it as a solitary peak. This also gives a fair choice of approach – from Glen Achall near Ullapool or Strath Mulzie in the north, from Gleann Beag in the south east, or from Inverlael in the south west. The first three approaches involve a considerable walk-in, although mountain bikes can be used, but perhaps the best option for the day walker is from Gleann na Sguaib near Inverlael.

If climbing Seana Bhraigh only, climb up through the forest to Glensquaib and then ascend the long nose of Druim na Saobhaidhe which forms the northern wall of Gleann na Squaib. A footpath follows the ridge, crosses over the Allt Gleann a' Mhadaidh and runs up the length of Coire an Lochain Sgeirich to the vast plateau north-east of Eididh nan Clach Geala.

Alternatively, Seana Bhraigh can be climbed fairly comfortably with Eididh nan Clach Geala to make a fine round which makes the most of some very good stalker's paths, one of which isn't shown by the OS. Walk up the length of Gleann na Squaib as far as the Eas Fionn waterfall where a cairn by the side of the track marks the beginning of a very good stalker's path which climbs the hillside to Lochan a' Chnapaich. Just before you reach the lochan, climb northwards on to the broad spur which emanates from Eididh nan Clach Geala, pass a small lochan tucked away in the heathery folds, and follow the broad ridge to the quartzy summit.

From there, broad grassy slopes lead north-east past the head of Coire an Lochain Sgeirich (your eventual descent route) and small lochans to the rim of the impressive Cadha Dearg, the Red Pass. I once sat here enthralled watching a golden eagle quarter the air space below me. This is a wild place of tremendous atmosphere, rich in botanical interest, with great crags forming its eastern and

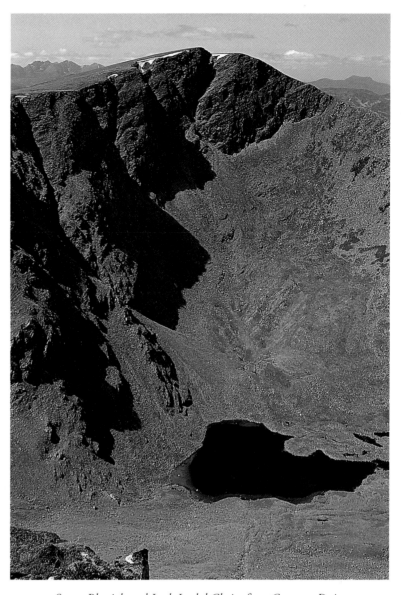

*Seana Bhraigh and Loch Luchd Choire from Creag an Duine*

northern extremities. The walking is easy around the great rim and then up grassy slopes, skirting the 906m bump and up final stony slopes to the summit – a breathtaking point with the windbreak cairn sitting on the very edge of nothing! The view across the void of the Luchd Choire to Seana Bhraigh's eastern top, Creag an Duine, is one of immense spaciousness with the whole of the North West arrayed before you in all its mountain glory.

Return by the rim of the Cadha Dearg and the footpath down Coire an Lochain Sgeirich.

# ASSYNT AND THE FAR NORTH

## The Munros:

### Conival    Ben More Assynt    Ben Klibreck    Ben Hope

If there is one area in Scotland which truly exposes the pointless nature of Munro-bagging it is this vast area north of Ullapool. Within a collection of smaller hills of the character of Stac Pollaidh, Suilven, Cul Mor and Cul Beag, Canisp, Quineag, Foinaven, Arkle and Ben Loyal we have some of the finest mountains in the country, and I'm afraid the Munros, fine as they are in their own right, very much stand in the shadow of their less-high neighbours.

So many Munro-seekers drive huge distances to climb these hills in quick bagging raids – many will climb Klibreck and Ben Hope in a day with a drive in the car in-between. I remember driving all the way north from Glasgow to climb Conival and Ben More Assynt and immediately driving all the way south again, looking out of the car window on the return drive just wishing I could stay in this incredible area for a bit longer.

Geologically, the area is predominantly gneiss, on top of which sandstone hills have weathered to create some of the weird and magnificent mountain shapes that are so typical of the region. From Inchnadamph the bare quartzite screes of Conival's upper tier contrast with the rich green of Gleann Dubh below, the bold greenness indicating the predominance of limestone. Below this surface lie caves, pot-holes and water courses and the well-known caves of Tralligill in Gleann Dubh.

Further north Ben Hope and Ben Klibreck are isolated hills surrounded by vast moorlands, a factor which greatly enhances their appearance, particularly the former.

**Route Summary:** Take the farm track, just N of the Inchnadamph Hotel, which runs alongside the River Tralligill. Follow the path to the Tralligill Caves, but stay on the NE bank. Opposite the caves leave the track and take to the slopes on the SW face of Beinn an Fhurain. Aim for the obvious col between Beinn an Fhurain and Conival. From the col the final slopes lead to a level ridge and the summit. Continue E along the rough ridge of scree and quartzite boulders to the summit of Ben More Assynt. The summit cairn is on the N top.

## Conival (154), 987m/3238ft, Ben More Assynt (140), 998m/3274ft

From Inchnadamph the grey quartzite screes of Conival tend to hide the bulk of Ben More Assynt, a rather secretive hill which is unusual in this area of normally bold mountains. These two hills are invariably climbed together, although a fine ridge walk over Conival and Breabag to the south offers great views of the superb corrie between Conival and Ben More Assynt which is ringed by sheets of grey quartzite screes and holds a sparkling green lochan. A diversion to Ben More and back to Conival involves only another three kilometres of ridge walking.

The normal route of ascent leaves the road a couple of hundred metres north of the Inchnadamph Hotel and follows the farm track along the north bank of the River Tralligill beyond the cottage at

*Conival and Ben More Assynt from the south-east*

Glenbain to a prominent copse of trees. Just beyond this point, a footpath crosses the river by a wooden bridge and continues towards the Tralligill Caves but unless you want to visit them, and they are worth the short diversion, stay on the north side of the glen and after a short distance follow a rising traverse up the south-west face of Beinn an Fhurain towards a col between Beinn an Fhurain and Conival.

From the col it's a straightforward climb up the broad north ridge, initially up quartzite screes and then through some small outcrops to the fairly level summit ridge and the cairn. A crest of broken quartzite blocks and boulders stretches east from the summit of Conival to the north top of Ben More Assynt, a distance of 1.5km. Although the walking is rough, there is a sense of spaciousness, with wide views both north and south. The ridge narrows dramatically in places, here and there it is very steep sided but there are no technical difficulties. In wet weather the quartzite blocks can be slippery, though!

The summit of Ben More is comprised of two rough bumps, the north one is the true summit.

**Map:** OS Sheet 15

**Access Point:** Inchnadamph

**Distance:** 17.6km, 1128m ascent

**Approx Time:** 4-7 hours

**Translation:** hill of joining; big hill of Assynt

**Pronunciation:** konivaal; byn moar assint

*Ben Loyal (left) and Ben Klibreck (on the right in the distance) from the summit of Ben Hope*

**Route Summary:** Cross the river and go E across the moorland towards Loch nan Uan. From the N end of the loch go SE up steep grassy slopes to the main ridge. Follow the easy ridge to a bouldery slope which leads to the summit

**Map:** OS Sheet 16

**Access Point:** A836 Lairg/Tongue road, GR545303

**Distance:** 11.2km, 792m ascent

# Ben Klibreck (190), 961m/3153ft

Another isolated hill rising high from the bare Sutherland moors, Beinn Cleith Bric, to give it its old name, is an 11km long, sinuous spine between Loch Naver and Loch Coire. The western aspects of the hill are in the most part steep and heathery with one prominent line of crags displayed just below the summit, Meall nan Con. The eastern side, overlooking Loch Coire, has more character, with the great grassy corries enclosed by bulging shoulders.

A number of expeditions can incorporate the ascent of Klibreck, from either the Crask Inn in the south or from Altnaharra in the north but the easiest approach, and the shortest, starts from the A836 road through Strath Vagastie. There is a good parking spot beside the river at GR545303 and once across the river, rough moorland rises towards the western slopes of the hill. Head for Loch nan Uan and from its northern shore the grass and heather slopes steepen quite dramatically towards the lowest point of the ridge above. From the outflow of the loch it's best to head south-east and so avoid the craggy ground below Meall nan Con.

Once the ridge is reached, a short ascent on good underfoot conditions lead to the summit boulderfield and the cairn.

## Ben Hope (253), 927m/3041ft

The most northerly of all our Munros, Ben Hope is most often climbed from Strath More up the burn north of the broch of Dun Dornaigil, which leads to the upper southern slopes. The western cliffs are a clear marker on the left and the summit is reached in a couple of hours. While it's an easy enough walk there is a fine feel of isolation, particularly since the eastern and southern slopes ease off into a watery wilderness and northern views follow the long thin arm of Loch Hope and the open spaciousness of the sea.

From the north the hill appears as a crag-girt wedge, but a long ridge gives easy access from the south from either one of two starting points.

Beyond the farm at Alltnacaillich, just north of the Dun Dornaigil (well worth visiting this ancient beehive-shaped building), the Allt na Caillich offers a line up past some fine waterfalls on to the ridge of Leitir Mhuiseil. Follow this northwards by an obvious cliff edge, all the way to the summit cairn.

Alternatively, a signposted route starts from an old shed a couple of kilometres north of Alltnacaillich and points a way to a breach in the western escarpment which offers a more direct, if steeper, line onto the broad terrace which runs up the hill to the east of the crags. Higher up the hill a line of cairns marks the route to a large cairn, and then the summit.

The more adventurous scrambler may wish to climb Ben Hope from the north. This route involves a walk-in from the head of Loch Hope towards the Dubh-loch na Beinne, a lochan which is situated just below the mountain's north western crags. Above the dark waters you can climb fairly easily to the mountain's north ridge where a section offers some exhilarating scrambling to the summit. The most difficult section can be avoided on the left (east) by climbing a gully which leads to the ridge higher up.

**Approx Time:** 4-6 hours

**Translation:** hill of the speckled cliff

**Pronunciation:** byn kleebreck

**Route Summary:** From the farm at Alltnacaillich go N for 1.6km and leave the road by a shed. Follow the stream and head NE to make for an obvious break in the crags which takes you on to a wide terrace above the escarpment. Turn N and follow the cliff edge which buttresses the mountain's summit

**Map:** OS Sheet 9

**Access Point:** Alltnacaillich

**Distance:** 6.4km, 914m ascent

**Approx Time:** 2-4 hours

**Translation:** hill of the bay

**Pronunciation:** byn hope

# SKYE AND MULL

## The Munros:

Ben More (Mull)    Bla Bheinn (Blaven)    Sgurr Dubh Mor
Sgurr nan Eag    Sgurr Alasdair    Sgurr Mhic Choinnich
Innaccessible Pinnacle    Sgurr na Banachdich
Sgurr a' Ghreadaidh    Sgurr a' Mhadaidh
Sgurr nan Gillean    Am Basteir    Bruach na Frithe

The islands of Mull and Skye are, somewhat surprisingly, the only two Scottish islands which can boast Munros. Ben More on Mull is an attractive hill and many Munroists keep it as their 'last Munro', making a celebration weekend out of it, sailing out across the Sound of Mull to Craignure from Oban, driving around to Loch na Keal for the walk and celebrating later in the evening in Tobermory. There have probably been more Munro celebrations in the restaurants of Tobermory than anywhere else.

There are regular celebrations in Skye's Glenbrittle and Sligachan too, celebrations that are tinged with a certain amount of relief. For many walkers, the Skye Cuillin is the dark side of their Munro ambitions. The fears that wake them up in the middle of the night with sweaty palms have much to do with exposure, knife-edged ridges, steep scrambles and of course the Inn Pin, the most technically difficult of all the Munros. These are the Munros that require not only fairly advanced rock scrambling, but rock climbing, and the Innaccessible Pinnacle requires knowledge and experience of how to abseil. Hence the relief for many walkers once they've successfully completed the Cuillin Ridge – they can get on with the rest of their lives without the dread of nightmares!

But in essence all that is required is an experienced companion – preferably a mountaineer with a rock climbing background, someone who is happy to belay you, and encourage you on the steeper sections.

Because of the unique nature of the main Cuillin Ridge, I've taken a different approach to describing it from the rest of this book. While the ridge breaks down naturally into four separate expeditions, I'm well aware that many may want to walk the entire ridge in one go, while others may wish to climb single Munros, depending on time available and the weather, which can be fickle to say the least. I've therefore described the ridge in one main essay, while describing a logical break- down of the ridge into four expeditions in the route summaries. I hope this gives a clearer picture of the options available.

*Sgurr na Gillean (sunlit on the right) from the south-east*

## Ben More (Mull) (185), 966m/3169ft

**Route Summary:** *Start at the foot of the Abhainn na h-Uamha and follow the S bank up the grassy Gleann na Beinne Fada to reach the col between Beinn Fhada and A' Chioch. Turn S and climb towards A' Chioch. Continue on the ridge over A' Chioch to Ben More. Descend by the broad NW ridge*

**Map:** OS Sheet 48

**Access Point:** Loch na Keal

**Distance:** 13km, 950m ascent

**Approx Time:** 4-7 hours

**Translation:** big hill

**Pronunciation:** byn moar

This hill seems to be gaining the reputation of the 'final Munro', as more walkers keep this hill as the last of their Munro round than any other. There are a number of reasons for this, the major one being the difficulty of access. You have to make a weekend of Mull's Ben More and if you're going to make a weekend of it you might as well make it a celebratory one. That's exactly what I did. I deliberately kept Ben More as my final Munro, took my wife with me, climbed the hill with her on a wet and cloudy day and retreated to Tobermory for a slap-up celebration dinner.

Other than those collecting the island's only Munro the Isle of Mull is curiously ignored by hill walkers, which is a pity for there are a couple of grand Corbetts and a lot of fine walking, albeit mostly on rough ground. If nothing else, Ben More offers a taster of what the island has to offer.

Perhaps another reason why walkers leave Ben More as their last Munro is to give them a chance to save up for it – it can be a costly weekend. Positioned near the west of the island it is a fair distance from the ferry at Craignure and you either have to take a car on the ferry from Oban, and drive to the starting point, or take a local bus to Salen from where you still have an 11km walk to Loch na Keal. A bike would be useful, and cheaper to transport on the Oban-Craignure ferry!

From the roadside at Loch na Keal follow the Abhainn na h-Uamha up the length of Gleann na Beinne Fada to the obvious col in the ridge between Beinn Fhada on your left and A' Chioch on the right. From the col turn south and climb increasingly steep and rocky slopes to the summit of A' Chioch.

The ridge to Ben More continues in much the same way, a steep and rocky descent to the narrow bealach then another steep, rocky climb to the summit wind break of Ben More. This final climb to Ben More looks difficult from the bealach but don't be discouraged, it's easier than it looks.

A word of warning – the summit of Ben More has much magnetic rock and compasses are notoriously unreliable. The best descent is down the broad and straightforward north-west ridge.

*The A' Chioch ridge from the summit of Ben More*

*Bla Bheinn from across Loch Slapin*

Route Summary: Leave the Elgol road at the Allt na Dunaiche just S of the head of Loch Slapin on its W side. Take the path that runs alongside the N bank of the stream through a wooded gorge, and then more steeply into Coire Uaigneich. Here the path becomes indistinct in places, but turns NNW up a steep slope just right of an obvious gully and soon reaches a distinct shoulder. Once this shoulder abuts on to the main ridge follow it in a WSW direction, following the rim of the ridge. As you climb closer to the summit dome there are one or two rocky obstacles to be scrambled over before more scree slopes lead to the summit

Map: OS Sheet 32

Access Point: Head of Loch Slapin

Distance: 6km, 940m ascent

Approx Time: 2-5 hours

Translation: possibly blue hill, or possibly warm hill

Pronunciation: blaa-vin

## Bla Bheinn (Blaven) (251), 928m/3045ft

In many ways Blaven is even more impressive than its celebrated cousins, the Cuillin. Standing at the head of Loch Slapin, Blaven and its Corbett neighbour, Clach Glas (the traverse of both mountains is a rock scrambler's delight) are set apart by the gulf created by Glen Sligachan and Strath na Creitheach. As such, the views are finer than any you'll see in the Cuillin, indeed on a stormy day of dark shifting clouds the views west and north-west from the summit of Blaven are distinctly Tolkienesque! Sherrif Alexander Nicolson, a local man and one of the early mountaineering pioneers on Skye, suggested Blaven was the finest mountain on the island. It has twin summits with the south-west top only a couple of metres lower than the main one.

Blaven is often climbed from Camasunary up the Coire nan Leac, or, less often, from the Am Mam between the A881 Elgol road and Camasunary. This route is less attractive as it involves a long haul up the mountain's stony south ridge. The 'trade route' is undoubtedly the often wet footpath which leaves the road near the head of Loch Slapin and follows the course of the Allt na Dunaiche into Coire Uaigneich.

Follow the path on the north side of the burn through some woodland and pass some lovely wooded waterfalls. Just past the falls, cross the stream and continue west. Soon the path steepens as you take more of a south westerly line up heather, then grassy slopes and into the secret corrie, Coire Uaigneich.

In the upper reaches of the corrie where the slope flattens out considerably start climbing in a north-north-west direction on the south flank of the east ridge. A rough path takes a zigzag line and

*Clach Glas and the 'Red Cuillin' from the summit of Bla Bheinn*

becomes clearer on the higher screes as it passes the top of the
Great Prow, which appears on the right before reaching a small top
on the hill's eastern shoulder.

The ridge is straightforward from here, as it
narrows and weaves gently to the left and
then to the right before becoming less
steep as it broadens out to the summit
trig point.

Descend southwards along the
summit ridge to a col. From here the
Great Scree Gully offers a fairly rapid
descent back to Coire Uaigneach. An
alternative descent is to head south
from the south-west top, which is
easily reached from the col, and then
follow the broad south-east ridge to
the upper slopes of Coire Uaigneach
and the footpath back to Loch Slapin.

# SKYE AND MULL

*The Cuillin from the north-west, across Loch Bracadale*

**The Cuillin Ridge:** Sgurr Dubh Mor (222), 944m/3097ft, Sgurr nan Eag (259), 924m/3031ft, Sgurr Alasdair (147), 993m/3258ft, Sgurr Mhic Choinnich (211), 948m/3110ft, Inaccessible Pinnacle (159), 986m/3235ft, Sgurr na Banachdich (186), 965m/3166ft, Sgurr a' Ghreadaidh (181), 973m/3192ft, Sgurr a' Mhadaidh (266), 918m/3012ft, Sgurr nan Gillean (187), 965m/3166ft, Am Basteir (236), 935m/3068ft, Bruach na Frithe (198), 958m/3143ft

Without doubt the finest way to climb the 11 Munros of the Cuillin is in one continuous expedition, starting at the south end of the ridge on Sgurr nan Eag, or even better Gars-bheinn, the most southerly top on the Cuillin ridge, and working your way north through the most spectacular mountain scenery in the British Isles to finish on the airy peak of Sgurr nan Gillean. The expedition is made up of 18 individual tops, 14 of which are over 914m, 11 of which are classed as Munros. Never dropping under 760m in its 11km, this is the longest ridge walk in Britain.

Most hillwalkers take about 10-12 hours for the trip, from Gars-bheinn to Sgurr nan Gillean, bivvying out somewhere on the Gars-bheinn to Sgurr a Choire Bhig ridge before setting off at daybreak. The record between the two tops is currently just under three-and-a-half hours!

Bruach na Frithe is most easily approached from the Sligachan end of the Bealach a' Mhaim track which crosses over boggy moorland between Sligachan and Glen Brittle. At a point about a kilometre short of the summit of the pass a cairned line diverts up to the Fionn Choire, from where a line can easily be worked out to the summit. Alternatively, the north-west ridge can be easily followed to the summit. This is certainly the easiest of the Skye Cuillin and the view from the summit will give a fine taster of the rest of the ridge. The Fionn Choire path leads to the Bealach na Lice, an easy pass, but the continuation into the Harta Corrie

**Sgurr Dubh Mor, 944m/3097ft, Sgurr nan Eag, 924m/3031ft**

**Route Summary:** From the camp site in Glen Brittle follow the track towards Coire Lagan but after 800m or so leave the path and cross the moorland in an ESE direction towards Sron na Ciche (Route A). Make for the edge of Coir' a' Ghrunnda by contouring around the foot of Sron na Ciche, and then climb into the corrie to reach the lochan. Climb to an obvious col on the main ridge between Sgurr Dubh an Da Bheinn and Sgurr Thearlaich. Climb easy slopes to Sgurr Dubh an Da Bheinn and from there follow the ridge E to Sgurr Dubh Mor. Return to Sgurr Dubh an Da Bheinn and descend S along the main ridge, traversing below the steep-sided Caisteal a' Garbh-choire on either its W or E side. Continue along the main ridge to Sgurr nan Eag

**Map:** OS Sheet 32

**Access Point:** Glen Brittle House

**Distance:** 14km, 1190m ascent

**Approx Time:** 4-6 hours

**Translation:** big black peak; peak of the notches

**Pronunciation:** skoor doo moar; skoor nan ayg

**Sgurr Alasdair, 993m/3258ft,
Sgurr Mhic Choinnich, 948m/3110ft,
Inaccessible Pinnacle, 986m/3235ft**

**Route Summary:** Approach is by the Great Stone Shoot in Coire Lagan (Route B) which takes you into the gap between Sgurr Alasdair and Sgurr Thearlaich. Alasdair is easily reached from the gap by an easy scramble, while the best way on to Sgurr Thearlaich is to descend for a short distance to the E of the gap and climb an obvious crack on your left. This takes you on to Thearlaich's S rib which can then be followed to the slabby summit. Descend rocky grooves to an obvious bealach and from here move up a little and then traverse round the W face by Collie's Ledge (moderate difficulty). A much more direct route for climbers takes the obvious corner of King's Chimney (difficult) on the S side. Walkers who don't wish to climb are best descending to Coire Lagan by the Great Stone Shoot between Sgurr Alasdair and Sgurr Thearlaich, regaining the ridge by the An Stac screes.

From the summit of Sgurr Mhic Choinnich descend NNE to the col above the An Stac screes. You have to drop down a little to reach a cairned path in the scree which leads up below the W edge of An Stac's tower. Staying close to the base of its wall climb to easier ground. Continue on the main ridge and climb the Inaccessible Pinnacle by its E ridge (moderate difficulty – rock climbing). On the tiny summit a convenient boulder provides an anchor for an 18m abseil off the W side of the pinnacle. Descend to Glen Brittle by Sgurr Dearg's W ridge

**Map:** OS Sheet 32

**Access Point:** Glen Brittle

**Distance:** 14km, 1680m ascent

**Approx Time:** 6-8 hours

**Translation:** Alexander's Peak (named after Sheriff Alexander Nicolson who made the first ascent in 1873); Mackenzie's Peak (named after John Mackenzie the first Skye guide)

**Pronunciation:** skoor alastar; skoor veechk chunyeech

**Sgurr na Banachdich, 965m/3166ft,
Sgurr a' Ghreadaidh, 973m/3192ft,
Sgurr a' Mhadaidh, 918m/3012ft**

**Route Summary:** Take the path above the Eas Mor waterfalls to the upper basin of Coire na Banachdich (Route C). From here a cairned route takes a devious line beneath the crags of Sgurr Dearg eventually turning left to reach screes which lead to a gap in the ridge N of Sgurr Dearg. To the N, across the Bealach Coire na Banachdich, steep rock and screes lead to Sron Bhuidhe, then two more 'tops' before the final pull to Sgurr na Banachdich. From the summit a short dip leads to the foot of Sgurr Thormaid. This is climbed by scrambling over large blocks and boulders. From the summit continue to the NE avoiding the 'three teeth' by traversing easy angled slabs on their left. Follow the short narrow arête which leads to a 120m scramble on good holds to the S top of Sgurr a' Ghreadaidh. Follow the very narrow ridge crest to the summit. Continue on the narrow ridge down into the gap known as the Eag Dubh. This is followed by another descent to a second gap, the An Dorus. From here scramble to the SW summit of Sgurr a' Mhadaidh, the only 'top' which is given Munro status. Follow the ridge NW which runs out to Sgurr Thuilm and drop down into Coir a' Ghreadaidh from the obvious col, returning to Glen Brittle

**Map:** OS Sheet 32

**Access Point:** Glen Brittle

**Distance:** 14km, 1340m ascent

**Approx Time:** 4-6 hours

**Translation:** possibly smallpox peak; peak of torment; peak of the fox

**Pronunciation:** skoor na banachteech; skoor a ghraytee; skoor a vaady

**Sgurr nan Gillean, 965m/3166ft,
Am Basteir, 935m/3068ft,
Bruach na Frithe, 958m/3143ft**

**Route Summary:** A footpath leaves the Carbost road just beyond the Sligachan Hotel (Route D). A good footpath crosses the moor as far as the Allt Dearg Beag. From here continue on the W bank of the stream to a bridge. Cross the stream and follow the path which heads S. Continue into Coire Riabhach past the lochan with the obvious wall of the Pinnacle Ridge on your right. A long pull eventually gives access to the crest of the SE ridge, which leads to the summit of Sgurr nan Gillean. Descend the W ridge steeply to the Tooth of Sgurr nan Gillean. A narrow cleft known as Nicolson's Chimney offers an abseil route to the base of the crag from where you can contour across the screes to regain the ridge E of Am Basteir. An easy scramble leads to the summit. Descend to the Basteir Tooth by way of ledges on the Lota Corrie (S) side and follow a terrace which inclines down towards Lota Corrie. Narrow shelves and walls lead to wider ledges at the foot of the cliffs from where you can climb screes up to the Bealach nan Lice. From the bealach climb over Sgurr a' Fionn Choire to reach Bruach na Frithe. Descend by the NW ridge to the Bealach a' Mhaim and Sligachan

**Map:** OS Sheet 32

**Access Point:** Sligachan

**Distance:** 14km, 1160m ascent

**Approx Time:** 4-7 hours

**Translation:** peak of the young men, meaning obscure, slope of the deer forest

**Pronunciation:** skoor nan geelyan, am bastar, brooach na freea and Glen Sligachan involves a long, awkward walk.

Sgurr na Banachdich is the easiest Munro from the Glen Brittle side of the ridge, and utilises a well-worn approach up Coir' an Each to gain the western slopes which run out to Sgurr nan Gobhar. Sgurr Alasdair, at 993m, is the highest of the Cuillin and the easiest approach is by the tiresome Great Stone Shoot from Coire Lagan. Unless you are a climber, forget the other routes, which are invariably barred by crags.

Sgurr nan Eag is probably the remotest of the Cuillin Munros, and can be reached by its bouldery south slopes after a long walk across boggy moorland from Glen Brittle. It's well worth traversing the ridge to Gars-bheinn, the most southerly top on the Cuillin ridge, but avoid Coire nan Laoigh for descents.

Coire a' Ghrunnda is a

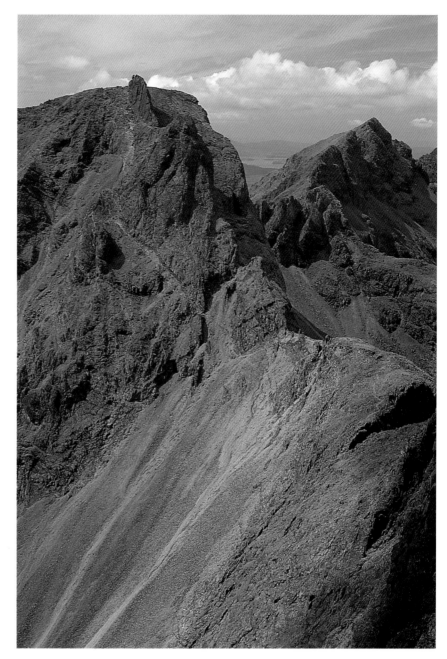

*The Inaccessible Pinnacle and Sgurr na Banachdich from Sgurr Mhic Chonnich*

fascinating place geologically but can be difficult to enter unless you're prepared to scramble a bit. If you are, then it's worthwhile linking Sgurr nan Eag with Sgurr Dubh Mor. This summit can be immensely difficult to find, never mind climb – it's positioned amid a great jumble of rocks and boulders and involves a fair bit of awkward scrambling to reach it. Try and keep it for a clear day. From Sgurr Dubh Mor a rocky ridge leads to Sgurr nan Eag, a route which is fairly straightforward, but the descent from Sgurr nan Eag westwards back to the Glenbrittle path is incredibly rocky and knee-jarring. My knees have never been the same since.

Sgurr a' Mhaidaidh and Sgurr a' Ghreadaidh can be climbed with some moderate scrambling from Coire a' Ghreadaidh. Being multi-topped, or, more accurately, multi-toothed hills, route finding can be extremely difficult. Sgurr Mhic Choinnich is a serious scramble, it is exposed and the rock can be extremely slippery when wet, especially on the summit slabs. It's usually climbed as part of the round of Coire Lagan, along with Sgurr Alasdair and the In Pinn and involves an exposed route called Collie's Ledge, a marvellous rocky promenade which appears to be carved from the rock face – it's actually a lot easier than it looks.

From its position just south of Sligachan, Sgurr nan Gillean is to most folks the epitome of the Cuillin. It is reached by a well maintained path from near the Sligachan Inn which weaves its way over and round low moorland hillocks, eventually crossing Coire Riabhach and curving round on to the south-east ridge of the hill. Higher up some scrambling is involved and the summit is extremely airy. Despite the scrambling this is the easiest route up the mountain. Am Basteir is usually climbed with Sgurr nan Gillean and can be difficult in misty weather. The summit crest is exposed and the route down past the Basteir Tooth to the Lota Corrie can be extremely tricky. Once the Bealach na Lice is reached, Bruach na Frithe can easily be climbed to give a fantastic trio of Munros.

Without doubt the Inaccessible Pinnacle is by far the most difficult of all the Cuillin hills, indeed of all the Munros. A narrowing blade of rock leaning against the summit crest of Sgurr Dearg, this impressive feature will either delight you, or scare the pants off you. It can be reached either by the path up Coire na Banachdich or from Coire Lagan, or from the ridge from Sgurr Mhic Choinnich.

There are two routes up the In Pin – the short steep western face which involves a rock climb of about V. Diff standard and the longer, east ridge, a moderate rock climb in technical terms but one which is seriously exposed. If you're an experienced climber then you'll romp up this eastern ridge, exhilarated by the position and exposure. If you've never climbed and are unhappy using your hands then you'll need a rope, climbing gear and an experienced companion. However you climb it, you have to abseil from the top, a 24m drop to Sgurr Dearg.

*'In wildness is the preservation of the world'*
*Henry David Thoreau*
*1817-62*

Far too many Munro collectors are put off by the In Pin which is a great shame, for while it may be exposed it is not technically difficult and it's well worthwhile swallowing your pride and asking some climbing acquaintance for help.

# MOUNTAIN SAFETY

Appropriate safety precautions should always be taken when venturing on to the Scottish hills. The number of serious injuries and deaths on the mountains has greatly increased in recent years, so it is very important to ensure that you are properly equipped whilst on a climb. There are a number of items which are essential for all climbers tackling a hill. Don't set off without packing waterproofs and spare inner clothing, food, a map, a compass, whistle and torch. It is also advisable to carry a survival bag for emergencies. Before you undertake a climb, make sure you have informed someone of the route you are taking and always report back when you are finished.

Remember that Scottish winter conditions can often be Arctic, and as severe as those on higher European mountains. They should therefore be treated with the utmost respect: an ice axe, crampons and specialist winter gear are necessary when climbing during the winter months, as is an understanding of any potential dangers such as unpredictable and severe snow conditions (particularly avalanches and snow cornices). When planning your outing make sure to pay attention to the weather forecast, and even if the likelihood is for fine weather it is important to be prepared for all outcomes, even during the summer months. Patches of snow left over from the winter are often still around in the summertime and should be avoided as they are likely to be hard, icy and slippery.

Anyone who is climbing in the Scottish mountains should be able to navigate accurately especially as tracks and paths are rarely signposted and can be difficult to trace on a map. The mountain weather can be extremely fickle and change very suddenly from bright sunshine to wicked storms, so consideration must be given to the possibility of routes becoming difficult or impassable due to variation of terrain and rising water levels in rivers and burns.

Scottish hillwalking and climbing courses are offered by numerous qualified instructors and guides and there are many such organisations operating in the Highlands. Guidance can also be found in the many magazines, pamphlets and other books published on the subject of mountaineering. To obtain information on mountaineering clubs and means of getting in touch with them you can write to:

The Honorary Secretary of the Mountaineering Council of Scotland,
IR, 71 King Street,
Crieff,
Perthshire PH7 3HB

The Scottish Sports Council,
Caledonia House,
South Gyle,
Edinburgh EH12 9DQ.

# ACCESS

Early in 1996, a Concordat on Access to the wild areas of Scotland was published[1] following an earlier review of access to Scotland's hills by Scottish Natural Heritage. The opening paragraph of this Concordat says:

> 'There is a longstanding tradition of access to hill land in Scotland – cherished by those who use the hills and long accepted by landowners and managers where this freedom is exercised with responsibility. As more people go to the hills, there is a growing need to encourage sensitive management and recreational practice. The Concordat aims to ensure that people can continue to enjoy access to the open hill in a way which shows consideration for the interests of others.'

While circumstances regarding access to Scotland's mountains are virtually the same post-Concordat as they were before, there is one major difference. There is now a general assumption of freedom of access, whereas before there was a tendency to believe that we could only go to the hills with the land-owners' permission. But the key words in the new Concordat are 'responsible access' and this means having due consideration for the day-to-day business of estates, especially during the deer stalking season. Hillwalkers shouldn't light fires, shouldn't leave litter of any sort, and should take particular care when crossing fences or walls. Most estates in the Highlands are involved in deer stalking to a greater or lesser degree, and ask hillgoers to respect the stag-shooting season which generally runs from 20 August to 20 October. Some estates may extend this season by a month or so. During this time span there are many upland areas in Scotland which are unaffected by deer stalking, like those reserves operated by Scottish Natural Heritage, and National Trust for Scotland properties.

The Mountaineering Council of Scotland and the Scottish Landowners' Federation jointly publish a booklet called *Heading for the Scottish Hills*, which contains useful information. Maps of the mountainous parts of the Highlands, Islands and Borders show the boundaries of the principal estates and lists are available which give details of estate contacts so that intending visitors can obtain information about estate activities and plan their expeditions accordingly. Sadly, in some areas local stalkers and keepers have gone ex-directory, no doubt fed-up with an increasing number of phone calls from hillwalkers. Obviously, if walkers can't get the information they need, they will just go to the hill anyway, and who can blame them? Despite several local problems, a chat with a gamekeeper or stalker will often result in a good compromise with the shooters chasing their prey on one side of the estate and walkers enjoying their hill on the other. The alternative to stalking on some estates could well be something much more unpleasant, like coniferisation or ski development, so a combination of dialogue, understanding and mutual tolerance is the only real way forward.

[1] *Scotland's Hills and Mountains: A Concordat on Access* (The Access Forum, SNH, Battleby, Nr. Perth, 1996)

# INDEX

| | | | | |
|---|---|---|---|---|
| A' Buidheanach Bheag | 91 | Ben Cruachan | 49 |
| A' Chailleach (Monadh Liath) | 135 | Beinn Dearg (Atholl) | 97 |
| A' Chailleach (Fannaichs) | 201 | Beinn Dearg (Ross-shire) | 204 |
| A' Chralaig | 164 | Beinn Dorain | 45 |
| A' Ghlas-bheinn | 166 | Beinn an Dothaidh | 45 |
| A' Mhaighdean | 194 | Beinn Dubhchraig | 26 |
| A' Mharconaich | 94 | Beinn Eibhinn | 85 |
| Am Basteir | 219 | Beinn Eighe (Ruadh-stac Mor) | 186 |
| Am Bodach | 70 | Beinn Eunaich | 51 |
| Am Faochagach | 203 | Beinn Fhada (Ben Attow) | 166 |
| An Caisteal | 21 | Beinn Fhionnlaidh (Appin) | 59 |
| An Coileachan | 198 | Beinn Fhionnlaidh (Glen Cannich) | 169 |
| An Gearanach | 70 | Beinn Ghlas | 38 |
| An Riabhachan | 171 | Beinn a' Ghlo | 96 |
| An Sgarsoch | 101 | Beinn Heasgarnich | 41 |
| An Socach (Glen Ey) | 103 | Ben Hope | 211 |
| An Socach (Glen Affric) | 168 | Beinn Ime | 16 |
| An Socach (Glen Cannich) | 171 | Beinn Iutharn Mhor | 103 |
| An Teallach | 192 | Ben Klibreck | 210 |
| Aonach air Chrith | 163 | Beinn na Lap | 82 |
| Aonach Beag (Lochaber) | 76 | Beinn Laoigh (Ben Lui) | 25 |
| Aonach Beag (Badenoch) | 85 | Ben Lawers | 38 |
| Aonach Eagach | 65 | Beinn Liath Mhor | 178 |
| Aonach Meadhoin | 161 | Beinn Liath Mhor Fannaich | 198 |
| Aonach Mor | 76 | Ben Lomond | 15 |
| | | Ben Macdui | 129 |
| Beinn Achaladair | 46 | Beinn Mhanach | 46 |
| Beinn nan Aighenan | 53 | Beinn Mheadhoin | 120 |
| Ben Alder | 88 | Ben More (Crianlarich) | 22 |
| Beinn Alligin | 182 | Ben More (Mull) | 214 |
| Ben Avon | 132 | Ben More Assynt | 208 |
| Beinn a' Bheithir | 67 | Beinn Narnain | 16 |
| Beinn Bheoil | 88 | Ben Nevis | 73 |
| Beinn Bhreac | 131 | Ben Oss | 26 |
| Beinn Bhrotain | 128 | Beinn Sgritheall | 156 |
| Beinn Bhuidhe | 19 | Beinn Sgulaird | 58 |
| Beinn a' Bhuird | 132 | Ben Starav | 53 |
| Beinn Chabhair | 21 | Beinn Tarsuinn | 196 |
| Ben Challum | 41 | Beinn Teallach | 138 |
| Beinn a' Chaorainn (Cairngorms) | 131 | Beinn Tulaichean | 22 |
| Beinn a' Chaorainn (Glen Spean) | 138 | Beinn Udlamain | 94 |
| Beinn a' Chlachair | 89 | Ben Vane | 16 |
| Beinn a' Chlaidheimh | 196 | Ben Vorlich (Loch Lomond) | 18 |
| Beinn a' Chleibh | 25 | Ben Vorlich (Loch Earn) | 29 |
| Beinn a' Chochuill | 51 | Ben Wyvis (Glas Leathad Mor) | 202 |
| Ben Chonzie | 31 | Bidean nam Bian | 64 |
| Beinn a' Chreachain | 46 | Bidein a' Choire Sheasgaich | 178 |
| Beinn a' Chroin | 21 | Bidein a' Ghlas Thuill (An Teallach) | 192 |

| | | | | |
|---|---|---|---|---|
| Binnein Beag | 69 | Creise | 57 |
| Binnein Mor | 69 | Cruach Ardrain | 22 |
| Bla Bheinn (Blaven) | 216 | | |
| Braeriach | 119 | Derry Cairngorm | 129 |
| Braigh Coire Chruinn-bhalgain | 96 | Devil's Point, The | 125 |
| Broad Cairn | 109 | Driesh | 112 |
| Bruach na Frithe | 219 | Druim Shionnach | 163 |
| Buachaille Etive Beag | 64 | | |
| Buachaille Etive Mor | 62 | Eididh nan Clach Geala | 206 |
| Bynack More | 122 | | |
| | | Fionn Bheinn | 181 |
| Cairn Bannoch | 109 | | |
| Cairn of Claise | 108 | Gairich | 151 |
| Cairngorm | 120 | Garbh Chioch Mhor | 148 |
| Cairn Toul | 125 | Geal Charn (Loch Laggan) | 89 |
| Cairnwell, The | 104 | Geal Charn (Drumochter) | 94 |
| Carn Aosda | 104 | Geal Charn (Monadh Liath) | 136 |
| Carn Bhac, | 103 | Geal-Charn (Loch Pattack) | 85 |
| Carn na Caim | 91 | Glas Bheinn Mhor | 53 |
| Carn a' Chlamain | 100 | Glas Leathad Mor (Ben Wyvis) | 202 |
| Carn a' Coire Boidheach (White Mounth) | 109 | Glas Maol | 108 |
| Carn Dearg (Loch Ossian) | 82 | Glas Tulaichean | 103 |
| Carn Dearg (Loch Pattack) | 85 | Gleouraich | 152 |
| Carn Dearg (Monadh Liath) | 135 | Gulvain | 143 |
| Carn Eige (Eighe) | 169 | | |
| Carn an Fhidhleir | 101 | Inaccessible Pinnacle (Sgurr Dearg) | 219 |
| Carn nan Gabhar (Beinn a' Ghlo) | 96 | | |
| Carn a' Gheoidh | 104 | Ladhar Bheinn | 153 |
| Carn Ghluasaid | 165 | Liathach | 184 |
| Carn nan Gobhar (Glen Cannich) | 171 | Lochnagar | 109 |
| Carn nan Gobhar (Glen Strathfarrar) | 173 | Luinne Bheinn | 153 |
| Carn Gorm | 33 | Lurg Mhor | 178 |
| Carn Liath (Beinn a' Ghlo) | 96 | | |
| Carn Liath (Loch Laggan) | 137 | Mam Sodhail | 169 |
| Carn Mairg | 33 | Maoile Lunndaidh | 176 |
| Carn a' Mhaim | 129 | Maol Chean-dearg (Torridon) | 181 |
| Carn mor Dearg | 73 | Maol Chinn-dearg (Glen Shiel) | 163 |
| Carn an Righ | 103 | Mayar | 112 |
| Carn Sgulain | 135 | Meall a' Bhuiridh | 57 |
| Carn an t-Sagairt Mor | 109 | Meall Buidhe (Glen Lyon) | 34 |
| Carn an Tuirc | 108 | Meall Buidhe (Knoydart) | 153 |
| Chno Dearg | 80 | Meall nan Ceapraichean | 204 |
| Ciste Dhubh | 161 | Meall a' Choire Leith | 37 |
| Cona' Mheall | 204 | Meall a' Chrasgaidh | 200 |
| Conival | 208 | Meall Chuaich | 93 |
| Creag nan Damh | 163 | Meall Corranaich | 37 |
| Creag Leacach | 108 | Meall Dearg (Aonach Eagach) | 65 |
| Creag Meagaidh | 137 | Meall nan Eun | 54 |
| Creag a' Mhaim | 163 | Meall Garbh (Glen Lyon) | 33 |
| Creag Mhor (Glen Lyon) | 33 | Meall Garbh (Lawers) | 38 |
| Creag Mhor (Glen Lochay) | 41 | Meall Ghaordie | 40 |
| Creag Pitridh | 89 | Meall Glas | 43 |

| | |
|---|---|
| Meall Greigh | 38 |
| Meall Gorm | 198 |
| Meall nan Tarmachan | 38 |
| Meall na Teanga | 141 |
| Monadh Mor | 128 |
| Moruisg | 176 |
| Mount Keen | 113 |
| Mullach Clach a' Bhlair | 116 |
| Mullach nan Coirean | 71 |
| Mullach Coire Mhic Fhearchair | 196 |
| Mullach na Dheiragain | 168 |
| Mullach Fraoch-choire | 164 |
| Mullach an Rathain (Liathach) | 184 |
| | |
| Na Gruagaichean | 69 |
| | |
| Ruadh-stac Mor (Beinn Eighe) | 186 |
| Ruadh Stac Mor | 194 |
| | |
| Saddle, The | 159 |
| Sail Chaorainn | 165 |
| Saileag | 161 |
| Schiehallion | 32 |
| Seana Bhraigh | 206 |
| Sgairneach Mhor | 94 |
| Sgiath Chuil | 43 |
| Sgor Gaibhre | 82 |
| Sgor Gaoith | 116 |
| Sgor an Iubhair | 70 |
| Sgor na h-Ulaidh | 61 |
| Sgorr Dhearg (Beinn a' Bheithir) | 67 |
| Sgorr Dhonuill (Beinn a' Bheithir) | 67 |
| Sgorr nam Fiannaidh (Aonach Eagach) | 65 |
| Sgorr Ruadh | 178 |
| Sgurr Alasdair | 219 |
| Sgurr na Banachdich | 219 |
| Sgurr Ban | 196 |
| Sgurr a' Bhealaich Dheirg | 161 |
| Sgurr Breac | 201 |
| Sgurr nan Ceannaichean | 176 |
| Sgurr nan Ceathreamhnan | 168 |
| Sgurr a' Chaorachain | 176 |
| Sgurr Choinnich | 176 |
| Sgurr Choinnich Mor | 77 |
| Sgurr a' Choire Ghlais | 173 |
| Sgurr na Ciche | 148 |
| Sgurr na Ciste Duibhe | 162 |
| Sgurr nan Clach Geala | 200 |
| Sgurr nan Conbhairean | 165 |
| Sgurr nan Coireachan (Glen Finnan) | 144 |
| Sgurr nan Coireachan (Glen Dessarry) | 148 |
| Sgurr Dearg (Inaccessible Pinnacle) | 219 |
| Sgurr an Doire Leathain | 163 |
| Sgurr Dubh Mor | 219 |
| Sgurr nan Each | 200 |
| Sgurr nan Eag | 219 |
| Sgurr Eilde Mor | 69 |
| Sgurr Fhuaran | 162 |
| Sgurr Fiona (An Teallach) | 192 |
| Sgurr Fhuar-thuill | 173 |
| Sgurr a' Ghreadaidh | 219 |
| Sgurr nan Gillean | 219 |
| Sgurr na Lapaich | 171 |
| Sgurr an Lochain | 163 |
| Sgurr a' Mhadaidh | 219 |
| Sgurr a' Mhaoraich | 157 |
| Sgurr a' Mhaim | 70 |
| Sgurr Mhic Choinnich | 219 |
| Sgurr Mor (Loch Quoich) | 150 |
| Sgurr Mor (Fannaichs) | 198 |
| Sgurr na Ruaidhe | 173 |
| Sgurr na Sgine | 159 |
| Sgurr Thuilm | 144 |
| Sisters of Kintail | 162 |
| Slioch | 189 |
| Spidean a' Choire Leith (Liathach) | 184 |
| Spidean Mialach | 152 |
| Sron a' Choire Ghairbh | 141 |
| Stob Ban (Mamores) | 71 |
| Stob Ban (Grey Corries) | 77 |
| Stob Binnein | 22 |
| Stob Coir' an Albannaich | 54 |
| Stob Coire a' Chairn | 70 |
| Stob Choire Claurigh | 77 |
| Stob Coire Easain | 79 |
| Stob Coire an Laoigh | 77 |
| Stob a' Choire Mheadhoin | 79 |
| Stob a' Choire Odhair | 57 |
| Stob Coire Sgriodain | 80 |
| Stob Dearg (Buachaille Etive Mor) | 62 |
| Stob Diamh | 49 |
| Stob Dubh (Buachaille Etive Beag) | 64 |
| Stob Ghabhar | 57 |
| Stob Poite Coire Ardair | 137 |
| Stuc a' Chroin | 29 |
| Stuchd an Lochain | 34 |
| | |
| Toll Creagach | 169 |
| Tolmount | 108 |
| Tom a' Choinich | 169 |
| Tom Buidhe | 108 |
| | |
| White Mounth, The | 109 |